WRITING SUSPENSE AND MYSTERY FICTION

Writing Suspense and Mystery Fiction

Edited by A. S. Burack

Publishers   THE WRITER, INC.   Boston

Copyright © 1977

by

The Writer, Inc.

Library of Congress Cataloging in Publication Data

Writing suspense and mystery fiction.

1. Detective and mystery stories—Technique.
I. Burack, Abraham Saul, 1908-
PN3377.5.D4W7   808.3'872   76-56430
ISBN 0-87116-104-4

Printed in the United States of America

FOREWORD

Mystery and suspense fiction continues to set new records in readership and sales each year, with many titles selling millions of copies and reaching best-seller lists. More and more of these are being sold to the movies or television. As a literary form, the conventional, tightly plotted mystery novel not only endures but flourishes. But it has undergone many changes in focus and emphasis, shifting from the puzzle worked out by cardboard characters to true-to-life fictional people with whom readers can identify. Some of these are detectives, but often they are the criminals, the victims, the suspects, or the survivors, and what is revealed about them and society goes beyond the crime itself.

While the conventional crime fiction of the Agatha Christie type is still tremendously popular, there has been a rapid growth in the demand for Gothics, which use many elements of the classical mystery, and for the police procedural story, which presents a detailed picture of how the police go about their investigations. In addition, we see more mystery and suspense books treated as important mainstream novels by reviewers, book clubs, and critics. There also continues to be a group of excellent writers who work in the tight disciplines of the short mystery and suspense story.

As the readership of mystery and suspense fiction has increased, so has the number of writers in these fields, but it is encouraging to note that although established authors of mysteries still attract large audiences, many new writers have risen to prominence in recent years, and their work appears in increasing numbers on bookstore and library shelves. The growth in outlets for paperback books accounts in large part for the often spectacular sales figures. Many of the bestselling softcover titles fall within the categories of mystery and suspense, Gothics, suspense-romance, and police procedural.

All types of mystery and suspense fiction writing are represented in WRITING SUSPENSE AND MYSTERY FICTION. Devising plots, developing believable characters, creating fictional sleuths, getting ideas, following exacting police procedures, doing careful research—all these techniques and methods are described here by masters of the craft. Most of these chapters have never before appeared in book form, but a few chapters from my previous volume (*Writing Detective and Mystery Fiction*) have been retained because the advice given is still important and valid. Also reprinted here are five chapters which have influenced the development of this genre and set it in proper historical perspective: "Detective Fiction: Origins and Development" by Dorothy L. Sayers (reprinted from her Introduction to the *Omnibus of Crime,* published by Harcourt, Brace & Company); "Twenty Rules for Writing Detective Stories" by S. S. Van Dine (reprinted by permission of Charles Scribner's Sons); "The Rules of the Game" by Howard Haycraft (reprinted from the author's *Murder for Pleasure: The Life and Times of the Detective Story,* published by D. Appleton-Century Company, Inc.); "Casual Notes on the Mystery Novel" by Raymond Chandler; and "Don't Guess, Let Me Tell You" by Ogden Nash (reprinted by permission of Little, Brown and Company).

The supplement, which contains "A Layman's Guide to Law and the Courts" and a "Glossary of Legal Terms," both prepared by the American Bar Association, provides writers of crime fiction with information on authentic procedures and proper terminology relating to law and the courts.

My thanks to all the authors and editors who generously granted permission to have their pieces included in this volume. The variety of approach and method—for there is no one way to write mystery and suspense fiction—will be of practical help to writers who aspire to work in this field.

Boston, Massachusetts   A. S. Burack

TABLE OF

CONTENTS

1 THOUGHTS ON PLOTS

by *Joan Aiken*

FOR A PERIOD of five years, I worked on an English short story magazine, and read, on an average, five short stories a day; say, 1,500 a year. About a hundred stories came into the office every week, and, except for the hopelessly illiterate, obscene, or handwritten, each had to be read by at least two people out of the editorial staff of five. If we thought a beginner's story showed promise but didn't quite make the grade for publication, we wrote and explained, to the best of our ability, why this was. Often the young authors were surprisingly grateful for our comments; not infrequently quite a brisk correspondence would spring up, stories and criticisms winging to and fro. Sometimes now a familiar name suddenly leaps out at me off a book jacket or TV screen, and I feel a delightful tiny spark of participation and hope that one of my bygone words of encouragement played some part in helping a young eagle to where he now perches.

Besides the stories, we received baskets of mail. By far the commonest letter was a heart cry that said, in one form or another: "I want to write, I enjoy writing, I am good at characters and descriptions, but I can't think of plots. Please tell me how." These letters—together with a large percentage of stories received which were not so much devoid of plot as they were evidence that the writers lacked awareness that there could *be* such a thing as a plot—convinced me that, while

1

some kinds of writing are instinctive, others really do have to be learned; and stories containing plots most definitely come into the latter category. Please note: it is no part of my intention to assert that plots are *necessary*; but I do feel it is necessary for a writer, before starting a piece of work, to be clear in his mind about the shape of it, and whether it is to have a plot or not. Inexperienced writers sometimes seem to confuse a *plot* with an *idea*. Some incident or character has seemed to them story-worthy, and they don't stop to reflect that as it stands it is only two-dimensional. The result, if written down, is often rambling and lacking in depth.

Fusion of ideas

In my magazine work, I also had the interesting task of interviewing a number of our established contributors about their writing techniques, and I shall always remember H. E. Bates, that master of the short story form, saying that besides inspiration and a lot of sheer hard labor, a story requires, for its germination, at least *two* separate ideas which, fusing together, begin to work and ferment and presently produce a plot. This tallies with my own experience: an idea can lie dormant in one's mind for months, sometimes years, until some apparently disconnected occurrence touches it off and starts the creative process working. And other writers I have compared notes with endorse this; their plots emerge through a juxtaposition of different elements, or from human conflict in combination with natural phenomena, or the jolt that occurs when two frames of reference collide. In short: a good plot, like a good casserole, needs more than one ingredient.

But how to assemble the ingredients? If you consult a textbook on creative writing, the plot chapter is likely to present a basic framework consisting of something pretty bleak, like this: *A character's intention—an obstacle—attempts to overcome obstacle—preliminary failure—ultimate success.* What could be more quenching? One can hardly bear the thought of a plot grinding along in such a mechanical way. Personally, I would find it almost impossible to launch a plot off a single character and his intention—whereas it is the easiest thing in the world to begin from a *situation*. X's urge to build a business empire doesn't stir a single impulse in me to write. I don't care if he succeeds or fails; but the thought of X pinned inside his car by a falling tree immediately sets my imagination working: Who will find him? What will he do? Perhaps he had no business on that particular road, and now he is trapped there. All his situation needs is another element of complication and you are away. (Some opening situations are practically surefire winners: injustice, for instance, or disguise, or a deathbed promise.) Stories should grow from the opening like living organisms, which is what they are.

I can still clearly remember achieving my first real plot, at the age of about twelve. I had been telling a story to my younger brother as we walked along a dull stretch of road, stringing together incidents in the way stigmatized by E. M. Forster as "And then—and then." With a sudden illumination, I saw that it would be possible to mold my story into a *shape,* to make it boomerang around so that the end reconnected with the beginning, giving a tweak to each connecting fiber and weaving them all together. Forgive the mixed metaphor; it arises from the vividly remembered feeling of terrific elation and power I had then. I have it still whenever a new plot begins to ferment. Whether the process is chemical, psychological, or is a message from elsewhere, which is what it feels like, it is the most rewarding part of a writer's experience, and makes up for the long blank periods when there is nothing to do but wait, hope, and keep in training.

Laying groundwork

Can one will this creative process to take place? I do not think one can, not entirely. But a lot of groundwork can be done which undoubtedly helps. One can—one must—keep a notebook. Mine is full of such entries as: *N. Cooke, aged 10, goes round filling up questionnaire on adults' private lives. X's character altered by car crash. Gout patients always carry colchicine. Father won't let daughter wear her glasses. Pickpocket finds test tube he has snatched contains tiny person. Heavy trucks get brake-fade on long hills. Old lady believes she will die if son digs up asparagus bed.*

Once you are in the way of noting down ideas for plots, they spring up everywhere: half-seen street signs, overheard remarks, dreams, news items. I used to find the personal ad columns very fertile sources. Sometimes, as an exercise, I set myself the task of combining two or three into a short story. Consider these: *Agile bagpiper with waterproof kilt wanted for party. Who would invite advertiser to haunted house? (Promise not to interfere with ghost's activities.) For sale: circular staircase. Model rhinoceros wanted. Would exchange gentleman's library for Jersey herd.* They are all genuine items from the London *Times* agony column. (I did in fact write a short story round the last one.) Another good exercise is to think of a title at random, say, *The Status Cymbal,* and write a story round it.

Of course a writer stands much more chance of acquiring useful ideas for plots if he is out and about in the world, holding down a job in factory or office (and therefore with less time for writing). This is one of the hopeless anomalies of the writer's life which he has to solve as best he can. But I don't believe that any writer under thirty—geniuses excepted—can stay writing in the attic forever without drying up.

So, having stocked a notebook with ingredients, what do you do? For myself, if I am in the rare state of not having anything I immediately want to write, I take hold of one idea, move slowly past all the others, hoping for reactions. If there are none, I go away and find some other occupation of a not too mentally absorbing kind, giving the subconscious time to tick. Mowing the lawn is good, for instance. Train rides

I find perfect for the germination of plots, because of the synthesis of rapid movement and a disburdened mind, but driving is no good. What else can be done to hasten the creative process? Coleridge took laudanum, Kipling sharpened pencils, Turgenev sat with his feet in a bucket of hot water, Michael Gilbert likes to go for a brisk walk on a downhill slope. If you can train your subconscious to work by such means, so much the better; if not, the only thing is to wait patiently; trying to hurry a plot can be a fatal mistake. Sometimes it will move along so far and no farther: A minor-seeming but insuperable snag arises and one's mind balks like a horse refusing a jump. You can patiently bring the horse back to the jump again and again, but I always take this refusal to mean that for some unperceived reason, the mind isn't ready yet to go on to the next stage. Leave it a little and, as likely as not, the problem will solve itself; you return to find the horse has flown the jump without your having noticed. Having several stories in progress simultaneously may be a help. If the first comes to a stop, you switch to a second. Ray Bradbury, another of my interviewees, said he always liked to have three stories under way: one straight, one fantasy, one science fiction. I, myself, prefer, while working on one book, to have the next in the middle background of my mind, rising gently like dough. Then I can relieve strain from technical problems with the current work by a refreshing spell on the vaguer, more flexible outlines of the future one.

I don't think one can lay down any rules about the structure of story plots. From my time as editorial reader, the two stories that linger most kindly in my mind are Irwin Shaw's *"The Kiss at Croton Falls,"* in which a woman has an indignant serial dream about the carrying-on of her perfectly blameless dead husband; and a story that we didn't buy (I would have liked to but I was in a very junior position at the time with no authority), about a young doctor who teased an unknown girl in a railway carriage by pretending to be mad and making her feed him grapes. Some years later they met again in strange circumstances. . . . Both these stories are quite unclassifiable, but it is plain in every line that the authors loved writing them, and that is the best criterion for success that I know.

Keeping the end in sight

Plots ought, certainly, to have a beginning, a middle, some sort of crisis, and an end; all these are important, but the end is *terribly* important. If it doesn't hit you like a flash of lightning and fill you with total conviction, then it is not the right end; go away and wait. Some writers create the end first, and work back; in the best stories the end is implicit from the beginning. Having a clear vision of what is to come keeps the story taut and moving in the right direction.

I have been talking about short stories; novels are so different that it is almost impossible to make any helpful generalizations about them. Most novels now eschew plots in the old-fashioned sense and rely on their own muscles, instead of somebody else's corsetry with a tidy shape and wind-up-all-characters conclusion. So what can you do if you are the kind of writer who enjoys plotting? You can write Gothics, or whodunits, or thrillers, or historicals, or children's stories. I do a mixture of all five, as I find something agreeable and soothing, like chess or embroidery, in working out the steps of a plot. But I haven't written enough yet to have an established routine. The main outline of each of my books was worked out in advance, but otherwise each seems to have evolved in a totally different way. Only one was plotted and written in a single uninterrupted operation; the others were to a greater or lesser extent interrupted by the exigencies of job, illness, children, family life. I began my most successful children's book in 1953, abandoned it after five days' intensive writing, and did not restart it for seven years. So one piece of advice I can wholeheartedly give is always to keep unfinished work; never throw anything out. If circumstances, or the work itself, should seize up on you, don't despair; it may be all the better after a bit of cold storage.

My thriller, *Dark Interval,* was an amalgamation of such different elements that it may be instructive—or at least serve as a warning—if I trace the process of its growth. Somehow from a tiny nucleus it snowballed in a totally unstoppable way.

It began in 1946 when one night I had a truly appalling dream. I dreamed I was the younger of two sisters, married, but come home to stay with my mother and sister because of a mental breakdown after the death of my little girl. I was completely out of my own character and into that of the girl, Caroline, but I could feel *her* identity slipping away, which was the chief horror of the nightmare—that, and the violently felt hatred of the mother and elder sister. I woke up stupefied with terror and had to wander about the house to reassure myself that I was I. It was a shock to get back into bed and find my husband there, still fast asleep. Next day I wrote it all down—three foolscap sheets, single-spaced—to get it out of my system, and I forgot it for eleven years.

Then, one day, on a solitary walk in Cornwall, prey to the germinal, pre-creative state which all writers will recognize, I thought how strange it would be to return to consciousness from a state of amnesia and find oneself thus wandering along a road, not knowing who one was, able only to see hands, feet, and clothes, with no memory, but a vague sense of being expected somewhere. I took this idea back to London and continued brooding over it; a couple of days later, walking home from the office, I suddenly realized that my amnesiac wanderer was Caroline, the girl of my dream. I had already established that the person who was waiting for her intended to murder her, and he intended to murder her *because* of the episode—a hit-and-run accident in which she had seen him kill a child—which had shocked her into the amnesia. But—aha!—he had never met her; so long as *she* didn't know who she was, *he* could not be sure he had the right victim.

The addition of more episodes from my dream gave me enough material for a story, but created complications. The death of Caroline's child caused her breakdown, the death of the second child made her relapse into amnesia, and a third child was due to turn up fortuitously and jolt her back to awareness, in time for some cat-and-mouse pursuit by the murderer. In fact, there were far too many children, I now see, but at the time of writing I was so personally involved, because of having experienced the dream, that I couldn't bring a detached literary judgment to bear and pick out the coincidences. I wrote it at 20,000-word length, called it *Hit and Run,* and sold it to a magazine. Seven years later, following the expert advice of the then editor of the Doubleday Crime Club, I expanded it into a book, *Dark Interval,* adding still more material from the dream. Some of this, a traumatic episode from Caroline's childhood—yet another child—I did have the sense not to use. Now, at some years' distance, I can see the plot's faults clearly, and they make me resolve to be more cautious in the future about using a dream-element in a book. Dreams can be as unbalancing to the sense of proportion as coincidence. "This is too improbable," an editor once said to me. "I like this story but it's just *too* hard to swallow." He was talking about the only story I ever wrote, flat, from real life, and it taught me a useful lesson about the risks of using unvarnished experience. I suppose these lessons are the writer's next best reward, after the act of writing itself, because they fill one with the impetus to start on another piece of work at once, and the resolve to avoid every pitfall and do it all much better this time.

2   THE THREE BASICS OF SUSPENSE

by *Charlotte Armstrong*

WHENEVER I THINK of gas-lit melodrama, the scene that leaps to my mind's eye is that of the heroine lashed to the railroad track. She is young and fair; the villain has tied her there. The hero is some place around.

I'd like to use this crude and elementary situation to illustrate, if I can, some points about the nature and technique of suspense. What we now call the suspense story is the lineal descendant of these old tales, after all.

Of course, if we were to come upon the scene *after* the train has passed by, we would be involved in a whodunit. So we may say the first requisite is, then, that somebody shall be tied to the railroad track. That is, there is something to fear. It has not happened yet. We, as readers, don't want to see it happen. We fear that it may. The nature of this something varies a great deal. It can be death or disappointment, financial ruin or moral injustice, capture by the enemy or no invitation to the party. It may be inverted, so that our hero is after something, and we fear lest he be prevented from getting it. There has to be something we are against.

But we are not going to be against it or be very much afraid if the girl lashed to the tracks is somebody we don't know anything about or if we don't much like what we do know. We just can't work up any steam unless we care, and we won't care

9

unless we know her and like her. Suspense is fear lest something bad happens to us, or to someone whose side we are on. So the second requisite is sympathy. So far, elementary indeed.

There are lots of stories in which a sympathetic character is caught in a situation of trouble or danger and goes through it as a simple ordeal. You've read them, too. The hero has a long hard journey to make. He suffers through and finally, after enduring many hardships, he gets to his destination. Or there is a physical battle between a good man and a bad one and after a while the author gets around to telling you which side wins. In terms of our illustration, we would see our girl in an uncomfortable and eventually dangerous position, struggling to get loose. She would twist and gnaw and after a while she would succeed and get out of her bonds.

Time limit

The ordeal is converted to suspense with the addition of a time limit. Suppose the hero has to get to the end of the journey with the news in three days or the fort falls to the Indians? Suppose the fist fight has to be won by noon or the papers will get out of the country? We can easily see that unless we know the railroad track has a train on it and unless we know the train is coming along within a time limit, we just aren't going to get excited, suffer though the girl may. By adding the time element we can play effort against time taken and work up a little something. But it is not yet enough.

It takes the hero, of course. It takes another force working on our side. What if we had the train on its way, the girl tugging futilely at her ropes, and just as the train is thundering down upon her, the hero leaps out of the shrubbery and snatches her to safety? This is surprise. It will be very annoying. Now, we'll want to know how in the dickens he happened to show up in the nick of time, and we'll have to listen to a long recapitulation to find this out and the whole feel of it is disappointing.

Even if we have had some clues and ought to have realized he was in those bushes, surprise is not much fun. The stage and the motion picture have no luck with it. The audience can't turn back to page forty-two and see the clue that wasn't noticed at the time, and it gets no satisfaction out of having been roundly fooled, as is possible in the "mystery." You mustn't keep a secret from the audience, they say.

No; to feel suspense, quite a different thing from surprise, we have to know all along that the hero is a possible source of help and know what he is doing. Then, as we begin to get worried about which is going to get there first, the hero or the train, our suspense is greater. But this is still too simple. There is still a question of waiting until the author gets around to telling us who won the race. It is suspense of a kind, but not the most excruciating kind.

So what more must there be? We already have someone we like in peril of something we fear, and there is a time limit, and we can see that the addition of hope is the significant factor. The technique of suspense is the juggling of these things. To juggle, you must have at least three balls. So we juggle hope, fear, and time, and it is the surging in and out of hope that does it.

Let's weave some suspense around our heroine now. We're crazy about her. She's a darling. The villain has tied her there and the train is coming. She struggles but cannot get away. What if the hero doesn't know a thing about it? He's right around the bend, in the town; he'd save her in a minute, brave fellow, but he thinks she's home doing the dishes or something. Ah-ha . . . throw in another character, the jealous woman who has seen the poor girl's plight. Will she tell? No, because she hates the girl. For a moment we hoped, but there is no hope in her. Wait . . . the girl's horse (this whole thing has a western flavor, somehow, so there should be a horse) . . . the girl's horse is loose and wanders toward the settlement. Surely somebody will figure she's on foot and maybe hurt. No, alas, it is the villain's henchman who finds the horse and hides it. Hope is dashed. . . . Hold on . . . the jealous woman has let on to an old bum. He, feeble, a character without credit, a born liar, is trying to convince the station agent that the train must not go through. Alas, the agent thinks he is drunk or crazy and time's a-wasting. . . . Just a minute . . . villain and hero meet, and the villain (egoist of course) is so foolish as to betray his triumph. Is the hero getting suspicious? Good, good, at least the hero begins to look for the girl.

But the train goes by the station and the old bum has been thrown out into the dust. No hope there. Yet, who but the hero (kindly, of course) picks the bum out of the dust and now is informed. Hope rises! Too late? No, now they can throw the switch and send the train on another track. . . . Wait, the villain has just found out that the jealous woman knows all and has told. With evidence so black against him he'd better rescue the girl and yet get rid of her just the same. The hero has caught the train by hard riding and swings up on the caboose. The villain is dragging the girl over to the *other* track, on which the train *now* approaches. The hero is working his way to the engineer's cab. Hope? Hope? No, the brakeman conscientiously starts slugging this unofficial passenger. Alas, alas . . .

The jealous woman is there at the tracks and she sees the villain apparently *saving* her hated rival. Is there hope in this? No, because. . . . Wait, yes . . . No. Yes . . .

That's how it goes.

Fear and hope . . .

There are all kinds of things wrong with this piece of fast ad-libbing, but ridiculous as the exaggeration may be, it serves as well or perhaps better than a more sober example to illustrate my contention that suspense is made out of fear, time, and hope, and the most important of these is hope.

Well, we'll leave the little lady on the railroad track. We must move into a world that is not gas-lit any more. Nowadays we would have to consider the engineer who is on the job and equipped with modern safety devices. We must add a lot of the "ologys"—foremost, psychology, and on top of that, technology, criminology, sociology, even economics and political ideology. There must be a deepening and a widening of the components of the story; there has to be a relationship to the real world as it is now. Yet the basic elements are still there.

The more this rising and falling of fright and hope depend upon character, upon action and reaction between people, resting solidly upon the kind of people they are, and less upon accidents of attention, or arbitrary rulings about the outcomes of fights and races, the better the quality of the suspense will be. When it is a question of a certain blindness of judgment and the reader is plugging for the hero to wake up and see the truth that he, the reader, knows already, or when it is a question of the villain betraying himself sooner or later by a weakness about which the reader is informed, or when it is a question of a latent heroism developing under stress—then we are pleased to lend ourselves to the manipulations of the author and enjoy it.

Our neon world is just as full of suspense as any other. Furthermore, although the riddle is spoiled when you've heard the answer, and the surprise surprises only once, a good suspense story operates, even though you've read the book before. So curious is the suspension in which he is held, the reader can know exactly how it all comes out and still be caught up in the razzle-dazzle of the proceedings.

3 TRICKS AND TRAPS IN WRITING SUSPENSE FICTION

by *Jean L. Backus*

DESPITE THE CRIES of some intellectual writers who often have nothing to say and say it beautifully, certain writers of suspense fiction continue to publish in a world where the market has grown increasingly crowded. Why is this? How do they manage to put out book after book which people buy eagerly and read with enthusiasm? And why is it that certain publishing writers fail when they turn to the suspense field? I think it is because they do not understand that suspense, while motivating all fiction, can be enjoyed for its own sake. A writer's ability to generate this special thrill of vicarious pain or pleasure in a reader depends on learning useful tricks and avoidable traps and applying them deliberately to any story material, right from the beginning.

The long realistic or straight novel can wind down to a quiet close if a writer wants it to, but not the suspense novel. Most of us have panted with fright as we cheered the hero or hissed the villain in a thriller, only to shut the book with a sense of disappointment because the writer has let us down with an ending of less impact than the story's problem demanded and unworthy of its development. Yet a simple trick can avoid this plotting trap. At the onset of an idea for a brilliant opening, incredible situation, fascinating character, or fabulous gimmick, the writer explores every possible ending, however unlikely, and selects the one which is realistically inevitable and won't let his reader down. From the very first word, the writer will know where the plot is going and will develop the material with the single purpose of reaching that goal. Never mind if readers hate the ending; reason and logic will convince them that this particular story could end in no other way.

On the other hand, the writer who begins with a perfect ending and then must find a story to go with it has the problem of providing a good opening. The sprawling family saga may start with a character's birth, but for a suspense novel, the moment just before, or the moment which actually precipitates the action is the moment to begin the story. Often a character arrives or departs, is sent on a mission, finds a body, is accused of a crime or plans a crime. . . . The variations are many, each one designed to lure the readers from TV or any other endeavor and engross them for several hours. In addition, planting the big clue to the solution as soon as possible is a trick almost certain to guarantee the reader will be fooled but will not feel foolish or betrayed when everything becomes clear.

Before the beginning

What about events leading up to and necessary to explain this critical moment of action? Flashbacks used soon after the opening take care of them, but there is a trap inherent in flashbacks: they may put so much information into the fabric of the story that it tears holes in the continuity, stops the action, and breaks the tension of the opening. Flashbacks must be compressed and confined to information essential for understanding the threat to the character, the nature of the story problem, and/or predicting the solution. Is there a special technique or trick that can be used to give essential information without using a genuine flashback? There is: *a glancing reference.*

Sometimes this is a paragraph or two of narrative; sometimes no more than a few words in the character's thoughts or dialogue. For example, "That part of the itinerary Sheila approved heartily. She and her ex-husband had stayed at the Carlton in London a year ago. Now it would take most of her first alimony check to pay for a suite, but she deserved a celebration." Unless the ex-husband threatens Sheila or influences what will happen to her, the reader doesn't have to know much more about him. Conversely, should the ex-husband be an important influence or be destined to appear later on in the story, this type of glancing reference throughout can describe and characterize him so thoroughly that his appearance, while it may come as a surprise, will not shock the reader.

There is also the *plot step,* the small propellant that ends a scene or chapter and sends the reader urgently on to find out what happens next. The opposite of flashback, this is foreshadowing with a vengeance, sometimes a page long, sometimes only a paragraph, or even a few words, such as, "Billy heard the shots in the distance. Coming closer." Can anyone bear not to find out if the guns are coming for Billy? Often the plot step can utilize speculation by a character, a good trick for misleading the reader. For instance, "She wondered if John would be calm or violent when he came home. Violent, probably, he usually was." It is acceptable then if the character (and therefore the reader) guesses wrong and John shows up in a calm mood.

Progressive complications

With the opening and the ending of a story worked out, the writer must still avoid the trap of creating complications that are fascinating but do not pertain to the main plot or lead to the chosen solution. "Because of this, that happened . . ." is a simple phrase, but it guarantees that each complication will evolve naturally and inevitably from the one before it.

I used that formula in plotting *Traitor's Wife.* Because Neal

Borden had murdered their son, his wife Della subconsciously wanted to kill him. Because Neal defected to the USSR, she agreed to accompany Peter Wing to a rendezvous arranged for their own reasons by the Russians. Because Peter was threatened en route, he killed his Russian contact. Because this aroused doubts of his loyalty, another agent was sent to kill Peter. Because this agent tried to rape Della, she killed him in Munich. Because they had to flee from the Bavarian police . . . and so on and on, until the end. Because Peter Wing's cover as a double agent was blown, the story ended happily. Did she kill her husband as foretold in the opening? No. But she had her reasons because of . . . .

This trick is extremely useful for developing or changing a character's motivation. Every detail from bald pate to gilded toenail may be necessary to show what the character looks like, but unless the reader understands why that character reacts as he does to the complications of the story, he won't come alive or convince the reader.

Take a ballerina, for instance, like my main character in *Dusha*. Kedrovna was dedicated to her dancing and devoted to Russia. She could conceive of no reason which would induce her to defect to the West. But because she was arrested and confined in a hospital, because her lover disappeared, and because she was threatened with banishment to Siberia (although innocent of all charges), she finally decided to abandon her homeland.

There is also a trick to choosing the right viewpoint character from which to tell a suspense story. The writer must examine the story material and discover the one person who is closest to the drama, most affected by the conflict, in the greatest danger, or who holds the key to the solution. Alternatively, the writer can choose the person from whom the most information must be hidden, who must go the farthest distance in solving the problem, or expend the greatest effort to bring the story to its close. Either way, the writer will have chosen the viewpoint which best exploits the material and generates the greatest drama.

Playing upon emotions

Next to plot and character motivation, the use of emotion produces the strongest suspense. Not only should the suspense fiction writer play upon various character responses, but also upon the responses of readers—their curiosity, anticipation, and their ultimate satisfaction. Readers must be made to experience vicariously the emotions aroused by the situation and by those who live through it. The trick lies in dealing honestly and realistically with the causes and effects of every action. The trap lies in dealing lightly with serious causes, or presenting effects out of all proportion to the cause. Sentimentality or melodrama or both can result if the writer does not avoid the overuse of adverbs, especially in action scenes, and exaggerated emotional effects in dramatic clashes. If a person tosses off an assault as a joke, or regards a missed appointment as serious as finding a body, false emotion will be generated. On the other hand, the judicious use of secondary causes can build more emotion than is otherwise possible. If the intended victim of murder is already condemned by a terminal illness, the effect of threat and approaching danger is doubled. But one should be cautious about piling it on until murder looks preferable to what the character already has to contend with.

Fair—and unfair—game

Achieving credibility in suspense fiction is one of the thorniest problems for writers. Readers will suspend disbelief to a certain extent, but it's unfair to ask the impossible of them unless the writer has made the impossible appear possible. The trick for accomplishing this depends on how much value a character places on life, property, power, revenge, or whatever, and how much he will risk to preserve or acquire his objective. If a boy climbs a dangerously steep cliff under no compulsion but his own desire to rescue a lamb, his climbing the cliff later to rescue a man who is being shot at will be credible. The trap of incredibility lies either in not showing the pattern of values and risks early enough, or in not showing it at all.

Writers may mislead readers *fairly,* with misinterpretation and misjudgment, disguise and diversion, or false deductions on the part of the characters, or by introducing new evidence or additional crimes; almost anything can be used—except a lie on the part of the writer. And almost anything can be told casually to the readers, if a startling development or a compelling piece of action follows at once, because readers, to one degree or another, read in order to be misled, or perversely, to trap the writer. But readers are subject to knee-jerk reactions as well. Show a character doing something foul, and right away the reader wants to hate that person and believe him guilty of every crime imaginable. But should such a character turn out to be the good guy after all, the writer had better have a reasonable explanation for the earlier bad behavior.

In a day when readers demand real blood instead of ketchup and real sex instead of drawn curtains and three dots, a writer has to decide for himself how much or how little of either to include in a novel. The trick is for the writer to make the sex or the violent scene, or any other scene, for that matter, earn its right to be dramatized. Let that scene reveal character, project future development, hide clues or plants, or end in a conclusive decision or act, but whatever it does, make it work to advance the story. The trap is to put in a scene purely for shock value, even if it stops the action and thus ruins the pace.

In the first draft, pacing should be ignored, since inspiration should not be sacrificed to reason. Normal rewriting and revision, the deepening and expansion of motives and explanations, the dramatizing of scenes passed over, plus the removal of excess wordage, repetitions, insignificant details, irrelevancies, or any other story stopper, usually takes care of pacing. But if the story seems to move too rapidly, the trick is to add complications, delay and retard the action, insert roadblocks to the solution, always making certain these are genuine and relate to the plot line. Conversely, if the story moves too slowly, remove excessive complications, combine those which closely resemble one another, and condense and cut once again. The story will then be so taut that not a single word could be cut without destroying the whole effect.

When planning is carefully and completely thought out, when writing is honest and realistic, suspense and tension are achieved by continuity, consistency, and clarity. Readers then unaware of traps avoided and tricks used will finish the story or close the book with a genuine sigh of satisfaction and pleasure.

4

THE MAN IN THE CLOSET
by *Cecilia Bartholomew*

THE *known is more suspenseful than the unknown.* Answer True or False. Offhand you'd say "false," wouldn't you? But there is nothing offhand about suspense writing—which is what we are really talking about. And, you were wrong: the opening statement is true. Take, for instance, the man in the closet.

What man? Well, that's just the point. You didn't see him go into the closet. You don't know he's there. You see Marilyn come home to her apartment with her escort. You see them say a tender good night at the door. Jeff wants to come in for a while, but Marilyn is a nice girl; besides, the landlord doesn't allow male visitors after midnight, and she says a firm no. Jeff leaves and Marilyn goes in, shuts the door, fixes the latch. She takes off her coat, walks into the bedroom, puts her hand on the closet door to open it, and out jumps the man.

Great stuff, you say. It made your hair stand on end. Your heart gave a big jump and is still beating hard. You could not wait to read on. Well, naturally, you were surprised. Nobody said you wouldn't be surprised. The unknown does surprise; it does shock. But we're talking about suspense. Suppose you *see* the man go into the closet to hide. You know he is there! All right, let's write it.

The apartment is empty; only one lamp is left burning. Marilyn has gone out for an evening on the town with Jeff. In the waiting silence, you see the fire escape window slowly open, and a man climbs over the sill. His precautions tip you off to the fact that he is an intruder. He hardly has time to look around the joint before you (and he) hear voices, and it is apparent that Marilyn and Jeff are returning earlier than expected. The intruder tiptoes hastily into the bedroom, jumps into the clothes closet, and closes the door just as Marilyn unlocks the front door.

It seems that our friend Jeff has been pushing things a little too fast, and Marilyn, being a nice girl, will have none of that. Jeff apologizes, says he should have known better, and won't she please give him another chance. ("Give him another chance," you hiss urgently, "Keep him around. There's a man in your closet.") Marilyn considers, decides to give him another chance. (You breathe a sigh of relief.) But not tonight, she says, tomorrow evening. ("You idiot," you shout, helplessly mute. And at the same time you're frantically coaching Jeff to charm her, to overwhelm her, to do anything that he has to do, but just stay around to protect her.) Jeff seems to catch something in the atmosphere; at any rate he hesitates, he wants to stay—but his cheek is still red. And Marilyn, innocent and a bit smug, determined to teach him a lesson, is closing the door in his face. ("All right," you mutter, "take the consequences. It's not my funeral." But the point is that you know the man is in the closet, and so in a sense it is your funeral.)

Marilyn takes off her coat and starts into the bedroom. ("Don't put it in the closet," you shout impotently. Well, thank God for small favors, she isn't one of those neat dames who have to hang up something the minute they take it off.) Marilyn drops her coat on the couch and goes toward the kitchen, but on the way, she notices the open window. You can see her thinking, did she leave it open? ("Of course you didn't," you warn her. "Think! What does an open window mean? Go for help!") But instead, she merely closes the window and goes for a glass of milk. (While she's at the refrigerator, you keep an eye on the closet door. You see it open stealth-ily, and you see the intruder slip out. Perhaps he'll exit without her even knowing he has been there, without doing what he came to do. Despite your relief from suspense, you're a trifle disappointed.) But Marilyn doesn't drink the glass of milk in the kitchen. She carries it with her. She'll drink it after she gets into bed. (*If* she ever gets into bed.) Hearing her foot-steps, the intruder pops back into the closet. (And you're back in that delicious agony again.)

The concealed and the revealed

We could go on stretching out the suspense just as long as your nerves will stand it. Every time Marilyn approaches the closet, you expect the intruder to jump out at her. You plead with her to stay away from danger. Before the writer is through with you, you don't care what happens, so long as the suspense is relaxed. That's the Known!

Obviously there doesn't always have to be a man in the bed-room closet, but there had better be something in the closet besides clothes, even Paris models. You will arouse more sus-pense if you will show early in your story what is there than if you keep it hidden, unknown, and let it jump out at the reader. To paraphrase E. M. Forster, if you have only sus-pense, you don't have a very good story; but if you don't have suspense, you don't have a story at all. Suspense, to me, is synonymous with plot. It isn't the unique province of the "sus-pense writer." All writers must live in that country.

Take, for example, that "practically perfect novel," *The Light in the Piazza,* by Elizabeth Spencer. (The quotation is from *The New Yorker.*) Where would the suspense have been if we had been kept ignorant, until after the wedding, of the pertinent fact that the bride because of a tragic accident had only the mind of a ten-year-old? But no one would dream of concealing that information, you say? Well, just for an experiment, get out some of your rejects and reread them. You may be surprised. Are you sure you have always allowed the reader to see the man hide in the closet? It is unbelievable how difficult it is sometimes to get a student writer (or any writer at times) to say what his story is about—to say it clearly, and openly, and as early in the story as possible; for the short story that means on the first page, in the first paragraph, in the first sentence.

Not "what" happens, but "how"

If suspense lies in the known, another truth emerges: the reader's interest then must lie not in what is going to happen, but how it is going to happen. I have no mind for figures, so I won't hazard a guess as to how many basic plots the experts say there are; but I do remember that they say there aren't many. I'd go further. I'd say that there is only one. When people use "formula" in the pejorative sense, they are speaking out of prejudice. Take any great love story, *Tristan and Isolde, Anna Karenina,* or the latest movie (good or bad). The formula is the known one: boy meets girl, boy falls for girl, boy fears he is going to lose girl, boy finally wins her, and they live happily ever after *or* he does lose her. If you substitute for the word "girl," job or fame, or "quest" for treasure or truth or life, I believe you will just about have taken care of all the story plots in literature.

The important step is that third one: boy fears he is going to lose. Here is the conflict. This is where the suspense lies. In other words, stories are about people, and people are interesting only when they are in trouble, or in conflict. (And that is a reflection that can stop us for a long echoing moment.) Classically there are three basic kinds of conflict: man against man, man against nature or conditions, man against himself. The important thing here is that the fighters must be evenly matched. No fight is any better than its principals. A thrown fight has no interest at all; neither has one that is too heavily weighted for or against one or the other combatant. We will feel sympathy for the underdog, but we have no interest in the fight; we just want it to be over.

It is the same in a story. Do your hero the courtesy of providing him with a worthy opponent, be it another man, the elements, or fate, or himself. In every good story (of whatever genre), there comes a place where the action hangs in balance, where the story can go in either direction, where the outcome is in question. This is the third step of the formula: boy (but let him be a man) fears he is going to lose. Will he or won't he? To be or not to be? Whether he is Shakespeare or the author of a thriller, the writer must make the reader question, worry. If the reader worries, if he identifies with the protagonist's fears, he will read on until he finds out what happens. So, prolong the suspense; stretch it out as far as you can, but—don't let it break.

The importance of timing

We speak of "timing" often in regard to performers. Timing is just as important for the writer as it is for the actor. Perhaps this goes back to the time when the storyteller narrated his stories by mouth, not typewriter, when he was an actor. You must play a scene for all it is worth, you must build the suspense as high as it will go, but you must not try to take it one step higher than the reader will go with you.

Put it another way. Remember the old story about the ghosts? If one ghost is scary, two ghosts will be twice as scary —but ten ghosts won't be scary at all; they'll be humorous, or ludicrous, or boring; they'll destroy the illusion and catapult the reader back into real life. Say that you have our interest because of your heroine's plight. Her husband, the heel, has deserted her with a small infant to care for. Suspense: Is she going to be able to keep the child or not? You can build the suspense by revealing that she has been accused of being unfit to raise a child; perhaps she is in a dubious profession. You might build the suspense further by making her physical condition precarious. She has never fully recovered from the difficult childbirth. *But* don't lay her low with cancer, or anything else truly critical, because, though this could happen in real life and we would give her our sympathy, in fiction our suspense will collapse. We know then for sure that she is not going to manage to keep the child.

A good story always has a man in the closet. In the entertainment story, it is enough to see the intruder hide in the closet and to wait with mounting suspense for the moment when he jumps out. In stories of more lasting value, the writer must make it clear why the man is in the closet, and the better the reason, the better the story.

The essence of tragedy is inevitability—when an irresistible force meets an immovable object (*Romeo and Juliet*). The essence of comedy is not so different. It is the breaking of the mold, but it is inevitable also. Take the clown in the circus: We know he can't ride the horse bareback, or walk the high wire. As soon as he gets up there, we know he is going to fall, and we wait for him to fall so that we can laugh. The wait during which he almost falls but doesn't quite is the period of suspense that makes the fall funnier.

The reader must be told in the very first paragraph what must happen; then it is the writer's task to keep him hoping against hope to the very last paragraph that it won't happen. This is the story that we'd all like to write.

5
ELEMENTS OF THE POLICE PROCEDURAL NOVEL
by *Rex Burns*

GIVEN THE development of the writer's sense of which words live and which don't—a development that for me comes as much through reading as through writing—I think the areas most pertinent to a successful police procedural are four: research, setting, plot, and character.

These divisions are, of course, artificial. As in any "recipe," the elements blend and influence each other; and in any art such as cooking or writing, the whole is greater than the sum of its parts. But though each writer must discover for himself this sense of life or wholeness, some of the basic elements contributing to it can be distinguished. Let's begin with research.

Research and the search for stories

The kind of research I favor is quite basic: my main source for information is the daily newspaper. I figure that if a newspaper article about a crime interests me, it will interest other readers. Naturally, the newspaper story must undergo a metamorphosis before it comes out as fiction. For one thing, there are the questions of libel and plagiarism; and, for another, too great a reliance on the facts as reported can cause a story to become quickly dated.

More important is the question of a good yarn—an inter-

27

esting newspaper article is only a germ, a bud. It provides a sequence of events and an indication of setting for the full-grown fiction. For example, the following paragraph from a UPI newswire release was the nucleus of a chapter of a novel I was working on: "The raids in Cordoba began when a small airplane, circling the city to apparently coordinate the attacks, threw a bomb that exploded without causing injuries near a provincial bank about 11 a.m." In short, a newspaper article can provide a rich source of actual what's, where's, and when's. The why's and the who's are the novelist's responsibility.

A second good source of information for the police procedural writer is court records. Affidavits, depositions, and transcripts—in addition to the writer sitting in on court hearings—help provide not only events and incidental tidbits for a story, but also the language of narration. Increasingly, a cop, especially a senior officer such as a detective, must understand the technology of the law. Every technology has its jargon, and this can be found in legal records and in courtrooms.

Both newspaper stories and court records are as valuable for what they leave out as for what they offer. To get some of that which is left out, read the story with the questions "how?" and "why?" in mind. For instance, that favorite phrase of reporters, "police, acting on a tip from an informant . . ." gives rise to such questions as: Which policeman? Who was the informant? What incentive did he have for informing? What kind of communication—telephone, written, conversational? Who believed the informant? Who didn't? How much time passed between the tip and the raid? etc., etc. These and similar questions come up when the novelist begins creating the fictional world which will embody any actual events he chooses to use.

Interviews

Though the writer's imagination furnishes the answers to such questions as those asked above, that imagination can be stimulated by a third kind of research which I've found to be most beneficial: interviewing. A policeman, like almost everyone else, enjoys talking about his work, and most municipalities have programs for bettering police-community relations. And a writer—despite what his neighbors may think—is a member of the community. In a larger town, check with the department's public information office. Departments in smaller towns tend to be less formal, and I think somewhat less accessible, perhaps because their manpower tends to be insufficient and the training less professional, generating a defensive attitude. The prosecutor's office and the sheriff's office are also worthwhile avenues of approach. For me, this interviewing tends to be quite casual and takes place during a duty watch; there's a lot of time for conversation during eight hours of riding in a patrol car.

Armed with some specific questions derived from reading newspapers and reports, the interviewer can start filling in those blanks found in the documents. The answers don't have to be related to the same cases read about—in fact, I like it better if they aren't. The novelist deals with probability, and patterns of common behavior offer more freedom for the invention of particulars than does the mere reporting of facts, which is where the journalist ends and the novelist begins. Unlike what takes place on most television talk shows, an interviewer-novelist should be a good listener, and speaking for myself, a copious but surreptitious note-taker. It also helps to train your eye for such minutiae as manufacturer's labels, model numbers, organization charts—in short, anything that gives quick specific detail for your story's setting. Interviewing also provides the latest slang and technical jargon.

The manner of introducing those technical terms into the narrative varies. If a character honestly might not know what a particular device or procedural is called, he can simply ask someone in the story. The character and the reader become informed together. I use this device sparingly, since my characters in the Gabe Wager books are generally professional and well-trained. (Moreover, as a reader, I get damned irritated when a story's development is continually interrupted by some idiot who needs everything explained to him.) Another means of introducing technical terms is to use the phrase in normal dialogue and let the descriptive passage carry the explanation: " 'Let me have the Kell-Kit,' said Wager. Sergeant Johnston handed him the small body transmitter. . . ." Or, for variation, the equation may be reversed: " 'Let me have the body transmitter,' said Wager. Sergeant Johnston handed him the small Kell-Kit." I'm not sure if police departments have yet surpassed the federal government in the use of acronyms and arcane initials, but these are an essential part of bureaucratic jargon. It is a rule of thumb in writing first to use the full phrase, then, in the next sentence or two, the more common initials: "Wager turned to his little book of Confidential Informants. The first C. I. was. . . ." No explanatory passage is needed, and the action moves without interruption.

Research, then, is the foundation for the police procedural, and on that foundation are built the setting, plot, and character. Setting is, of course, easiest to create if it's well known to the writer. For the Gabriel Wager stories, that means Denver. Ironically, my editors more than once pointed out that a street which I invented wasn't on their map of Denver, or an odd-numbered address should be on the north rather than south side of a particular avenue. But the familiarity I mean is as much in flavor as in fact, and its manner of presentation is—for me—impressionistic. The single well-chosen detail that captures the flavor of the setting and gives focus and life to an otherwise sketchy scene is part of the economy I associate with the "grittiness" of a police procedural. A Gothic, a novel that explores states of mind, or a sci-fi fantasy may call for more sweeping and panoramic descriptions to create a mood or sustain a romance. But I find harmony between a spare style and the realistic police story. Since this descriptive technique tends to emphasize action rather than setting, and since a police procedural is akin to a report—and a report is usually about "what happened"—the emphasis on concrete and concise detail feels right to me.

What happens and why

The concern with what happened brings us to plot. Plot is not just *what* takes place but *why* it takes place. The police procedural may or may not use the mystery as the basis of suspense. If the police do not know who the perpetrator is, then unraveling the mystery becomes the plot—i.e., the gradual revelation of motive and opportunity. But often, in life as well as in fiction, the police do know who the villain is, and the plot centers on gathering enough evidence for a viable court case. The manner of getting this evidence is quite tedious and even dull—questioning fifty or a hundred witnesses, long hours of surveillance, studying accounting records. The problem for the storyteller in the police procedural field becomes one of remaining true to reality without boring the reader. One technique that fits the police procedural is focusing attention on new methods of surveillance or on the ever-changing avenues of legal presentation. Here, research is indispensable. Another device is to give your detective more cases than one. This is by no means unrealistic, but a good story requires that the cases somehow work together toward a single conclusion. That's the old demand of art for unity, a unity seldom apparent in real life.

Another very familiar technique for maintaining interest is the foil—someone who offers by-play for the protagonist. A foil should serve a variety of purposes, all contributing toward the unity of the novel. The character used as a foil—a rookie, for instance—may be not only a device for explaining police procedure, but can also reveal the protagonist's character through his reaction to the foil's activities.

Character development

I try to make character as interesting as case. The strongest novels are those with living characters to whom the action is vital, and this holds true for any tale, even plotless ones. But whether it's a who-done-it or a how-to-prove-it, the police story is fundamentally an action story, and in it the development of character should not impede the action. Ideally, character development and action should coincide; but where they do not, I tip the balance in favor of action, possibly because I envision the Gabe Wager series as one long novel of perhaps fifteen volumes, and this view gives me plenty of room to let the character grow.

There are several other concrete devices that aid the quick presentation of character without interrupting the action. One device especially useful for creating secondary characters is the "signature"—a distinctive act, speech pattern, or habit of thought that identifies and distinguishes one character from another. This signature may be simple: one secondary figure in my *The Alvarez Journal* smokes cigars, another has an old man's rumbling cough, a third speaks administrative jargon. Or, if the character is of more importance to the story, a combination of signatures may be used to flesh him out. At its worst, this device generates cliché characters—the western bad man with his black hat and sneer. At best, the signature makes the character become alive and individualized—the girth, thirst, and cowardice of Falstaff. The problem, of course, is to characterize without caricaturing—unless your aim is satire. The novelist's ability to create real characters can be improved by reading other writers who are very good at it: Shakespeare, Flaubert, Faulkner. Another means is "reading" friends and neighbors: What exactly is it that distinguishes one of your acquaintances from another? Given universal human qualities, what makes one individual different from another?

Minor and secondary characters, while absolutely necessary, do not give life to the action. Rarely can any story, police procedural or other, do without a protagonist. Again, because of the importance of action in police procedurals, the writer is faced with the need for an economical development of his main character. The technique I have chosen for my Gabe Wager series is by no means new: It's the familiar "recording consciousness" of Henry James, the restricted third-person point of view, in which every event and concept in the story is presented from the perspective of a single protagonist. I've found several advantages to this device: the action proceeds and the protagonist's character is revealed at the same time. The reader is faced with the same limitations of knowledge as the protagonist, and thus the element of suspense is heightened. Using third person rather than first person puts distance between the reader and the protagonist and offers another dimension to the story, which helps carry the reader through those necessary and authentic but often slow stages of a case's development.

This narrative technique also has shortcomings. The author can't give the reader any information that the protagonist does not have, thus leaving little chance for irony or depth. For this point of view to work, the author must also have a total understanding of the protagonist, which, while it may not be relevant to the story, nonetheless is necessary to having the character's actions consistent.

First-person narration achieves many of the same results but brings an even closer identification between author and character. Think of the popular image of Mickey Spillane, for example. I prefer third person because it enforces objectivity and quite possibly because, unlike Gabe Wager, I'm not a good cop.

Focusing all the action through Wager's perspective, then, contributes to a unity of action and characterization in which action dominates but character development follows quite closely and, I hope, unobtrusively. I try to achieve this by placing a heavy emphasis on dialogue. By its very nature, dialogue is dramatic—the characters are onstage talking rather than being talked about by a narrator. Again, the signature is very important, and I play a little game of trying to see how many lines of dialogue I can put together without having to state who is speaking. The idea is that each character's voice should be distinct enough to indicate the speaker.

I place the police procedural in the category of literary realism. The contemporary, the probable, the routine, determine my choice of a realistic subject. Once I select my subject, the elements of research, setting, plot, and character are indispensable, and in my Gabe Wager police procedurals, all of these elements must contribute to the action.

6

RESEARCH AND THE MYSTERY WRITER

by *Frances Crane*

NOT LONG AGO, I read a piece by a successful mystery writer in which he said, "The only research I need for a novel is a good non-fiction article about my background and a map." I was filled with envy. The novel he referred to was laid in Hong Kong, and I was at that moment up to my ears in research for a Hong Kong story, even though I had spent three weeks there. When I was in Hong Kong, however, I had not planned to use it as a background for a story. I had kept my usual notes—not a diary, just impressions of the city and items of interest from day to day. Just by chance, I had also talked with the Superintendent of the Criminal Investigation Department of the Hong Kong police. After leaving Hong Kong, I stopped in London for two months. When I reached New York, my editor suggested I do a story with a Hong Kong setting. Remembering my packet of notes, I said I could.

Authentic backgrounds

Backgrounds for me must be as authentic as possible, but no two people see a city in the same way. Also, cities change every day, especially a city like Hong Kong, where there is very rapid change in sections frequented by travelers. I like to use genuine places, streets, hotels, and so on. This gives substance and reality to a story. In my Hong Kong book, my hero stayed at the Peninsula Hotel in Kowloon, across the harbor from Victoria, the capital of the Colony. To many thousands of travelers, the Peninsula means Hong Kong Colony. Many beautiful new hotels have been built, but none has the associations and history of the Peninsula.

I had still another reason for having my hero stay at the Peninsula. So many of the attractions are on the Island of Hong Kong and in or around Victoria that he had constantly to use the Star Ferry for pedestrians. In Victoria are many of the more famous restaurants, night clubs, the stair-stepped passages called "ladder streets," markets, the Tiger Balm Gardens with their Chinese horrors in paint and plaster, the Wan Chai section where the sailors hang out. The Peak Tram goes at a dizzying angle to the top of the Peak with its superb views of the harbor and of many other islands. Around Hong Kong Island are fantastic colonies of sampans in which the Boat People live. Near these are the Floating Restaurants. And every time one uses the ferry, one has fresh views of the harbor and the cities around it.

The huge lobby of the Peninsula is itself fabulous. People of all races and colors, often in their national dress, sit around this lobby having tea or drinking martinis, Scotch, or the Hong Kong tipple called the gimlet. It's a good show just to watch, and many do.

When in Hong Kong I was doing tourist things as a tourist. But when I go to a place with a story in mind, I make notes specifically for that purpose. I plan the story either before or after I get there. But in this case, since I had not intended to set a story in Hong Kong, I made notes, out of habit, and collected booklets and maps and such for my own use.

Some English friends rushed me around to places I might not otherwise have seen. One day they took me to the South China Seas Club where the sailors of all nations meet. There was an American carrier in the harbor just then, and thousands of our boys in their whites were to be found everywhere. When I left my friends, I noticed across a narrow street a tall white building, police headquarters for the Colony.

The British take great interest in police procedure. The police issue booklets and write articles about their work. These can usually be had for little or nothing, and I crossed the street to the big modern building to ask what was available. When I said I was a writer of "thrillers," a clerk at an information desk sent me up to the Criminal Investigation Department. A Chinese policeman in uniform showed me to an office with a Superintendent's name on the door. This is a rank in English police organization a notch or two above Inspector. The Superintendent—an Englishman—received me most cordially, asked if I would like tea, and in a moment large cups of black tea, with milk and sugar, were brought in.

It was eleven in the morning, an hour in which the Peninsula lobby would be filled with both Westerners and Orientals, many drinking pale tea from tiny cups without handles. Tea is always *de rigueur* at any hour in Hong Kong. The English Superintendent was, however, having his own variety of tea.

I always call on the police of a particular city when I plan to set a story there. In this case, however, I felt I shouldn't take the Superintendent's time. I stayed a very short while. He said that homicide was not a major problem in Hong Kong, commenting further that in an American city of that size, there would have been many more murders. He also said that booklets on all kinds of local activities, including one on police organization and their work in the previous year, could be had at the main post office. I thanked the Superintendent, went on my way, and later on picked up the police reports along with other booklets about Hong Kong.

In one way or another, I accumulated a lot of printed matter, just in case I might need it; I had my hotel ship all of this material home, along with my personal notes. And when I arrived home—after telling my editor I would do a Hong Kong story—the printed matter was there. But I never received my notes.

I felt lost. I have a photographic memory for places, and a very bad one for the names of streets, or how much time is necessary for this or that. I began to read everything I could about the Hong Kong Colony. The public library was especially useful in getting material for me from the Merchants and Mechanics Research Library in San Francisco. I ordered from Hong Kong the newspapers covering the period of time I decided to use, and I bought three handsome volumes on customs and superstitions, also printed in Hong Kong. From these expensive volumes, I found only one half-page of any use. Burial urns, in which the bones of Chinese wait for transportation to various ancestral graveyards, stand along the border between the Colony and Red China. I intended to use one of these for something nefarious. That didn't work out. My costly information on burial urns wound up as a spot of atmosphere.

In a very short time, I had too much material, which may be almost as bad as doing a fictional story based on somebody else's factual article and a map. But much of this research was necessary to confirm and revive my remembered impressions.

Some may say of foreign backgrounds, "Why bother? Most readers will never go there, so why does it matter?" Well, it matters to those who *do* go. And, as a writer, it matters to me.

Even when a story is to be located in the next town, county or state, I find it essential to visit my intended background and to check on police procedure (which differs from place to place) in cases of murder. Arrangements can be made to visit the crime laboratories of large city or state police departments to learn about actual methods of criminal investigation. Usually in small towns and rural communities, the county sheriff handles homicide. In a city large enough for an extensive police force, such a job may go to a chief of police or the homicide department. But recently, in Phoenix, Arizona, a large city, I found that the sheriff investigates murder anywhere in the city and county. In some states the state patrol takes charge. All units may cooperate; the Federal Bureau of Investigation comes in when a case falls into one of its special categories.

So when I visit a place to learn how it looks, sounds, smells and feels, I also go to talk to the police. They will all tell me that fictional crime is a far cry from the real thing, but I've never had an instance in which they didn't like to talk about their own investigations.

Book research fills in where personal experience stops. (I personally need both.) Some knowledge of human anatomy, as well as facts about poisons, ballistics, and other information regarding murder methods, is useful and can be found in books —the best being those from medical libraries. (A doctor or lawyer in the family can be very handy.) But remember—most experienced crime writers stick to simple means of doing away with their imaginary victims. It is easier that way than to devise some unheard-of method for variety.

An affiliate membership in the Mystery Writers of America in New York City brings you their newsletter, "The Third Degree," which often includes articles by experts in crime investigation. In addition, there are many books on police procedure and criminal investigation available in the public library. A few of these titles follow:

MODERN CRIMINAL INVESTIGATION. *By Harry Soderman and John J. O'Connell. 5th Ed. Revised by Charles E. O'Hara.* (Funk & Wagnalls)

PRACTICAL FINGERPRINTING. *By B. C. Bridges. Revised by Charles E. O'Hara.* (Funk & Wagnalls)

THE HUMAN BODY. *By Isaac Asimov.* (Houghton Mifflin)

TWELVE AGAINST CRIME. *By Edward D. Radin.* (Collier Books)

LEGAL MEDICINE, PATHOLOGY, AND TOXICOLOGY. *By Gonzales, Vance, Helpern, and Umburger. 2nd Ed.* (Appleton-Century-Crofts)

MOSTLY MURDER. *By Sir Sydney Smith.* (Doubleday)

TECHNIQUES OF CRIME SCENE INVESTIGATION. *By Arne Svensson and Otto Wendel. 2nd Revised and Expanded American Ed.* (Elsevier)

SCOTLAND YARD: *A Study of the Metropolitan Police. By Peter Laurie.* (Holt, Rinehart & Winston, Inc.)

ENCYCLOPEDIA OF MYSTERY & DETECTION. *By Chris Steinbrunner and Otto Penzler.* (McGraw-Hill)

7

THE "I-CAN'T-PUT-IT-DOWN" FACTOR

by *Babs H. Deal*

ALTHOUGH I have published eleven novels and only three of them are, strictly speaking, in the suspense genre, almost always when I meet readers at a literary gathering they'll say to me, "Oh, yes. You write suspense novels, don't you?" At first, this may seem to be a put-down, but it is not: Americans are inordinately fond of suspense novels, as a glance at the best-seller list will tell you. More than likely, the speaker has read one of my three suspense novels and possibly some of the others, too. But it is the suspense novel he or she remembers.

Actually, any good or successful novel should qualify as a suspense novel. It should have the elements that keep the reader burning the midnight oil—the narrative drive that keeps him turning the pages. I would define a suspense novel as one in which the author knows something the reader does not and conceals it from the reader as long as possible. This is true whether the book is a murder mystery, a spy story, a ghost story, a Gothic romance, or has that more indefinite quality which might simply be termed Menace.

Some authors write suspense exclusively; others, whose main body of work is the mainstream or straight novel, produce an occasional suspense novel.

Almost everyone would agree that the I-can't-put-it-down factor is the most vital element in the suspense novel. How

41

does a writer inject this into a novel? I'm not sure I have the faintest idea. I've been reading Agatha Christie since childhood and think I've read all of them twice, even though murder mysteries are supposed to be one-time things. One of my happiest moments came when I saw the movie of her *Murder on the Orient Express;* although I remembered "whodunit," I'd forgotten the intricacies of the plot and was able to enjoy them all over again.

Christie is, of course, a puzzle writer, and it is her amazing and unique ability to give you all the pieces and still lead you down the garden path. She fools you—and makes you like to be fooled. You feel cheated if you figure the puzzle out before the end.

John D. MacDonald, on the other hand, whose fifty-plus books I have also read, makes no attempt deliberately or diabolically to construct this elaborate jigsaw. The puzzle is there, but he seems to be saying, "O.K., figure it out if you want to. I don't care; I've got you hooked anyway." And he has.

Beginning with a character

The initial ideas for my suspense novels tend to be characters, though often the characters and what they are going to do are so interwoven, it is hard to say which came first. For my suspense novels, the beginning idea is more likely to contain plot than my regular novels are. For most of my novels, I can vividly remember the first moment I became aware of their presence. This is certainly true of my first suspense novel, *Fancy's Knell*. I had spent a summer which turned my thoughts generally to a kind of life and happening taking place in America today. But the idea itself came to me instantaneously as I was waiting on a boat dock for my husband to come in from a day's fishing. He was very late, and I was worried because he was alone and there were no lights on his boat. As I gazed out over the darkening water, I realized I had the whole first chapter, the title, and the two main characters—one dead at the beginning of the novel, the other alive and ready to carry the story. The rest followed.

My second suspense novel, *The Crystal Mouse,* had a very similar inception. This time I was sitting on my terrace at dusk, looking out at a new high-rise. As darkness fell and lights began to come on in the neighborhood, I saw that there was only one lighted window in all that expanse of concrete and steel. One occupant for that enormous building! *The Crystal Mouse* grew from that point, although my character Sara came to me along with the initial idea as the only possible person living in that empty building.

Waiting to Hear from William, my latest suspense novel, began a little differently. The two main themes in it had been in my mind off and on over a period of years: one a private literary joke, the other a basic concept of ESP. I had never before considered turning either one into a novel. But again, several things occurred: a change of scene, a different tempo from that of my everyday life, and an encounter with a particularly charming and fey child who made me think of my own daughter and yet in no way resembled her. The two children began to haunt my mind so vividly I had to hang pictures of both on my office wall. *Waiting to Hear from William* was well on the way to coming to life, but that did not happen until a friend said, "Why don't you write a book with a happy ending?" *Voilà!* Everything came together, and I had another year's work ahead. Which is to say, it is very well to have an inspiration, but then you have to make it work.

The way it had to be

How does a writer accomplish this in a suspense novel? In some ways it is infinitely harder than writing a straight novel because of the necessity to hide facts from the reader. You simply cannot say in chapter one, "This is what I'm talking about; now I'll tell you how it happened." Instead, you have to keep your reader hanging on, page after page, chapter after chapter, and you hope that when he reaches the last page, he will not feel cheated, but will put the book down with a sigh and say, "Yes, that is the way it had to be!"

The best way to accomplish this is the same in writing any kind of novel—through character. If readers are interested in a character, they will be interested in what happens to her or him. They care and keep trying to find out how things are going to end for this new acquaintance, who is in a situation of danger, romance, horror, and menace.

With interest in the character established, the second thing you have to do is make the menace felt. The way to do it is to keep taking another trick out of the bag. If your basic character is good and your basic situation is valid, making readers feel menace is easier than it sounds. You'll find that different menaces keep popping out. However, it is not a good idea to bring out too many at once—save a few for the end of the chapters. This old Saturday serial effect still works, as it did in the days when we waited breathlessly to see what Fu Manchu was going to do to Nayland Smith next week.

In writing a suspense novel—as in all novels—there is the inevitable sag point, which usually occurs when you're about two-thirds of the way through the book. You've introduced the characters, you have the plot underway, you know how it's going to end. But you need another fifty pages or so Right Here. Now is the time to pull the rabbit out of the hat—to introduce a completely new twist. This can be a new character, a new or different way of looking at the situation, or even a hint, but only a hint, of what is going to happen at the end. It is well to be prepared and to know that at a certain point you are going to need that rabbit. Sometimes, you may even have to stop writing while you wait for him, but if you are really a writer, the rabbit will appear.

Now, you've found the rabbit, you're on your way to the solution, you've kept the readers with you all the way. You must not disappoint them. This does not necessarily mean you have fooled them, except, of course, in the puzzle mystery. But it does mean that you have not revealed everything to them. Let your readers feel, as they read your last chapter, that your ending was in the cards, but they couldn't have known it until the final deal.

Today, many readers want a message with their menace. This is fine. I wouldn't want to write menace without message; if you agree with this, you should try to interweave the message in a way that will not sound preachy. After all, fiction has always been a method of sugar-coating the pill. In *Fancy's Knell,* I tried to say something valuable about small towns, overaffluent families, permissive child-raising, and the over-expectations of the American dream. What I wrote was a suspense novel with elements of the puzzle-murder mystery. In *The Crystal Mouse,* I attempted to make a valid comment on high-rise apartments, widows, the plight of the woman with no resources of her own, dependent on the male. What I wrote was a suspense novel about one woman against loneliness and terror. My message in *Waiting to Hear from William* concerned ESP, writers, people who haven't learned to make commitments, and the dangers of prejudgment. What I wrote was a ghost story. What I am saying is that messages are fine, but don't let them kill the medium.

Suspense without violence

One more thing: There's a lot of talk about the prevalence of violence, and, admittedly, many suspense novels do contain violence. Mine don't. In fact, readers and reviewers note this one thing about my work—suspense without violence. It *is* possible to achieve this combination; whether a writer cares to do so or not is up to him. I might add, in spite of the fact that all of Agatha Christie's books are about murder, they are in essence non-violent.

My most successful novel, *The Walls Came Tumbling Down,* I do not consider a suspense novel at all, but many other people do. It is about seven women, one of whom put a dead baby in a sorority house wall during a long-ago summer of her youth. This book is to me a study of American marriage in seven incarnations. As I originally conceived the novel, any of the seven women could have committed the deed. I intended to keep the question of which one did unanswered, so that the readers could decide which one it was. The publishers felt that this was cheating the readers, and I rewrote the book with clues that pointed toward one particular woman as the person who did it. To this day, I receive letters from readers asking me which one it was. Does this mean that I, the writer, revealed in such a way as to conceal, and thus remained true to my original concept? Or does it mean that you can't change the life of the novel once it has begun to develop? It's interesting to speculate about this, but, like the novels discussed here, it remains a mystery.

8

IRONY AND SURPRISE
by *Stanley Ellin*

I AM A READER and writer of mystery stories who thinks that the works of Sir Arthur Conan Doyle are a monument to boredom. A pox, I say, on the posturing Holmes and the goggle-eyed Watson. Anathema to The Baker Street Irregulars, that unholy gang of worshipers at the shrine of Sherlock. The next time they drink a toast to him, may their wine turn to sarsaparilla in the glass!

Do I stand alone in this matter? I do not think so. A secret agent (he is allowed to keep ten percent of the information he brings me) recently mentioned other symptoms of revolt in the ranks, but I am not overly optimistic about them. The sad truth is that we anti-Holmesites are a rabbity breed of iconoclast, indeed, and I admit to being as long-eared and cotton-tailed as any. Not long ago, I let fall an unfavorable comment about the Master in the presence of a fellow mystery writer. Before I could say another word I was pierced by a look so terrible that I immediately slunk away to find solace among the potato chips and beer, and was mightily glad that I outweighed the enraged writer by some thirty pounds, or, as Holmes would say, two stone and thruppence. At even weights I was a goner, and knew it.

The trouble is that I discovered Holmes much too late in life. Sir Arthur is, of course, a highly satisfactory writer for the youthful audience which, in its innocence, may readily mistake

47

his cardboard figures for People, his tedious declamations for Dialogue, and his heavy-handed devices for Plotting. But the reader who is introduced to all this for the first time in his middle years will only be distressed by it. This reader is not only likely to be suffering from tired blood and constriction of the income tax; he has also had the chance, over the years, to read some mystery stories written for the adult audience. He will, after his initial plunge into Holmes, come to the surface wondering if someone is not playing a joke on him.

That is what happened to me. At the age of thirty-five— *midway in life's journey,* as Dante, a noted Italian mystery writer, phrased it—I was led by a friend to take the plunge. So keen is my regard for this man that he could have the Hathaway shirt off my back and the patch from my eye merely by crooking a finger at them, but before I was halfway through his Collected Works of Doyle I knew that even a friendship like ours had its limits. I returned his book and explained that he would have to take me Doyle-less, or not at all. We are still friends, I am glad to say, but no thanks to Sherlock Holmes for that.

Now, what is it about the Works which could lead to such a crisis? It is not, strangely enough, those little matters of characterization and style previously referred to, although they were certainly hard to take. But, I must confess, I read Henry James and Theodore Dreiser with pleasure, and there are times when they make Doyle's technique look positively graceful. No, what is lacking in Doyle is something of much greater importance. In a nutshell, his stories are all built on *surprise,* and, at the same time, are totally devoid of *irony.*

Surprises with significance

There is a vast distinction between surprise and irony. When you read *Gulliver's Travels* as a child (in a nicely expurgated edition, I trust), you read it for surprise, and through Swift's inventive genius you were provided with that on one page after another. When you reread the book as an adult, you read it for irony, and Swift's merciless opinions of 18th-century mankind provided that in full measure. You may gather from this that the difference between surprise and irony is akin to the difference between child and adult, and so it is. Or, in terms of the classic mystery story, it is the difference between Sir Arthur Conan Doyle and Edgar Allan Poe.

Doyle wrote a massive collection of short mystery stories, and there is not a glimmer of irony in them. Poe wrote four little mystery stories—the four from which the entire *genre* flowered—and they are replete with an irony that invests them with true literary worth. That is not to say that the reader can be counted on to consciously seek out or find the irony underlying a piece of fiction. But if it is there he will somehow sense it, and he will know that he is seeing something more than a man pulling rabbits out of a hat.

When you have the chance, reread Poe's "Murders in the Rue Morgue" and "The Purloined Letter." The first implies very sharply that when an ape batters a woman to death he is acting remarkably like a man. The second makes note of a universal human characteristic: when a human being searches for a lost object, the last place he will look for it is right under his nose. These are dramatic ironies. These are the elements which, underlying the factor of surprise that the mystery writer must weave into his story, give that surprise its deepest significance.

I am afraid that most of those writers who are bending their efforts to the mystery story for the first time are not aware of this. Or, if aware, are concealing the awareness stoically. They are so intrigued by the horrific nature of crime itself, and by all the appurtenances which can be crowded into a story about a crime, that they approach their maiden efforts in somewhat the spirit of a boy getting to work on his first Erector set. The difference in the long run is that while the boy knows his bridge isn't a real bridge, the hopeful writer doesn't know that his story isn't a real story. It *looks* like a real story, doesn't it? It has everything in it that a mystery is supposed to have, doesn't it? Then why does it keep bouncing back in the mails like something attached to a rubber band?

What makes a real mystery story?

My answer is intended only for those who have a lively imagination, an ability to create plausible characters, a sound plotting sense, a command of the English language, and a typewriter.

First, what *is* a mystery story? And I mean by that, how would you define the term "mystery story" in the present-day sense? Do not rush to answer that; there are pitfalls ahead. The wise course is to get an armful of various mystery magazines—with emphasis on *Ellery Queen's Mystery Magazine* and *Alfred Hitchcock's Mystery Magazine*—and to spend a few weeks of time reading them. Ready now? All right, put down your definition and compare it with this one:

A mystery story is a short prose fiction that is, in some way, concerned with a crime.

That's all there is to it. It's as vague and all-inclusive and generally infuriating as that. And if your definition departs far from the above, if it glitters with fine-sounding technicalities and criminous terminology, you will please write on the blackboard one thousand times: *I was completely out of touch with what mystery magazine editors wanted.*

The fact is that your story can be one thousand words long, or ten thousand. It can have a detective, a victim, clues, and deduction, or none of them. It can have a mystery, secret or not, just as you choose. It can be savage or tender, mocking or serious, coarse or delicate. It can, in brief, be anything you want to make of it, as long as it has some concern with a crime.

To the writer who has been becalmed in the horse latitudes of rejection slips, this information sometimes comes as an unpleasant shock. At least, while he was becalmed he knew where he was. Now he has the feeling that his otherwise snug—albeit unprofitable—craft has slipped her moorings and is drifting off into a fog. Especially is this true of the writer who has been grinding out variations on the ancient Dead victim-Omniscient detective-Clever clues theme. The one which ends up with: "You, Jenkins, are the killer, and here, madame, are your jewels."

But once the initial shock passes he will find that he is drifting, not in a fog, but on wide, inviting seas. There is virtually no limitation on what he may use as story material, or on how he may organize it. A writer is at his most confident and capable when he deals with things familiar to him. Now our mystery writer is free to discard the brilliant police detective and the tough private eye, who were remote and unlikely acquaintances of his at best, and turn to the people next door, the people in the office, the people in his home. They may not be the exact material around which a given story should be constructed, but they will serve as guides to the people and ideas which will finally kindle genuine inspiration.

We have now come full cycle back to the matter of irony. Dramatic irony, that is. In a way, the names of Ellery Queen and Alfred Hitchcock should have indicated the inevitability of that, because to the informed their names are synonymous with that word "irony." Give them a story which in some way invokes the ancient spirit of Hubris—the ironic self-destruction inherent in the act of flouting the gods—and they are the happiest of men. They like surprise, but they will buy irony.

Dramatic impact

If finding a proper definition for the modern mystery story was difficult, finding a proper definition for dramatic irony is a hundred times more difficult. Anyone asked to do it in so many words will soon find himself in the position of the man asked to define a corkscrew. The hands then draw spirals in the air, examples and comparisons flood the mind, but the exact, neat definition remains elusive. It is best to go directly to the examples themselves.

One such example is provided by the story of a lynching. The classical formula would suggest that we have a victim killed by a lynch mob, whereupon a wise and sternly just sheriff manages, through courage and clever deduction, to apprehend the leader of the mob. A pretty good story could be written around this framework, and a few have been.

But the finest story written about a lynching—the lynching of a Negro in the Deep South in this case—is by John Steinbeck. He was not interested in the brute scene itself, in the mob, in justice being done. He was interested only in one of the men who attended the affair, and who, very probably, did not even take physical part in it. And the entire story is about the small episode wherein this man returns to his home and is greeted there by his wife who does not know where he has been. Then she takes one look at him, and flies into a fury. He has just been to bed with another woman, she rages, and she knows that—because of the expression on his face!

Another example is provided by Somerset Maugham's "Miss Thompson," the short story later dramatized under the title, *Rain*. It is too familiar to warrant outlining here, but suffice it to say that its naked revelation of Reverend Davidson's true character at the end is a classical example of tragic irony.

And, finally, we have one of the greatest short stories ever written, "The Procurator of Judea" by Anatole France. Two old friends meet, after years of separation, at the baths in ancient Rome. The story is simply their dialogue during the few minutes of their meeting. Old politicians both, they reminisce about political affairs long dead and forgotten. One of the men is named Pontius Pilate, and he is full of pleasant recollections of his younger and heartier days. Slowly, the talk turns to the time when he was administrator of the outlandish province of Judea, and slowly, as we know it must, it moves toward a reference to the Christ. It is the friend who makes the reference, and he waits while Pilate muses over it.

"Jesus?" Pilate murmurs at last. "Jesus—of Nazareth? I cannot call him to mind."

That is the final line of the story, and you can read that story, and reread it again and again, and still get the same terrible impact from that line. It is not surprise which gives it to you, because once you know any story it can have no further surprise to offer. But it is irony—the peak of tragic irony—which is the deep, abiding chord under the small note of surprise.

If any of the three stories used as examples here arrived in manuscript, unknown and by an unknown writer, at the offices of *Ellery Queen's Mystery Magazine* or *Alfred Hitchcock's Mystery Magazine,* they would be bought on the spot. Almost no other magazine editors—and, irony of ironies, I include those who originally published them—would today give these tales the eager reception which the best mystery magazine editors would.

Does this mean that the writer who cannot hope to equal Steinbeck or Maugham or France at his best must, perforce, give up the idea of writing mystery stories altogether? Obviously, it does not. If it did, we would all be out of business tomorrow, perish the thought. But it does mean that the neophyte must stop right here and take careful stock.

No editor will buy pale carbon copies of wearily familiar stories—the routine stories which are accepted by the heedless as synonymous with mystery writing. On the other hand, no editor really expects to find another "The Procurator of Judea" in his slush pile tomorrow. What he would like to find there, however, are stories which try to achieve the impact and irony of that masterpiece, no matter how far below it they may fall. He knows that the writers of such stories are his writers of tomorrow.

9 A METHOD TO MYSTERY

by *A. A. Fair*

A WRITER KNOWS that simply because he has written a few fairly successful mystery stories, he is in no position to give advice on the technique of writing the mystery novel.

A mystery writer who receives a request, however, to write on this subject can't keep his fingers off the keyboard of the typewriter.

Therefore, vanity having triumphed over discretion, let's see just what we're letting ourselves in for. By feeling our way along cautiously, we may be able to prove each point as we make it and thereby keep from sticking our necks out too far.

One thing is certain—a mystery story to be any good at all must be interesting and entertaining. People dutifully read the books "everyone is talking about." They catch up on their "must" reading. Some of them are satisfied with that.

Thousands are not.

Some minds, and they're usually the brightest, demand relaxation, a measure of excitement and lots of interest. These people want a puzzle story told in terms of interesting events, exciting enough to hold a work-weary mind and give it relief, clever enough to appeal to trained minds, real enough to be convincing.

It's not easy to create such a story.

Types of mystery novels

As far as technique is concerned, it varies with the different types of mystery novels a writer may want to write.

There is the hard-boiled mystery. The hero is usually a private detective, big, tough, and with an almost unlimited capacity to absorb and dish out punishment. During the course of the story, everything is thrown at him, including the kitchen sink. He takes it all in his stride, and in due time, polishes off the villain with several well-placed shots from his six-shooter, grabs the heroine and kisses her on the mouth—hard.

Another is the intellectual type of story in which the British influence predominates. There is a murder y'know. And, dash it all, something just doesn't fit. Some little clue that's out of place, and the bally clues just *won't* fit into the proper pattern. During the course of this story, there is ample opportunity for the reader to review everything that has happened. The detective usually prepares a chart along about the middle of the book, showing where everyone was at the time of the murder. The detective and some bosom companion sit up late of nights in smoke-filled rooms, discussing the possibility that each of the persons involved may have committed the murder, marshaling the facts against each suspect in turn, and then offsetting them with at least one apparently insurmountable obstacle.

Then there's the marooned-in-a-snowstorm mystery, set in the big country house, with ten or twelve people gathered for a nice quiet weekend. The wind begins to blow, the heavy laden clouds start pelting the place with heavy, moist snowflakes. By midnight, it's the worst storm the countryside has seen in fifty years. The wind is howling and shrieking around the corners of the house. The last belated guest arrives with the cheerful information that the road is blocked. He had to leave his car half a mile down the road, and then barely made it to the house. About two o'clock in the morning, the first murder takes place. The frightened occupants of the house try to call the authorities and can't. The wires are all down, and the howling wind mocks at their puny attempts. The host decides to get the police at any cost. He turns the handle on the door. A ninety-mile wind blows it open and it takes the combined efforts of two strong men to close it, following which, the hall is filled with snow that was blown in. The remaining guests (the corpse, of course, excluded) gather for coffee in the kitchen, only to find that one of their number is missing. A hasty search reveals the second corpse; whereupon, all of the guests begin to look at each other with suspicion. About daylight a shriek is heard over the howling of the wind, and the third corpse is discovered. Thereafter, the survivors agree that under no circumstances will they straggle off into isolated parts of the house. They determine to remain together for mutual protection. One of them is the murderer, but there's safety in numbers. Following this decision, they all do exactly the opposite. The heroine wonders if Auntie's shawl wasn't really a significant clue and leaves on a tiptoed quest for evidence. The hero sees her go and wants a word with her. The electric wires go down under the gale, and the big house with its creaking boards and furtive footfalls is in darkness.

In the sophisticated mystery novel, the police officers are frankly puzzled. The district attorney is utterly bewildered, and "my friend the gifted What'shisname refuses, at first, to be interested because he's working on his treatise concerning the application of glaze in the Ming Dynasty." But at length, he is persuaded to accompany the district attorney to the scene of the crime, where he is terribly bored by it all, being infinitely superior to all of the characters in the book—as well as the reader, by implication. He smiles at the district attorney, makes some enigmatical remark, and returns to his investigation of the Ming vases. Whereupon, it turns out that his enigmatic remark, which was disregarded by the exasperated attorney, is the most significant clue of all, and the district attorney finally gets him back on the case for another half hour and another cryptic remark.

Popular, too, is the romance-suspense type. There must be a romantic plot sufficiently compelling to hold the reader, even if there weren't any murder. That's quite an order. It usually is an oil-and-water emulsion of love story and murder mystery. The reader who likes the murder mystery may be bored stiff by the love story angle. The romantic reader who is attracted by the love story is repelled by the mystery. But if the story is well enough done, both readers will start it and will finish it—which is probably the reason that romantic-suspense novels sell by the million in paperback.

Pace, puzzle, and plot

It is possible to write the stories classified under each type in a variety of ways. There is what has been so cleverly tagged as the "had-I-but-known" style of presentation. There is the first-person, naive type of narration in which the heroine is so extremely innocent that the reader wants to yell at her, "Don't go there. Don't meet him in that deserted house," but the heroine pushes blithely on. Not until she gets in the old house, and suddenly realizes that it is a trap, does she fully awaken to the horror of the situation. Then it is too late. There are no lights. The dark silence of rooms cluttered with cobwebs is broken by the ominous sound of someone breathing——.

Personally, I like a story that is just a little short of the hard-boiled school. A mystery story that has an element of humor, a puzzling plot, and a style of narration that makes for swift action. You play perfectly fair with the reader. You give him not only the facts that the detective has, but you let him see the approximate significance of those facts; and you throw the story at him with such a bewildering rapidity of pace that he loses his breath about the second chapter and never gets it back until he turns the last page.

That, of course, is the ideal toward which I strive, the goal I seek to attain. Probably better than anyone else, I realize how far I miss that goal. Chapters which, when I write them, seem to have drive and punch sound strained and artificial when I read them a few days later.

This is perhaps the most disheartening experience an author can have. It isn't the fact that he realizes his writing is lousy, because it goes deeper than that. He knows absolutely that he had a smashing climax in his mind. If he could only have achieved the effect he wanted, he would have brought the reader to the edge of the chair. But the steam leaked out of his pipes. Somehow he has put on paper only a very faint hint; he has perhaps aroused the reader's interest, but has failed to arouse his emotions.

That, I think, is the danger of the rapid style of telling a story. You *must,* you simply MUST carry the reader along with you. You can't let him get ahead of the story; but definitely, you can't leave him behind. If you move the story so fast that you jerk the yarn out from under him, you leave him with a bewildered feeling of painful irritation. On the other hand, once having committed yourself to a fast-moving type of story, you simply don't dare to let the reader get so much as one paragraph ahead of you. You have to keep the story moving at such a pace the reader can just keep up.

This is another goal for which the writer must strive. If he cannot attain it, some of the readers are bound to feel that the story has been jerked out from under them; others are bound to get a thought or two ahead.

Reread and revise

Although I have been fortunate in the reader reception given to my mystery novels, I am always painfully conscious of the shortcomings of each book. I read and revise the manuscript half a dozen times before it goes off to the publisher. The editor usually wants more revisions. When I finally finish it, I think, "Well, I've done the best work that is in me. I simply *can't* improve on that." When I see the book in print several months later, I realize that while I had a whale of an idea in mind, the book fell short in its presentation and expression of it. For a while, I'm discouraged; then I go to my typewriter with grim determination that I can do a lot better—and that, by George, I'm going to on my next book!

My two detectives are entirely different in character. Bertha Cool is big, greedy, confident, hard-boiled, realistic. Donald Lam, junior partner, is no superman physically. He's not exactly frail, but he's a pushover for the big bruisers who occasionally shove him around; but Donald has an unquenchable, unwavering spirit, and a smoothly functioning mind. What's more, he is a real fighter in the sense that he has the courageous convictions of a scrapper. He doesn't have the physical stamina to back them up, but he has the intestinal fortitude to stick to and by his guns.

To me, those characters are exceedingly real. I know everything about them. I see them clearly. They are more real to me than many of my friends. If I could *only* get them on paper the way I see them.

And so I keep on plugging away, conscious of the goal I have in mind, realizing my shortcomings—and grimly determined to make this book the best that I have ever written.

All of which means that all I know of the technique of the mystery story is that I'm studying it, too, and hope some day to know more about it than I do now.

10 HOW TO DEVISE AN INGENIOUS PLOT

by *Rosemary Gatenby*

BECAUSE I write suspense fiction, people often say to me, "You must be very imaginative." I don't think so; if I were, I'd be able to sit down and think up a dandy plot at will. Other writers may well do that, but for me it's a matter of waiting till a suitable idea comes along. I don't do Gothics, or procedurals, or private-eye books, or any kind of series, so sometimes it's quite a wait.

My decision to settle on mysteries was the result of an unscheduled and lonely stay in a hospital in a strange city, years ago. It was a stack of Agatha Christies that got me through the ordeal. The cozy fireside teas; clandestine chats in the garden; visits with old friends; impending dangers; shocking murders; tantalizing puzzles . . . I don't know what I would have done without all these for company. I decided that writing mysteries was not mere frivolity—they were needed. And so I set to work.

I haven't yet gotten to writing about cozy fireside teas; I have felt quite at home with mysteries and love doing them. Since I started writing, mysteries as a class have changed—mine along with many others of the genre. They have become less the formal puzzles of some years ago; they are concerned more with characters and background in a suspense form. They are closer to being mainstream novels. Bringing me back, as time goes on, closer to what I wanted to do in the first place —write for-real novels. With the passage of time I have, in fact, acquired some measure of those things I lacked when I started—*some* philosophy of life, *some* ability to cast light on the relationships between people. These things have been finding their way into my books as I, along with mysteries, have evolved.

Recognizing a good idea

Usually the subject for a book comes to me without warning—most often from a newspaper story, but sometimes from an incident I've heard about. I recognize it as a book idea by the instant feeling of excitement it generates, and by a certain "inevitability" of the story.

Remember when Howard Hughes disappeared from his high-security living quarters in Las Vegas, resulting in much speculation in the press? From this incident sprang my novel *The Season of Danger*—which was not about Howard Hughes. It's largely an action story set in Texas and Mexico, its concern a wealthy, reclusive novelist who's been taken prisoner by his own guards. It came of my wondering about the possible risks of living hidden away behind a private security system.

Another book of mine stemmed from some remarks about an apparent suicide. "She wasn't the kind of person who would have killed herself," her neighbor told me. "And her husband behaved so *oddly* . . ." But when I wrote *Hanged for a Sheep*, the story was the reverse of what I thought the truth might have been. The husband was the hero, but suspicion of him caused much of the book's action.

The important thing about a book idea is that it be a good one—with potential, with momentum. I test mine for the following:

1. It must be something that has not already been done—that is new to *me*, at least.

2. It must be *interesting*. There must be excitement and an

element of mystery in the events that are to take place, and the protagonist(s) must be of sufficient stature to be worth the reader's attention.

3. The idea must have sufficient potential for ongoing action and a progression of developments.

4. The story must present a challenge to me as a writer.

What to do with a suspense plot

Each author has his own methods, certainly, of working out a plot. Also, the needs of one book will be different from another. However, I can give you several suggestions which usually work for me.

STEP 1. *A double strand*. I start with a double strand—the crime filament and a man-woman situation. Conflict between the sexes makes for more interest, and the possibility of eventual romance is an added element of suspense.

STEP 2. *A story line*. A good idea or situation is one in which the beginning contains the possibility of a fascinating ending. This is what I meant by a certain "inevitability." So when you begin the story, you already have somewhere to go with it. My story *never* follows or parallels that of the true-life occurrence which set me off on it. Often my characters themselves determine which way things go—which is one reason I don't outline more than the first half of the book before beginning. I do have, however, a general idea of where we are going to end up.

STEP 3. *A double version*. The plotting method that often works best for me is to figure out the story as it first came to me, with the crime, the perpetrator and his motive; then think of someone else who could have done it, and then start over, creating a second string of relationships and happenings for this person in his new role. The second version thickens the plot, gives more material with which to work.

In *Deadly Relations,* for example, I wrote of a politician whose wife stands in the way of his ambitions. Until almost the end, the crimes all seem to belong to this man. Not so. The one responsible is the woman Bruce once loved, who tries to further his career in the belief that she will get him back from his wife. The politician turns out to have been mostly a victim. Bruce was my *original* villain, Iris the second version.

STEP 4. *Red herrings.* Red herrings seem to appear spontaneously, from the tendency of subsidiary characters in going about their business to do so in a suspicious-seeming way.

STEP 5. *Deceptions.* From successful deception springs surprise. And surprise is what makes your plot "ingenious."

One way to mislead is to give a fact, or an incident, and immediately have your protagonist make an assumption about it which points in the wrong direction. The pull of the story line should drag the reader along on this mistaken path instead of letting him think for himself. Even if the reader suspects this is the wrong way, he will be uneasy (this, too, is suspense) about the hero's persisting in his misguided course—and will be happy later to have his original guess proved right.

In another means of deception, nothing is presented which isn't true, but much is left out, thus creating a faulty context in which certain things will be read. The reader, knowing nothing of the gaps, is trapped by his own logic into making assumptions that are incorrect. I use this technique when I have placed the reader in the mind of a character who's guilty of something. For instance, Dwight, in *The Season of Danger,* worries about the hazardous mission Jack has undertaken. The reader assumes he's worried about his friend Jack—but later will look back and realize that Dwight was worried for fear his own part in the conspiracy would be discovered. Much is *trompe l'oeil* in a suspense book; the reader is tricked into seeing something different from the actuality.

I sometimes use "magic tricks" to delude readers. A basic

technique of magicians is to keep the audience so busy watching some inconsequential bit of action that they miss the important part of the trick. I tried this in *Evil Is As Evil Does.* The security of the bigamous "heroine," who walked away from her first marriage when she survived a train wreck, is threatened by a man who was on the train. The reader is kept so busy watching Betty squirm for fear Harry will give her away that Harry's actual role in the story goes unnoticed until late. *He* has more to hide than *she* does, because he murdered his father-in-law during the wreck—as Betty at last deduces. (And only she knows he was on the train.)

This method achieves its effect by emphasis—by presenting important facts as if they were only background details instead of key plot pieces, and by keeping attention riveted on what *seems* to be the main action.

Another magic trick is one done with time. In *Hanged for a Sheep,* my murderer, Joel Davis, was above suspicion: how could he have killed Enid Weir when he'd never heard of the woman until after her death? He supposedly hears of her only *because of* her death, which triggers the revelation by Joel's wife of her own long-hidden secret, an illegitimate child. Twelve years before, Jeanette had given the baby to her cousin Gil and his wife Enid, who lived in another town. Now, with the foster mother dead, Jeanette hopes to get her child back; at last she finds the courage to tell her husband about little Margaret. The reader watches—the dramatic interest centered on how Joel will take this news about his wife's past. There is a long scene, and then:

> He had put his hand over his eyes, as though shielding them from some harsh light. "Why didn't you tell me?"

And so it is established that he has never been told, and therefore knew nothing about the baby or its foster mother, Enid Weir. The reader is sure he knows the facts, because seeing is believing; what you see, surely, is more reliable than what is told you, which after all might be a lie. The truth behind the scene above is that Joel had known all along about the baby and about Enid Weir; his father had had Joel's fiancée investigated before their marriage.

It is essential, when misleading the reader, to be convincing. To this end, it is sometimes wise to use forestalling tactics. If you fear a piece of deception will not pass muster, have your protagonist suspect it and seemingly dispose of possible doubts. Or if you think the reader may guess in any case, tell him as much of the truth as you have to, and lead him down the nearest garden path as to what the relevance of this truth is.

STEP 6. *Difficulties*. The most devious plot twists can be spawned out of desperation—the desperation resulting from your story's hitting a snag. *Deadly Relations* would not work out the way I planned it. It's a boy-gets-girl, boy-loses-girl, boy-gets-girl story. Steve meets the politician's wife when she has fled from her failed marriage. They fall in love, but she disappears. He traces her, and then according to my original plan, the two of them were supposed to work together to expose Bruce's corruptness. Trouble was, the action ground to a halt the minute Steve found Marian again, in her old home town. After the love affair, it was anticlimactic for them to settle down together to amateur detective work. And the moral values were all wrong; this pair weren't the kind to carry on adulterously right in her husband's shadow. I almost gave up on the book.

Then from difficulty came inspiration: I would keep the romantic pair apart, and Steve could go on alone with his investigations. I'd always intended to have the attempted murder of Marian at some point—now I knew where to put it. So Steve reads in the paper that she has been killed by a bomb planted in her husband's car. When he tries to look into the matter, he himself is almost killed. The police, when they discover his relationship with Marian, suspect him of killing her.

Next, he receives a mysterious phone call from Marian and believes she is, after all, alive. Now how could that be? Fact is, in order to escape a second time from her husband, Marian had persuaded her hairdresser to take her place—just long enough for her to get away. But long enough for the hairdresser to be killed instead of my heroine.

One thing led to another, with twists and reversals I couldn't have foreseen. I could never have dreamed them up if I hadn't had to think long and hard about how to get my hero out of an impasse—and my heroine out of his embrace.

So from adversity comes complexity. This is true not only for the writer, of course, but also for the writer's hero: make things hard for him and you will have a better story.

STEP 7. *Spliced endings.* The "wrap-up" of a book is the most exciting part to do. I finish writing, and then I cut and splice the final segments much as a film editor must do a movie—trying for the most suspenseful effects.

Put off unveiling the villain as long as you can. As the end nears, subplots can be finished off, red herrings explained, and loose ends tied; but keep the main thrust of the tale going as long as possible.

When the identity of the villain *must* be revealed, either manage to end the book promptly or see to it that the hero or heroine is at this point hopelessly in the killer's clutches. Any remaining filling in of motivation or past events can then be done while the excitement is still going on. Though *not* by means of a long explanation from the villain while he holds poor Janet at bay with a gun or cleaver; this method is a cliché, and simply not believable.

I generally use the cliff-hanging technique for the final scenes; cut from the imperiled heroine to the hero, just uncovering the last piece of evidence which has the killer's name on it; back to the *more* imperiled heroine, alone with the villain and with her predicament suddenly worsened; back to the hero who is desperately looking for the heroine in the wrong place and figuring out at last why the villain *has* done all this; and will he ever reach Janet in time . . . ? Although an explanation for everything that has happened must be given or at least suggested, and a resolution of the action must be reached, it works well to leave, perhaps, some component of your plot unresolved. In *The Fugitive Affair,* my villain, though his identity is established beyond reasonable doubt, is not brought to justice because he is untouchable—an irony commensurate with the state of law enforcement today, and thoroughly believable.

Surprising and believable

Surprise and believability are the things most essential to an ingenious plot. Surprise comes from your having effectively concealed the true motives and actions of your evil-doers. Believability comes from carefully laid groundwork—all those little details whose relevance goes undetected until the denouement, when they then must serve to convince the reader of the ending's truth.

The most memorable last page is inevitably the one that projects into the future, leaving your reader with the impression that your characters are not shut up within the book covers he has just closed, but are continuing on with their lives in the setting you have made for them.

11 EXCITEMENT FOR SALE

by *The Gordons*

WHEN Liza Minnelli sings, she's more than a singer. She generates an excitement that sweeps and holds her audience.

In putting words on paper, we are in the business of attempting to create and market the same kind of excitement. Our goal has always been a simple one: to write a novel you will find difficult to put down once you have started reading.

Some years ago, we were prowling about in the colorful market place of Marrakech, an exotic oasis on the northern fringes of the Sahara, where the caravans begin and end their long, hot treks. Here the nomadic peoples of the desert, the merchants and traders and camel drivers, gather to hear the news and exchange stories and gossip.

Many cannot read. So there are professional storytellers, as in ancient times. Crowds gather about to listen, no matter how intense the broiling sun. They listen raptly, not missing a word or an expression. If the story is good, they toss in coins. If it doesn't hold their interest, they drift away.

So as we go through the laborious process of writing a book, we keep imagining ourselves storytellers in far-off Marrakech. Every chapter of the way, we ask ourselves, "Are we holding the crowd? Or at this point are they about to wander off?"

But how to hold them was the question when we first started writing. We knew we must have interesting characters and situations, since without these two basics we could not develop the suspense a novel must have. We remember how we would sit around trying to conjure up plots and characters out of thin air. Eventually we discovered we must put down a few words on paper first of all—almost any words that would suggest an idea, a development, a plot. Maybe only one word, maybe ten, but from there we could begin to work in specifics.

Finding plots

We did some extensive but enjoyable research into this business of "selling" excitement. We read Charles Dickens and Victor Hugo, some favorite modern suspense novels, and "Dear Abby," a strange collection with one factor in common: You can't put any one of them down.

We found that the plots we liked best came out of the (1) personal experiences of the writers, or (2) out of the times in which they lived. Now Jack London and Joseph Conrad and Ernest Hemingway had experiences most of us don't. Or do we? Well, not swashbuckling, buccaneering ones, but we all do have experiences of a quieter but dramatic nature. Even a cat does. The adventures of our cat, D.C., were the basis of our novel and the Disney film, *That Darn Cat,* and later, another novel, *Catnapped.*

Most of our suspense novels, however, have come about as a result of the times in which we live, of reading the newspapers. Most of our plots are from newspaper stories. Once we have a basic idea that appeals strongly to us, we start dreaming, letting our imaginations run riot. But there comes a moment of reckoning when we pull ourselves up short. We study the pages of notes we have made while we were speculating, to see if we have strong suspense. Now we are getting down to the bare mechanics, a subject that in our early years we shied away from since it seemed so commercial and unliterary. Surely Shakespeare would never have stooped that low. But didn't he? Outline any of his dramas, and the mechanics jump out at you. In fact, most editors today would send Shakespeare a rejection slip. They would scribble on it: "Overplotted."

We recognize that there are inherent dangers in taking plots from the newspapers. The story may have shock value (a rape, a sniper killing of an old woman, etc.) but not the kind of suspense that would hold up for several hundred pages. Also, the news story may be unbelievable for fiction. This is a cliché but one that shouldn't be ignored.

You may read a news story so great you are tempted to use it even though you do not have a feel for the people. We find this matter of empathy with our characters terribly important. We know that a writer doesn't have to be a race driver to write about one, but he must have an understanding of a race driver, an insight into his thinking and reactions and his whole gamut of emotions. We didn't have to be a criminal attorney, an extortionist, or a terrified secretary to write *Night Before the Wedding,* but we did have to know what motivated them, and even more important, how they felt about life, their problems, their loves, their fears, their ambitions—all of that.

We have tackled novels and have even been well along with the preparatory work before discovering that we had no feeling for a key person. This matter of empathy is something we cannot explain. Sometimes we develop it for characters we have known only scantily in actual life, and sometimes we don't have it for people around us. For this reason we always write biographies of our principal characters before starting a novel. If we don't "feel" for a key person after finishing his biography, we forget the project.

It is reasonable to ask if you can be sued for libel if you use a news story. Yes, of course (and there have been such actions), if you copy it verbatim. But no hardworking, conscientious writer would do that. He starts changing the plot, maybe to add to the suspense, perhaps to tone down an unlikely episode. He creates his own people, and they themselves change the plot as they react to developments. He thinks for them, and feels for them, and in the end, only the basic idea remains, an idea common to thousands of similar news events the papers have reported over the years.

But a story from out of our experiences, or taken from a newspaper headline, is only good when we apply coldly and unemotionally this test: Is it a good "continuing suspense" situation, or if not, does it have the basics for a "chain of suspense events"?

Categories of suspense

The kind of plot we call "continuing suspense" is one in which someone finds himself or herself in one single life-and-death situation from beginning to end. War stories are good examples. At any moment a soldier may be captured or killed. This is true with a kidnapping or an extortion case. The basic situation, of course, doesn't have to be an action one. A man suffers a heart attack and through the rest of the novel we wonder when and if he will die from another.

This is the kind of suspense we used in *Ordeal*, a novel about a girl flyer whose plane crashes in Arizona's Navajo country with half a million dollars aboard, and the predators who move in on her. She is in danger in every chapter, sometimes mildly so, sometimes extremely. This is what we mean by "continuing suspense." She can't escape her predicament until the wind-up, the climax.

The other kind, equally as exciting in the hands of a master storyteller such as Alistair MacLean, might be described as a chain of events in which one suspense episode follows closely on the heels of the last. Here again, the mechanics, the need for outlining exactly what will take place, are essential. Here, too, is an example of the basic tenet for a strong, exciting, entertaining kind of novel—a story that has a beginning, a middle and an ending.

We must admit that it's the middle section that often gives us the most trouble. We can come up with a strong beginning and an exciting ending, but unless the story has sufficient developments—such as we find in the "continuing suspense" and the "chain of events"—we discard it.

Sometimes a counterplot—interwoven but independent of the main plot—will provide the tangents and developments needed for that hazardous middle section.

Checkpoints for excitement

Here are some of the checkpoints we use to check and recheck our novels before we are satisfied.

1. *Does our story have reality?* Can we see the place we are describing? Do we know this character, have we met him? Is the episode believable? Would it actually happen? Here we are afraid to trust to chance, so we don't conjure up characters or places or even situations. We use people we have known, change their habitat, age, looks, and otherwise camouflage them. And we always use locales and backgrounds we know. In *Operation Terror* (film title: *Experiment in Terror*), we even used our own home, our street, and our neighbor's dog. And the plot is based on a case that actually happened some years ago. Even the opening, in which our heroine is waylaid by the criminal as she drives into her garage late at night, was drawn from life.

2. *Does our story have suspense?* Is it so gripping, or a character so fascinating, that the reader will stay up long after he should have been asleep? This is when we travel back to Marrakech to ask ourselves, "Will the people walk away?" Suspense, of course, is a necessary ingredient in every type of writing. Suspense is build-up; it is timing; it is many things. It is vital to humor, to melodrama, to action, to storytelling in general.

3. *Does our suspense mount steadily?* That is, do we have merely a string of action scenes, like peas in a pod, rather than a well-motivated series of events which build toward a climax? On the other hand, does any one event eclipse or overpower the climax?

To illustrate, half way through *Catnapped,* the villain specified that the girl whose cat he was threatening to kidnap should meet him alone in an oil field at night. She had tipped off the security officers, and they were ready to move in. Here we had the makings of a scary suspense episode, but if played out, it might overpower the ending. So, just before the bad guy gets to the girl, he falls into an oil slough and is bogged down. This solved our problem, and at the same time provided some humor.

4. *Do we get our suspense thread underway right at the start?* Or do we slow down the beginning of the story with too much background and too much characterization when these could be woven into the fabric as we go along? We believe in "interweaving," and not throwing entire chapters of background and characterization at the reader.

5. *Do we have sufficient developments to keep the story moving?* By this we do not mean action scenes but the kind of everyday developments that keep our own lives interesting. And are these developments in a fairly simple, direct story line? That is, are they arranged so they will not be confusing? For some reason, we've discovered that we have an unexplainable fondness for flashbacks when flashbacks are not needed. So we keep reminding ourselves: tell the story in the present unless there is some vital reason to flash back, such as briefly to show an incident in a character's childhood.

6. *Is our plot as simple as possible?* Repeatedly we write in characters and scenes that only tend to confuse the story. We make one careful trip through the manuscript to strike out such clutter.

7. *Is our principal character sympathetic?* In this age of realism, when a "slice of life" is so often taken from the sordid, we still hold to the old principle that a character must have sufficient good qualities for the reader to feel for him, to want to "pull" for him. That doesn't mean he should be a knight on a white horse. He may have many weak, even bad qualities, but he must be "simpatico."

8. *Is there sufficient contrast in our characters?* Or is there a sameness about them? Have we modeled them too much to our own way of acting and thinking, or have we managed to crawl outside our own craniums and into the lives of others?

We like to pick at least one unusual character for each book. When we were plotting *Operation Terror,* we remembered an old character we had known in Chicago. He was a likable crumbum on North Clark Street who lived by buying and selling "news." He would learn that the police planned to raid a bookie joint and sell the news to the bookie, or he might learn of a crime about to be committed, and market the information to the police. We called him Popcorn in the book, and as the novel took shape, we became very fond of Popcorn. No matter how many books we may write in the future, we'll always have a warm spot for him. So it is with characters.

9. *Have we dramatized our episodes properly?* Or have we let them drift aimlessly? Have we intensified the emotional impact where we should have? Have we muffed any chance to produce a shock effect? This, of course, is a matter of elemental storytelling. One person will relate an anecdote that causes you to roar; another, telling the same story, bores you. So often it is *how* something is told, as well as the content.

10. *Have we overlooked any conflict between characters that would be there in real life?* We find that we have a tendency to soften situations. We're just not the belligerent type, and in dealing with aggressive people, we have to remind ourselves that their philosophy of life is different from ours.

11. *Have we failed to draw humor out of situations or characters where there would be humor?* We feel strongly that the tension and suspense should be relieved with humor—not only for its entertaining effect, but because it adds to the realism, and gives us a chance to ease up on the suspense. Thus, what follows may be even more exciting. Drama, of course, must have valleys. It cannot be lived entirely on peaks. And humor helps take care of the valleys.

12. *Is the ending satisfying?* We like a story to end when it ends, and not to take an extra chapter at the climax to unravel the plot to its last thread. But it should not end too abruptly. We should let the reader enjoy the satisfaction of "seeing" and "feeling" that there is a rightness to the ending.

Does our manuscript meet these requirements? If it does, we have excitement for sale.

12 SHORT FICTION—WITH A DIFFERENCE

by *Joe Gores*

A MYSTERY story," writes Stanley Ellin, "is a short prose fiction that is, in some way, concerned with a crime."*

Brief and simple as this is, it successfully spans the immense variety of the short mystery since Poe and makes you want to hustle over to the old portable and peck one out. Just lift a crime from today's newspaper, dream up a couple of side-of-the-mouth characters, crank out a few pages of one-sentence dialogue in the Hammett manner. . . .

It didn't come out so well? Didn't . . . hold together?

Defining the short mystery story doesn't make us able to *write* one. Especially when the definition seems, at first glance, to give us only a single element to set apart the mystery (whether novel or short story) from the mainstream of fiction: a crime.

Let's begin with our crime, then, be it art forgery or stealing someone's good name or murder. We immediately see that the crime leads us logically and inescapably to a new element: a solution. If we have a crime, we must have a solution. This is absolute bedrock to the short mystery.

I can see the boys flicking open their switchblades to cut me up. How straight can you get, man? Don't you dig obscure?

---

* See Chapter 8, "Irony and Surprise."

Don't you dig the anti-hero and black humor and existentialism?

I dig. But despite the fact that fiction can probe deeper and talk dirtier than ever before, can, since Sigmund Freud, glibly mouth *psychosis* and *id* and *ego,* the successful story still must have a resolution. No resolution, no story, whatever other merits it may have as a piece of prose. And if it is a mystery story, implicit in that resolution must be some solution to the crime. It doesn't matter if your bad guy triumphs over your good guy, or even if your bad guy *is* your good guy; there still must be some sort of solution.

After the crime and its solution, however, the mystery short story starts getting tricky. (Here you are, folks, all those whodunits and howdunits and whydunits, and suspense and thriller and crime stories, and private-eye capers, and procedural and formal mystery and locked room and spy stories and Gothics. . . .)

Not at all.

"Telling" or "plotting"

By getting tricky I don't mean all the possible ways to make a reader believe the butler dunit—or didn't dunit. We are going to get tricky by making the necessary distinction between *telling* a story and *plotting* a story. It is precisely here that the "serious" writers who condescend to walk down our dingy little street of crime so often step on the banana peel. They have never learned how to plot.

This distinction between storytelling and story plotting is simple—and vital. E. M. Forster once defined a story as "a narrative of events arranged in their time sequence."

It might now be helpful to analyze a mystery short from first conception to finished manuscript, to show how a story originally conceived as a straight fiction tale became a mystery short story through a deliberate building-in of suspense elements.

As a junior in college, I wrote a story, "Epitaph," following the lingering death of a deeply loved and respected grandfather. The story, which contained a good deal of youthful anger and sorrow, opened with a doctor walking downstairs from a sickroom in which Chris Miller's father lies dying of cancer:

> "Well?"
> "Your father—he—he's very ill." His moon face was drawn up into what was supposed to be condolence, and his fat gut still quivered from the stairs.
> I shrugged. "Ya, ya, cut the crap. Is he going to live or die?"

Chris is an inarticulate man in his mid-twenties, a ne'er-do-well who spends his time hunting and fishing. As a result, neither his mother, his two sisters, nor his brother Rod, who works at the local bank, understand his deep, unspoken emotion at his father's terminal illness. A few days after the old man's death, Chris and his brother go up to the casket at the funeral home to view the body:

> "Looks just like old dad, doesn't it?" Rod said with a quaver in his voice.
> "No, it looks like hell to me."

Afterwards, the mourners follow the casket out to the cemetery ("moving at a proper funeral pace, to show the world that we were sad"). As they return to town, Chris looks back: the snow "had stopped melting on the coffin; it laid a soft blanket over it and . . . would cover the old man up from this shallow mess of humanity that had carried him out here." Chris skips the wake; he knows that no one will miss him there.

> No more jump-shooting mallards down in the bottoms or deer-shining out of season in the hardwood belt across the

creek . . . (But) I knew a good rabbit woods across the highway from my shack, where the snow wouldn't be too deep for
the dog. The old man would like that, I thought. He always
loved rabbit hunting.

After reading "Epitaph," my writing instructor told me that
funeral stories were hard to sell, and suggested that I put it
away for a while. I did. For fifteen years, in fact. But the story
kept bugging me; there was a wealth of honest emotion in it
despite my college-boy hostilities and shallow philosophizing.
Later, I tried a rewrite with Chris as an older man, about
thirty-five now, an ex-convict returning home after his release
from prison. I blue-penciled his sisters, gave Rod a wife, and
began the story with Chris's arrival in town:

   I got off the Greyhound and stopped to draw icy Minnesota
   air into my lungs . . . I caught my passing reflection in the
   window of the old-fashioned depot: a tall, hard man with a
   white and savage face . . .

Chris, who calls the old man "Pops" inside himself, remains
at his father's side for the thirty-seven hours until the death,
despite open hostility from the family.

   I could see the old man's arms hanging limply over the edge
   of the bed . . . The upper arm, which once had measured an
   honest 18 and had swung his small tight fist against the side of
   my head a score of times, could not even hold a cigarette up in
   the air. It gave me the same wrench as finding a good foxhound
   that's gotten mixed up with a bobcat.

As the image suggests, Chris has retained the earlier version's love of the outdoors. His father's eyes, "translucent with
imminent death," are to Chris the "pure, pale blue of birch
shadows on fresh snow"; and when he and his father reminisce,
the old man goes "way back . . . to the big white-tail buck that
followed him through the woods one rutting season until he
whacked it on the nose with a tree branch."
Chris goes to the funeral home and the grave, but leaves

"when the preacher starts his scam." He gets a long-barreled .22 target pistol from the house ("Pops and I had spent thousands of hours with that gun"), takes the jeep to drive down into the woods.

> There was a flash of brown as a cottontail streaked from under a deadfall toward a rotting woodpile I'd stacked years before. My slug took him in the spine . . .
> I left him there and moved out again, down into the small marshy triangle between the hills . . . Finally a ringneck in full plumage burst out . . . I squeezed off in mid-swing, knowing it was perfect even before he took that heart-stopping pinwheel tumble . . .

Chris returns to the cemetery and, in the dusk, lays the dead rabbit and pheasant on top of the casket. He stands in silent contemplation for a minute or two ("The wind must have been strong, because I found that tears were burning on my cheeks"), then leaves town (again by bus), taking the .22 with him because "Pops would have liked that."

I began submitting the story, to find my ex-teacher's judgment still valid: stories about funerals don't sell. Finally, despite the lack of crime in the story, I sent it to *Ellery Queen's Mystery Magazine*. After all, I rationalized, I had a criminal. Ellery Queen's editorial reaction was swift, crisp, and pointed.

> It is (not) a crime story simply because it has a criminal in it. A detective story is not necessarily that simply because it contains a detective. There would need to be some detection.
> Suppose Chris managed a prison break in order to get to see his father before he dies . . . (It) will have much more suspense if the cops are after him . . . He would need to leave some sort of red herring that would send the cops off in a different direction . . .

I decided to revise the story along the lines suggested. Into the opening paragraph, for instance, went a second reflection in the bus depot window:

. . . one that froze my guts: a cop in uniform. Could they already know it was someone else in that burned-out car?

That was my red herring. An old farmer (with whom Chris hitched a ride after the break) has been killed when the car has gone off an icy road. Chris has poured gasoline on him and lighted it, so the police will think that the body is Chris. But Queen still was dissatisfied.

You're missing the point . . . Your red herring throws the cops off completely . . . The dramatic situation can't just be left hanging; it needs to be resolved to make the story complete . . .

On reflection I knew Queen was right; so revision included references to the search Chris knows must be fanning out behind him. My ending was dramatic, with Chris dodging downhill between the tombstones for a presumably fatal shoot-out with the arriving police.

Ellery Queen's Mystery Magazine offered to buy this version. But now the essential difference between a great editor and an editor who merely buys stories from writers became apparent. He wrote:

I will, of course, run the present version if you wish me to. But I still think that the last scene is not as strong and dramatic as it could or should be . . . He should . . . turn to leave—and see the cops and/or detectives standing there, waiting for him. I think this stark, sudden, final ending is what this particular story needs.

Please think it over, Joe, and if you agree, send a revised last page.

I thought it over, and sent a revised last page to them. It read like this:

I turned away, toward the jeep—and stopped dead. I hadn't even heard them come up . . . I tensed, my mind going to the .22 pistol that they didn't know about in my overcoat pocket. Yeah. Except that it had all the stopping power of a fox's bark.

If only Pops had run to hand guns of a little heavier caliber. But he hadn't.

Very slowly, as if my arms suddenly had grown very heavy, I raised my hands above my head.

Tone and title

A straight short story that wouldn't sell had become a mystery short that would, and did. But one other change first was necessary. The original title, "Epitaph," no longer fit the tone of the story. Out of the ending of the earlier version I had constructed what may be the best paragraph I have ever written; and from it came *the* absolutely perfect title.

> Goodbye, Pops. Goodbye to deer-shining out of season in the hardwood belt across the creek. Goodbye to jump-shooting mallards down in the river bottoms. Goodbye to woodsmoke and mellow bourbon by firelight and all the things that made a part of you mine. The part they could never get at.

In May, 1970, my story, "Goodbye, Pops" was given the Edgar Allan Poe Award by Mystery Writers of America as the best mystery short published in America that year. But whenever I notice that statuette glowering from the bookshelf, I have the nagging feeling that I should somehow share my Edgar with the *Ellery Queen* editor. Because it was he, as editor, who reminded me, as writer, that only when the mystery short follows the simple formula of crime, solution and logical plot can it be wholly successful.

13 MAKE YOUR READER WONDER

by *Naomi A. Hintze*

FOR ME, it all started when a young friend handed me a book to read. Don't ask me what it was called. I can no more remember those titles than I can remember the jacket drawings of all those frightened girls posing against turreted castles looming out of mists. "Read it," urged my young friend. "She's my favorite author—I read everything she writes." (At that time I had been writing for years and selling almost everything I wrote—my bank balance a dismaying confirmation that Edna Ferber knew her statistics when she said that the average income for a full-time writer was right up there with that of the full-time clam digger, a cool $2,200 a year.)

The book recommended was about some ninny who left her warm bed at midnight, going all by herself (naturally) to investigate mysterious moans in the castle dungeon that were none of her business. Or maybe it was the tower . . . chapel? Well, whatever. The only reason I was able to struggle through to the end was my perplexity as to why my young friend should be this writer's devoted fan.

I went to the library and lugged home armloads of books by this and other rich authors of similar novels. A bewildering procession of ding-a-ling females climbed miles of cobwebbed stairs, crying a lot, inviting disaster to the point where this reader hoped they'd end up with their throats cut on the last page.

Also in the field of mystery-suspense were some excellent writers I could never hope to emulate. But the awful-awfuls were what turned me on. It seemed a field that one of modest talent might break into. I sharpened my pencils. My family rallied round, doing the housework and bringing me food. And in eight weeks I had written *You'll Like My Mother.* (My next two books took me a year each to write.)

For one new to the field, I had some luck. But when I was asked how I build and maintain suspense, it alarmed me to find that I really did not know. It seemed good to be forced to sort out my thoughts on the subject. This is what I shall try to keep telling myself: You must give your reader something to *wonder* about.

Lures

Although title is the least of all you have to worry about, try for one that will pique curiosity and not get lost among the hundreds of sound-alikes. This may serve little purpose beyond catching the editor's eye, so don't be surprised if you have to change it.

Do pick a setting that you know, one that's not been done to death, a place on the globe, if possible, that people have wondered about. If you should choose a foreign setting, bear in mind that your chances for sale in this country will be better if you start with an American protagonist.

Do spend time on characterizations, writing dossiers of each person, including not only physical characteristics, but qualities of mind and emotional hangups.

Do try to construct a plot (fully realized characters will help you) that's not hackneyed. The only way I know to do this is to read and read and read what's been published in the field before you ever begin. Read at least some of the bad; study the good.

Take a look now at the way Shirley Jackson lures you at the beginning of *The Haunting of Hill House:* "No live organism can continue for long to exist sanely under conditions of absolute reality; even larks and katydids are supposed, by some, to dream. Hill House, not sane, stood by itself against its hills, holding darkness within . . . and whatever walked there, walked alone."

Could you read Daphne du Maurier's description of the lost loveliness of Manderley without wondering what had happened there? In her dream, the never-named heroine of *Rebecca* gives such tantalizing glimpses that even those who dislike flashbacks simply must go on.

Consider this description that sets the scene in *Wuthering Heights:* "One may guess the power of the wind . . . by a range of gaunt thorns all stretching their limbs one way as if craving alms of the sun." And also, ". . . grotesque carvings lavished . . . about the principal door; above which, among a wilderness of crumbling griffins and shameless little boys, I detected the date '1500.' "

These writers are among the masters of the art, and we may as well have a further look at them as they go on to catch the reader's interest with characterizations. Emily Brontë's Cathy is still marvelously believable as she spits at young Heathcliff at first, then becomes much too fond of him. "After behaving as badly as possible all day, she sometimes came fondling to her father to make it up at night. 'Nay, Cathy,' the old man would say, 'I cannot love thee; thou'rt worse than thy brother. Go, say thy prayers, child, and ask God's pardon.' " Later, the mercurial Cathy says, " 'If I were in Heaven, Nelly, I should be extremely miserable.' "

The shy protagonist of *Rebecca* immediately enlists our sympathies. Her sense of humor keeps her from being masochistic, although she is used by her employer, Mrs. Van Hooper, with her "fat, complacent laugh," and later driven to despair by the housekeeper who seeks to destroy her.

In *The Haunting of Hill House* we read, very early, these lines about Eleanor, the 32-year-old spinster who has been invited to spend the summer in an old house whose supernatural manifestations are to be investigated: "The only person in the world she genuinely hated, now that her mother was dead, was her sister." Could you stop reading? I couldn't.

Davis Grubb, author of *Night of the Hunter,* gets us into the characterization of the Preacher by showing us his tattooed hands: "The fingers of the right hand, each one with a blue letter beneath the gray, evil skin—L-O-V-E. And the fingers of the left hand done the same way only now the letters spell out H-A-T-E. What kind of man? What kind of preacher?" We wonder too.

In this book, we are given a gimmick to wonder about. After the first few mentions of the old, rag doll which little Pearl, "stony silent as a graveyard cherub," carries with her always, we know that the doll figures importantly, but we don't at first guess how. The child hugs the doll, breathes into its matted wig, sleeps with it clutched tight against her flat little chest. You may guess the secret of the doll before you are told—it's probably good for the reader to be allowed the satisfaction of guessing right about a few things—but that doesn't keep you from chewing your nails right up until the end of this superbly plotted book.

Begin by wondering

How does one go about plotting a suspense story? It may well start with a writer's wondering about a real-life situation, or an interesting personality. It may even start with wondering what would have happened in someone else's book if a different tack had been taken.

Barbara Jefferis, an Australian writer, once wrote a charming book, *Half Angel,* about a little boy who found and hid a Siamese cat. I wondered, somewhat idly, if it would be possible to hide a baby. Several years later I adapted and used this idea when I wrote *You'll Like My Mother.*

My wondering about a certain stone slab found on a Connecticut hillside led to my writing *The Stone Carnation* long after I had moved to Virginia. I was poking through a tumble-down boundary wall searching for a flagstone to complete a small terrace. One stone, which seemed to be about right for my purpose, was about the size and shape of early gravestones, and in the short time it took me to turn it over I wondered what I should do if I found lettering on the other side. It wouldn't be right to walk on a gravestone, would it? It was the perfect size to top a small cocktail table, but if I were to take it into the house, might I not have the eerie feeling that the house was thereafter haunted? It was only an ordinary, flat stone, but before I heaved it over, I had the plot for a short-short story (which never got written) and eventually, a full-length book.

During the writing of it, I realized that here was the perfect use for something else I had wondered about for many years. One summer at my parents' home in Illinois, a country neighbor sat with me on the steps while I told her about the quaint inscriptions on some of the gravestones my father and I had seen that morning in an old cemetery. Quite casually, she remarked that the bones of one of those interred there rested in an outsize coffin. "She had been sewn between two feather-beds, you know, and that was how they buried her. Bitten by a mad dog, poor thing, and that, of course, was how they used to restrain them in the final throes of hydrophobia."

That was the extent of her knowledge on that macabre subject; my parents never had heard of such a thing. I delved into old books of weird "cures" and practices without finding another word to back up this intriguing scrap of information.

But when I was writing *The Stone Carnation,* I had that little thrill that all writers know when something finally jumps into place: Here was where that ghoulish bit belonged.

What is your reaction when you get one of those letters in the mail that says you hold the lucky number that entitles you to a cozy income for life, or a trip around the world, or even a free lot at some lake? Mine, too. I wonder if all these things are on the level. Although my third book went through many title changes before it finally became *Aloha Means Goodbye,* my working title was *You May Already Have Won.*

Bearing in mind that nobody is going to empathize with a pure fool, I tried to have the girl in this story, and also her skeptical father, collect some good solid reasons that seemed to prove that her winning of a trip to Hawaii was on the level. I did, however, mean for my readers to have their doubts.

It's difficult to reveal just enough to have your readers saying, "No, no, don't go—," or, "Hurry, hurry, get out of that house—," without making the protagonist seem to be a dumbdumb who should have known better all along. This is where adequate motivation comes in. Back to *The Haunting of Hill House*—the reader knows perfectly well that Eleanor shouldn't even go into Hill House. Eleanor knows it too: "The house is vile, it is diseased. Get away from here at once." But the reader also knows of the sterility of Eleanor's life, her interest in the occult, and her pathetic gratitude that such fascinating people wanted to include her in their investigation. She *has* to go in.

My wondering took me into parapsychology: I wondered what ever happened to those who had been a nine-days'-wonder in the newspapers, focal points of the poltergeist phenomenon, and I wrote *Listen, Please Listen.* I wondered if hypnotic regression to one's early childhood could have any validity, and the Majorca-based *Cry Witch* was the result. *Maya,* with a Mexican locale, began as a result of my interest in precognitive dreams.

Escape reading

The market for escape reading is a huge one with much variety. Straight detective stories with their cluttering of clues wear me out, but a friend, brighter than I, likes them as mental exercise although, halfway through, she usually spots the murderer. Reader loyalty to those books with the plastic people I deplored earlier must indicate a need, not so much for escape, perhaps, as for identification. Addicts like my young friend may find it easier to identify with heroines who have no bothersome personalities to interfere with vicarious journeys, as, safe in bed with a good light and the doors all locked, these avid readers take romantic chances that in real life would frighten them silly.

I know that there must have been many times when I have failed to make my readers wonder, care enough to be lured into page turning. Although I find balm in the words of flatterers who say one of my books has deprived them of a night's sleep, a certain tactless comment, bluntly honest, is the one I should frame and place over my typewriter:

A stranger asked what I had written and I mentioned my most recent effort. "Oh, yes," eyes glazed, "I started that. . . ."

14 PLOTTING THE MYSTERY SHORT STORY

by *Edward D. Hoch*

WHERE DO YOU get your ideas?"

I suppose you can't consider yourself a really professional writer until you've been asked that question at least a dozen times. I'm always expecting it when I meet new people and the conversation turns to my writing, and yet I'm never quite prepared to answer it. With some 425 published short stories, mainly in the mystery field, it stands to reason that I've come up with at least 425 different ideas in the course of my writing career.

Where *did* all those ideas come from, and how did I go about developing them into salable short stories?

Because I read a great deal, ideas often come from something I've read. One of my stories, "Five Rings in Reno" (published in *Ellery Queen's Mystery Magazine* under my pseudonym R. L. Stevens), grew out of my reading E. L. Doctorow's *Ragtime* and John Dickson Carr's *The Life of Sir Arthur Conan Doyle* in the same week. *Ragtime,* of course, encouraged me to try a story using real people in a fictitious situation. Carr's biography yielded the fact that Conan Doyle had been invited to referee the world championship fight between Jack Johnson and Jim Jeffries in Reno in 1910. Conan Doyle tentatively accepted the invitation but later changed his mind and declined.

What would have happened if he had come to America, to Reno, to referee a prize fight? In my story he does come, and solves a murder. Since Conan Doyle actually did investigate a real-life murder in England, this seemed not so farfetched as one might think. In plotting the crime itself, I made some elements of it similar to a plot device in a Sherlock Holmes story, thus giving both Conan Doyle and the reader an opportunity to solve it.

Though the story ends as the fight itself begins, I fleshed out my plot with a confrontation between the fighters, and a conversation between Conan Doyle and Jack London, who reported on the fight for two newspapers. The result was a satisfying and different sort of mystery plot.

Crimes past and present

Only relatively few of my stories have been set in the past, though a current series of mine involves a country doctor in the 1920's. However, the past can occasionally be used in other ways. Famous crimes of the past can be updated with a modern twist, and hardly a season passes without some story presenting a new version of the Jack-the-Ripper legend. Even classic short stories can serve as a jumping-off point. Cleveland Moffett's famous riddle story, *The Mysterious Card** (1896), was updated by me to form the basis of my story, "The Spy

---

* According to the *Encyclopedia of Mystery and Detection* (Chris Steinbrunner and Otto Penzler), *The Mysterious Card* by Cleveland Moffett (1896), originally published as two short stories in *The Black Cat* Magazine, is said to have used for the first time the familiar plot of an innocent person who meets suspicion, anger, horror and persecution when he shows people a message written on a card in a strange language and asks them to translate it. Color blindness is used as a clue (also possibly for the first time). The second part of the story, "The Mysterious Card Unveiled," offers a supernatural explanation of the Jack the Ripper murders, using the Jekyll-Hyde theme. When the book was first published, as a sales gimmick this part was sealed, and purchasers were offered a refund if they returned the book with the seal unbroken.—*Ed.*

and the Mysterious Card," published in *Ellery Queen's Mystery Magazine*. Another story of mine is an updated version of the classic story, "The Problem of Cell 13," by Jacques Futrelle (1875-1912).

But ideas are not to be found only in the past. For the mystery writer, the daily newspaper can offer an endless variety of plots. I look not for the routine crime, or the well-publicized one, but for obscure little oddities in the news. Writing a story based on the latest terrorist kidnapping or skyjacking is likely to result only in one more such story landing on the editor's already crowded desk.

I rarely write about people I know or have met, and very little of my personal life finds its way into my stories. Once when I broke a wrist, I wrote a story about a detective who breaks his wrist, but as a general rule only places I know personally—not people or events—figure in my stories.

A tried-and-true method of developing a good plot, especially for a mystery, is to take a number of unrelated characters and incidents and try to work them into a plot relationship. An unusual setting, such as a car wash, could be combined with a bandit who struck only on rainy days and an insurance agent making collections from his customers, as in my Captain Leopold story, "The Rainy-Day Bandit" (*EQMM*). By the time you've worked out the relationship among these elements, you have a plot.

Where is the story going?

But important as it is to get an idea and develop it, much more important is knowing where you're going with it. Some mystery writers will tell you it's not necessary to know the end of a story when you start writing it, and that's perfectly true— if the story is a suspense or crime type that depends solely on a clever twist at the end. You can write the story and then think about the proper sort of twist ending it needs. But if you're writing a detective story, with clues along the way and a solution at the end, it's necessary at the beginning to know where you're going.

This does not mean that a goal can't be changed along the way. Some of my best stories have resulted from changing course in the middle of a story, rewriting the beginning, and ending up with something quite different from the original concept.

Occasionally, even with the bare bones of the plot and characters before you, a story will fail to jell. Something is lacking, and quite often it's a unifying theme. Almost by definition, a short story's action should ideally occur within a brief span of time—a few days or a week at most. In a recent story with which I was having trouble, I decided to change the time span from a few vague days in summer to a long Fourth of July weekend. At once, the story took on new life. Was my detective working on a holiday weekend when he'd rather be somewhere else? Was the crime connected with the holiday in any way? Was the killer using the long weekend to some advantage? Banks and offices are closed, there is no mail delivery— were these facts aiding or frustrating the killer? By the time I'd worked out all these answers to my satisfaction, a difficult story had turned out well.

Where do I get my ideas? One place I don't get them is from friends who have a "great plot" for me. Very few of these ever work out, and I can think of only two of my stories that were directly inspired by plots from friends (one was from my wife), though occasionally editors have made suggestions which proved valuable in developing plots, especially concerning series characters.

Writers of short mystery stories derive many benefits from developing a series character. The series character offers special advantages when it comes to plot development. The writer knows his or her background and habits, and simply by placing the series protagonist in an unfamiliar or menacing situation, a plot can begin to take shape. A forgotten figure from the past appears, or a close friend asks the protagonist's help, or he may merely go away on vacation. Gatherings like reunions or conventions provide natural settings for dramatic action.

Plot patterns and gimmicks

The plotting of a formal detective story follows a pattern that makes it at once easier and more difficult to write than most other types of fiction. In the opening pages, word of the crime, be it murder, robbery, kidnapping or arson, must reach the protagonist. Because of his official position—or because the crime involves him or her in some way—it becomes necessary for him or her to solve the mystery and bring the guilty party to justice. There follows the investigation phase, in which suspects are questioned and clues are examined. Then comes the revelation and solution. There's very little room in a short story for a second crime or multiple red herrings such as often turn up in novels, though certainly a second crime can be included if the plot calls for it.

Given that simple outline, how does one keep the mystery short story from falling into a predictable rut? Skilled authors always seem to find a way to hold our interest. As early as 1912, R. Austin Freeman's *The Singing Bone* pioneered the inverted detective story, in which the first part is seen from the criminal's viewpoint and the suspense is not in whodunit, but in how the detective will prove it. A modern example of the inverted detective story is NBC-TV's *Columbo*.

A mystery can be straight or inverted. The plot need not concern itself with murder, and surprisingly enough many early mysteries did not. A glance through some of the Sherlock Holmes stories like "The Red-Headed League" and "A Scandal in Bohemia" shows that bank robbery and blackmail can be just as diverting as murder. Readers and editors today seem to prefer murder, but there's always a market for a good con man or a clever robbery story.

An important part of any plot is the gimmick—the clue or surprise or oddity that makes it different. It can be an unusual setting or character, a bizarre crime, or simply a little-known fact which allows the story to be resolved. I think it's most important to choose a gimmick that is new and different to the author—one that would grab his interest if he came upon or a clever robbery story.

The same can be true of the plot's denouement. It was Stanley Ellin who once wrote that the closing lines of a mystery are more important than the opening lines, and no one can argue with that. When approaching the ending of a story, I often sit back, stare at the typewriter, and try to imagine the conclusion which would be most satisfying to me as a reader. Not the easiest to write, or always the most logical, but the most *satisfying*. This is not to say that every plot must be resolved happily, or even that the reader must be left feeling good. But he must feel satisfied at the outcome.

If the original ending can't accomplish that, it's time to go back and rewrite the story.

Postscript

Mystery writers occasionally wonder whether a "new wave" in mystery writing is on the way. In editing for the second time the annual *Best Detective Stories of the Year* (Dutton), I've had the opportunity of reading everything being written in the short mystery field today. It seems to me that the "new wave," if and when it comes, must originate with publishers of original anthologies, rather than with magazine publishers. And thus far no book publishers have shown a serious interest in anthologies of original mysteries.

But if by "new wave" one means a loosening of plot structure, a formlessness often seen in mainstream fiction, I think its time has not yet come in the field of the mystery. Perhaps no other genre of writing demands such adherence to the conventions of plot. In the short story, especially, characterization can be minimal, fancy writing can be nonexistent, but plot is all-important.

Where do I get my ideas?

Well, there's this writer sitting at his typewriter doing an article about plotting, and he happens to look out his window and sees a shoebox on the grass beneath a neighbor's window. And he wonders who put it there, and what it might contain. . . .

15 THE CHANGING MYSTERY NOVEL

by *Joan Kahn*

EDGAR ALLAN POE started the mystery story proper about 120 years ago, though ever since Cain and Abel, with a few people like Lady Macbeth along the way, there's been a certain amount of interest in who killed whom and how, with special emphasis on the individual killing. The problems of the poisoned arrow and was-he-pushed or did-he-fall have always been more intriguing, when one is considering the extermination of one man, than thousands of deaths by famine or flood.

From the time of Poe till about thirty-five years ago, mystery novelists enveloped their plots in games and puzzles. They asked the reader to find out whodunit and how it was done; they weren't very much concerned with the personality of the victim or the culprit. Mystery novels then were fairly formularized and formal. They followed fairly set rules, and they were very often not especially well written.

The rules ran this way: Readers were allowed to feel they were brighter than anyone, because though the police seemed to think it was Mr. Blumph who had committed the crime, readers knew Aunt Martha had really done it. Readers remembered that Aunt Martha's alibi had been that she was at the grocer's while the murder was being committed, and they knew they were the *only* people who remembered that the murder was committed on a Sunday when the grocery store was closed. (Though that alibi would work in the states where, these days, many grocers *are* open on Sundays.) Of course, readers didn't *really* think it *could* be Aunt Martha—they'd have been terribly disappointed when they came to the end of the book if they *had* been able to guess correctly early in the story. Readers were delighted when the murderer turned out to be someone that not even they had suspected, and they were particularly enchanted if they could go back over the novel and find the places where there had been clues pointing to the real murderer that they'd missed in the first reading.

The end of sleight-of-hand

That sleight-of-hand game was fun for, well, over a hundred years. Sometimes it was played with originality and with skill —sometimes it was clumsy and repetitive. And eventually it began to be played out. There are only so many possible and plausible puzzles: once you've used the murderer leaving the scene of the crime with his shoes on backwards, or had the murder weapon be an icicle which would then melt, or once the reader had learned the trick of the pebble stuck under the gas pedal—well, it all became a little *déjà vu*.

From the mid-1920's to the end of the 1930's there was a very popular novelist who called himself S. S. Van Dine and wrote novels that featured a detective named Philo Vance. His credo, "Twenty Rules for Writing Detective Stories,"* begins: "The detective story is a kind of intellectual game." (Detective stories, as he saw them, do not include "secret service tales," i.e., books that concern themselves with "international plotting and war politics.") Of his twenty rules, I think only one is still very valid—#10: "The culprit must turn out to be a person who has played a more or less prominent part in

---

* See page 267.

the story—that is, a person with whom the reader is familiar and in whom he takes an interest. For a writer to fasten the crime, in the final chapter, on a stranger or person who has played a wholly unimportant part in the tale, is to confess to his inability to match wits with the reader."

Matching wits with their readers is less important for suspense writers these days, for though there's much that's still intellectual about the mystery-suspense field—including its readers and writers—there is now very little of the game approach. And although I liked Van Dine when I read him years ago, I find I now cannot reread him.

Dorothy L. Sayers, on the other hand, whom I not only can and do read happily these days and whose books I'm proud to publish, has written an essay† on the origins and development of detective fiction that I recommend highly, though I disagree with her occasionally, as when she says of detective story writers, "The most successful writers are those who contrive to keep the story running from beginning to end upon the same emotional level, and it is better to err in the direction of too little feeling than too much." She's also somewhat perturbed by the love interest in detective stories, and says, "Far more blameworthy are the heroes who insist on fooling about after young women when they ought to be putting their minds on the job of detection." Oh, Miss Sayers! What would Lord Peter and Harriet have to say about that!

And still another eminent critic writing about detective fiction, Howard Haycraft, in "The Rules of the Game,"‡ said something that is still valid: "Structurally speaking, the first thing to know about the detective story is that it is conceived not forward developmentally, as are most types of fiction, but *backward*."

---

† See page 221.
‡ See page 273.

Beginnings and endings

I don't think you actually have to start with your ending, but how a mystery novel starts *is* very important. If you start off badly, you're dead. No one's going to read you, for one thing. (Except perhaps an editor, who may shake his or her head at the bad beginning but still may jump hopefully to the middle—and then, not so hopefully, will look quickly at the end. And if things haven't improved, the editor will send the manuscript back. It's the editor's job to read more than the opening—a book buyer doesn't have to.)

A good opening for a mystery novel is pretty easy to write. You can start with something marvelous and incredible and exciting—but when you have to, eventually, explain how that splendid opening came to be, then there's often, very often, trouble. Many manuscripts that seem as if they might be publishable when one starts to read them, aren't, when one gets to the end. So, even if you don't start at the end, you'd better have a really good idea of exactly where you're coming out when you go in.

The beginnings and endings of mystery-suspense novels have changed in the last forty years or so. Here are just a few examples:

Let's start with one by Anthony Berkeley (c. 1929) who was also Francis Iles and a member of the English Detection Club (no detective writer was eligible for membership who willfully withheld vital information from the reader). He says in his introduction to *The Poisoned Chocolates Case,* "How long can the detective story expect to maintain its present popularity? Always, I think, provided that it moves with the times."

Here's how his novel opens:

Roger Sheringham took a sip of the old brandy in front of him and leaned back in his chair at the head of the table. Through the haze of cigarette smoke, eager voices reached his ears from all directions, prattling joyfully upon this and that and connected with murder and poisons and sudden death. For this was his own, his very own Crimes Circle, founded, organized, collected, and now run by himself alone. . . .

He turned to Chief Inspector Moresby of Scotland Yard, who, as the guest of the evening, was sitting on his right, engaged, a little uneasily, with a positively enormous cigar.

"Honestly, Moresby, without any disrespect to your own institution, I do believe that there's more solid criminological genius in this room (intuitive genius, I mean; not capacity for taking pains) than anywhere in the world outside of the Sureté in Paris."

Here's how it ends:

"I have ascertained that immediately preceding the crime, this woman, whose name by the way is Jane Harding, stayed for two nights at the Savoy Hotel and left London, on the morning the chocolates were delivered, for Africa. Where she may be now I have not the least idea. Nor, I should say, has anyone else. But she came to London from Paris, where she had been staying for a week. . . .

"It would be simple to ask this other lady to post the parcel in London, as the parcel postage is so heavy from France, and just as simple to ensure it being delivered on the morning of the lunch appointment with Mrs. Bendix, by saying it was a birthday present, or some other pretext—and—and—must be posted to arrive on that particular day."

I'm going to skip a few paragraphs which are rather more of the same here, up to the ending:

Mr. Bradley was the first to get a grip on himself. "So we did have a practicing criminologist amongst us after all," he drawled, in a manner that was never quite Oxford. "How quite interesting."

Again silence held the Circle.

"So now," asked the President helplessly, "what the devil do we do?" Nobody enlightened him.

That was an opening and a closing in 1929.

In 1936 Patrick Quentin (also a pseudonym—in the mystery-suspense field they do abound) wrote *Puzzle for Fools*. It opened:

> It was always worse at night. And that particular night was the first time they had left me without any kind of dope to help me sleep.
>
> Moreno, the psychiatrist in charge, had given me one of those dark, impatient looks of his and said, "You've got to start standing on your own feet again, Mr. Duluth. We've coddled you long enough."

And it ends:

> "But you got the right man," I said.
>
> "Ye-es." The director's voice was rather hesitant. "I came upon the correct solution eventually. But, to tell you the truth, until this evening I was suspecting someone quite different."
>
> "You were?" I asked, suddenly alert.
>
> "I knew from the start that we were dealing with a very sane, very talented and very intelligent person. . . . I do not make a practice of taking patients into my confidence on sanitarium matters. I only did so in your case through a scientific miscalculation far more unpardonable than your own."
>
> "But who did you think . . . ?"
>
> "I did not see how it could be anyone but yourself, Mr. Duluth."

We'll skip here, since they continue to get along with each other swimmingly, to the end.

> At last the door opened and I sprang to my feet.
>
> "Iris . . . !"
>
> "Peter . . . !"
>
> She didn't move. Neither did I. We just stood there, looking at each other. I don't know why or how, but I guess it was the same way people in love have looked at each other since the world started spinning on its cock-eyed axis.
>
> Or—in our particular case—like a couple of nuts.

The shape of the mystery-suspense novel was, clearly, changing. In 1949, William Krasner opened *Walk the Dark Streets* this way:

> The yellow fog was already creeping up around the Marne Hotel, mingling with the white breath from the sewers, carrying west the faint, sweet, rotting scent of the Ohio River. It was not thick yet, only a gentle curdling of the atmosphere, but it laid damp greasy fingers on the crumbling granite, on the pavement, and on the windshield of the coupe that Detective Captain Sam Birge of the Homicide Squad was pulling to the curb. . . .

He ended his novel in the following way:

> "Charley," Birge said. "Charley—do me a favor. Follow her. See that she's booked properly and has what she needs."
>
> "And Charley—," he raised his hand again. "See what you can do there. You know—see if you can make it a little easier for her."

And the final paragraph:

> He looked at his watch. It was late now. It was time to be on his way home. Time to go home, to Edna, and to his son. He got up.

Things continued to change, a little here—a little there—front and back. In 1957, *Gideon's Night,* by J. J. Marric, opens:

> In the early, misty dusk, Gideon stepped out of his house and closed the door on brightness and music. It was not yet six o'clock. His family, except Matthew, who was out, would spend the evening gathered round the fire, the television, lesson book, and if Pru could make the others sit back for half an hour, her violin.

And it ended:

> "Thought I'd catch you," greeted Matthew eagerly, and he leaned against the window but showed no desire to get into the car. "Just wanted a word, Dad. I thought you ought to know.

When I got back last night I couldn't help talking about where I'd been, and I thought I might as well strike while the iron was hot, so I told Mum what I'm going to be doing for a living. She didn't seem to mind as much as I thought she would. Do you know what she said?"

"No, what?"

"She said that she'd be a happy mother if I ever turned out to be half as good a copper as my father! So I told her I'd have a damned—I mean a darned good try."

I wouldn't advise trying this sort of opening and closing unless one knew a great deal about police procedure to use in between, and unless one had created a Gideon of Scotland Yard. Which isn't as easy as you might think.

Then let's look at 1964 and see how a writer named Dick Francis opened a book called *Nerve!*

Art Matthews shot himself, loudly and messily, in the center of the parade ring at Dunstable races.

I was standing only six feet from him, but he did it so quickly that had it been only six inches I would not have had time to stop him.

The book ends;

"I waited for you to have a fall that looked fairly bad, and then I used sugar."

And, further finally:

I took the torch from the gatepost and walked up the path to the quiet cottage, to sweep it clean.

Forgiveness, I thought. That was something else again.

It would take a long time to forgive.

As we move along—and I trust you can see how it's moving along—to 1972 and *Box 100,* by Frank Leonard, which opens:

It was nine-thirty in the morning, and I was sitting alone in the shabby little office of the Box 100 section of the New York City Department of Investigation. I was supposed to begin work as a special investigator and I was waiting for someone to get there and explain the job to me. At age forty-six I was starting what I calculated to be my twenty-seventh job and my first as a gum shoe.

Box 100 had been set up by a previous mayor. Any citizen could write in to Box 100 with a complaint about wrong-doing in city government.

And *Box 100* winds up with:

"I complained about her but nobody paid attention so I took the law into my own hands," said Castori, an unemployed laborer.

I walked past the rubble-strewn lot with the model cities sign dangling from the fence.

I decided to get on the subway and go down to the office. What I really needed to cheer me up was to read a big batch of new letters to Box 100.

The suspense novel grows, changes, shifts with the times, and I think the shifting toward the contemporary helps keep the suspense field a vital, entertaining, continuing part of to-day's fiction. The excerpts below are from *A Death in the Life* by Dorothy Salisbury Davis, a 1976 novel set mainly in one of the tougher midtown sections of New York.

It opens:

"What am I doing here? What am I doing here . . . ? There's a fly upon the wall, how I wish that he would fall. A fly in the Doctor's office? Never. A mote, a beam. There's a crack in the ceiling. It gets bigger and bigger every session. Twenty-one floors of psychoanalysts are going to come down on top of me. Julie à la Freud."

"Doctor?"

"Yes?"

"What's going through *your* mind at this minute?"

"What do you think is going through my mind?"

"That I've got skinny legs and no breasts."

We are then taken on through a strong and suspenseful novel to this ending:

> "Why didn't she commit suicide?"
>
> "I don't like pat answers, but I do think her murder of Mallory was a kind of suicide, and she did keep the knife—but where? It is too—Freudian. If I am appointed by the court, I will see her. Whether I shall know more than I do now, I can't say. And for what I'll be able to say then, there are undoubtedly persons as eminently qualified as myself who will say the opposite. It takes me years to know a patient. I hope I'm quicker in helping patients to know themselves."
>
> "I'll bear witness," Julie said.
>
> "Be careful it isn't false witness."
>
> Doctor picked up her appointment book. "Now you want the month of June off to go to Paris. . . ."
>
> "You bet."

There is a psychiatrist in both Dorothy Salisbury Davis's 1976 novel, and in Patrick Quentin's 1936 novel, and each of the novels is well worth your attention. But each of them smells and tastes forty years different from the other.

The shift to people

As is evident from the tone of voice of the excerpts—concentrating on the beginnings and endings—when the mystery novel shifted to the suspense novel, the game side became less important, and the *people* involved in the story became more important. I started to work as an editor in the mystery-suspense field as the shift was being made, and I do prefer people to puzzles. I get tired of games pretty quickly and doubt that I could have spent as many years in the business as I have, if the whodunit had not turned into the suspense novel when it did, with the primary focus on the perpetrators rather than on their deeds and the mechanisms by which their deeds were done.

At Harper's, when we started the suspense department, we said we intended to handle suspense novels the way we handled non-suspense novels, with the same attention to production, advertising, and editorial assistance. And we said we were interested in the quality of the writing and the credibility of the characters and the situations in which the characters were involved. We've continued to feel that way.

It turned out that the writers in the field were glad to have a chance to break away from the formulas of the game, were glad to use their writing skills as fully as possible, were glad to be taken seriously.

We were not, of course, the only publishers who realized the time for a change had come—though some publishing houses even now still restrict the suspense novel. Some publishing houses even now still feel their books must not go over (or under) a certain length, and insist that they have only a minimum of sex, and that they must watch their language. I don't intend to publish pornography. I'm certainly not keen about verbosity or padding for padding's sake (quite often writers, readers and even critics confuse length with strength in fiction, of any kind), but I think a suspense novel has to be able to move freely in the manner that suits it best. All I ask of a book is that it's good reading, believable, and the best the author can do at the moment.

Suspense novels today are, free of the puzzle bondage, breaking out happily in all directions. They are still, of course, novels of entertainment—meaning that they are agreeably diverting occupiers of the mind. Odd to remember that they are primarily entertainment even when they are concerned, in almost every case, with that most serious of crimes, murder. But their purpose *is* to entertain, not to instruct or exhort or expose or reveal. Even so, now that the writers in the field are using their writing skills and their imaginations more fully and are bringing whatever special background knowledge they may have acquired into their books, the books are more firmly and fully fleshed, and no longer (oh, sure, there are still exceptions) just books to spend time with while traveling or to fall asleep over.

They are good reading. Even after all the years I've been reading novels of suspense, I'm still excited by the new books coming along. And I'm sure I wouldn't have been able to spend thirty years reading part of ("part of," if the book is really awful) or all of two hundred suspense manuscripts a year (I read other manuscripts, too, but my main job is with suspense manuscripts), if they'd been just puzzling. Goodness knows, not *all* of those two hundred were always a complete delight. But I've found about fourteen a year that delighted me enough so that I published them. That makes over four hundred Harper suspense novels so far that have given me pleasure. And though there are days when I wish no one was ever let near a typewriter again, I expect to go on reading suspense novels eagerly, because I think they are getting better all the time. Established writers are moving from strength to strength, and newcomers come hurtling in over the horizon from everywhere, with fresh, new ideas, fine, new approaches, and brand-new backgrounds.

And *if* anyone can think up a new (and believable) puzzle —I'd be happy to see it. It's fun to be fooled, and I'd be absolutely delighted to be dumbfounded. I like being frightened, too, on paper. So there's still room for some good mysteries in among the good suspense novels, *if* the author can find a room of his own.

16 SETTING FOR SUSPENSE

by *John Lutz*

RAIN BURST in violent clichés against the windowpanes, wind whistled hackneyed through the ancient eaves, and thunder echoed redundantly across the boiling night sky.

The proper background for a mystery story? Sure—in a clichéd, hackneyed, redundant way. Of course a background conducive to mystery and suspense is an integral part of every mystery, but among fledgling practitioners of the art of mystery writing, background is not wholly understood.

The beginner often overlooks the most important point: The story's characters must not be set *against* the background; they must be *of* the background. The characters must move through the story's background with a familiarity and ease in order to make both the background and the characters—indeed every facet of the story—seem plausible. In an English manor house, perhaps the French windows would casually be thrown open to admit the scent of the well-tended garden. At a stakeout in Chicago on a windy, rainy night, a puddle of muddy water may be used to extinguish a smoked-down cigarette. In a swank restaurant the character may possibly ponder for a moment over the use of the proper flatware, or in James Bondish, man-about-town fashion, tip the maître d' five dollars for a good table. These instances are not necessarily digressions from plot or action, but image-evoking incidents that link character to background and so give each the dimension of realism.

Without real characters there can be no real suspense, and real characters cannot exist on their own within a piece of fiction. Neither character or background can exist independent of the other. It is not enough to sketch in verbally here and there the correct details and descriptions that suit your story's action. In so doing, you will describe but you will not produce the atmosphere or mood necessary to suspense.

Visual and three-dimensional

The writer must use background and its trappings for his character in much the same way an accomplished actor uses background and its trappings to bring to life the character he is playing on screen or stage. There is a silent language of face and body known to actors and directors that it would be wise for a writer to learn: methods of entering a room to convey certain moods; the choice of, and manner of sitting in, a particular piece of furniture to indicate personality; the slightly louder click of coffee cup against saucer to indicate nervousness; an affinity for corners or walls to convey insecurity; etc.

Develop a critical eye for top-rated movies often shown on television featuring accomplished actors or actresses. Observe the performances of these adroit players three or four times, concentrating on their methods of putting life into their character portrayals. You'll be surprised how much more you notice with each viewing of the movie: the distinctive handling of certain props, physical actions involving setting (Sydney Greenstreet's method of gliding through a doorway and beckoning in *The Mask of Dimitrios*)—all give the character a seeming familiarity with his background that increases believability. Your character must seem to fit and belong to his setting.

This brings us to one of the roots of the problem. The word

"background" is in itself slightly misleading, two-dimensional, suggesting the movement of the story against its environment. One wouldn't depict a fish set against water, so why a character set against the story background? Instead of thinking in terms of *background,* try the more visual and three-dimensional words, *surroundings* or *setting.* As we live out our lives moving amidst our surroundings, so must the fictional character move within his fictitious world.

Creating character is one of the more important aspects of setting. Remember, in most cases you are not merely describing background or surroundings; you are describing your protagonist's *perception* of those surroundings. The same setting might convey two entirely different moods to two different protagonists, depending upon the particular character or story situation.

A hospital room is an example. The room can be restful, or claustrophobically confining; reassuringly neat and efficient, or possessed of a terrible precision and mausoleum-like coolness; a place of safety and optimism, or of horrible apprehension. Same room, same physical details, but seen through the eyes of different characters. And as your character perceives his surroundings, your reader will be perceiving the nature and individuality of your character—evidence that to a larger degree than many suppose, character is delineated through setting.

A scene in a published story of mine offers an extreme example of setting used to substantiate character traits. The protagonist, an inmate of a mental institution, stands in the institution's lounge, unconsciously hearing the ticking of the wall clock. To him, the clock is ticking lazily and out of rhythm (suggesting his bizarre perception of the way time is passing at that point in the story), while to the young psychiatrist who talks with him in the lounge, there is apparently nothing unusual about the clock. The mood of the story was to be one of uncertainty and imbalance, so the out-of-rhythm clock fulfilled the double function of helping to establish both the precarious mental state of my protagonist and the desired atmosphere of the story—at the same time only incidentally introducing a solidifying detail of the lounge.

Setting can also be used to lift the reader out of possible complacency during a flat part of your story. Suppose your main character is sitting in a taxi going over in his mind important details that you think must be repeated for clarity of plot, but that many of your readers might find merely repetitious. If the story is about a wife-murderer, you might have your protagonist glance out the taxi window and notice a man and woman arguing violently on a street corner as they wait for the traffic light to change. Thus you've introduced an interesting though brief scene that increases the interest of your story and relates to your protagonist's chain of thought about the depth of emotion possible in husband-wife relationships that might lead to murder. Again, the thing to remember is that there must be a blend of character and background to lend the story depth, for the basis of suspense is plausibility.

Ties to the familiar

Even when a character in your story is purposely presented in conflict with his background, this blend, this oneness, must exist. When your character finds himself in an environment to which he's unaccustomed, he must still display a familiarity with those few things with which he would naturally be familiar.

Suppose I have a character named Louis Bratten, a hard-drinking ex-chief of homicide who has also lost his private investigator's license for his uncompromising and rebellious behavior. He is expert and sincere, but he is sloppily dressed, sarcastic and devoid of manners. He is called upon by extremely wealthy friends to conduct an investigation at their home. Within this setting of formality and opulence, his character is all the more distinctive by element of contrast. He would hardly be distinctive in the milieu of Mickey Spillane's Mike Hammer, or on the mean streets down which Raymond Chandler's Philip Marlowe walks. But in the drawing room he glows like a fuchsia moon.

Yet even in these surroundings, to provide plausibility Bratten exhibits familiarity with his setting as he slouches in a chair with one leg draped over its arm (for a bargain-basement recliner and a collector's item are both, in the final analysis, chairs). And the first thing he asks for is a glass of Scotch (for mellow Scotch of the highest quality is still Scotch whiskey). And Bratten's irreverent insults seem to zip through the elegant atmosphere with all the more speed and bite (a #XX!#X# is still a #XX!#X#, even if he resides in a sprawling mansion).

Playing your character in conflict with your setting can be effective, but only if you obtain the same blend of character and setting that you can obtain with the conventional method. Whichever method you employ, if you are not utilizing setting to help delineate character, you are missing a very important but often neglected trick of the trade.

Secondary to this technique is the well-practiced art of selecting certain details in your setting to heighten suspense. No denying that while the heroine is anxiously bolting the old country house's doors and windows, it serves the writer's purpose if there is a violent storm outside, complete with banging shutter. But the storm will be on the outside of the story as well if it is not skillfully woven in with the script's other elements of character and situation.

Let's have the blue sky of that morning gradually cloud all day to coincide with the heroine's growing sense of foreboding. Introduce early in the story her child-like fear of lightning. Whomever she dreads has a pattern of striking under cover of a storm. And it is the storm that has washed out a bridge and isolated her from possible rescue. Bring into being some conditions like that, and you will have a real storm, and a much more real heroine and country house. And just maybe your reader will really flinch a bit when lightning topples the old stone chimney and the lights fail.

There must be an interrelationship to substantiate everything that occurs. If during the course of your story a message is found inside a Ming vase, the Ming vase must be mentioned earlier so its existence is established in the reader's mind beforehand. If a character's car is to stall and leave him stranded on a narrow railroad trestle, the incident must be foreshadowed by having the car sputter several times the previous day (because of the character's negligence in maintaining it— if that is the type of character you are trying to create), or possibly by having the character merely mention the aggravation of persistent car trouble. In the incident of lightning toppling the old stone chimney, the chimney (slightly atilt) should have been included in an earlier description of the house and its surroundings.

The necessary subtlety to accomplish these delicate interrelationships effectively without being too obvious comes only with practice and concentration. The writer constructing a successful mystery story is something like the master chef concocting his specialty dish. To be a success, each finished product must have the correct blend of the correct ingredients at the correct time. And the ingredients must be mixed so skillfully that only another chef can discern them individually by sampling. Therefore, your setting should be blended thoroughly and unobtrusively with the other aspects of your fiction, with nothing to jar the reader's sensibilities from the carefully sustained illusion.

Fiction does not lean entirely upon the world of fact for plausibility; it must establish its verisimilitude within itself. The "where" of your story is extremely important, because it relates to every other element in the story. And no element of fiction stands at maximum effectiveness if it stands alone.

17 PLOTTING SHORT MYSTERIES

by *Margaret Maron*

ROBERT FROST once said that, for him, writing poetry without form was like playing tennis without the net; and he defined poetic discipline as "moving freely in harness." For me, his words are just as applicable to the craft of writing short mystery/suspense fiction.

There *is* a form, and you are bound by it, if you wish to sell. It's a form as old as the first tales told around some cave fire eons ago; it moves in a linear fashion proceeding logically out of circumstances you have contrived; and its prime function is to keep your reader wondering, "What happens next?"

For entertainment only

If you resent this type of discipline, if you'd rather experiment with mood pieces or introspective sensitivity of higher moral significance, then you probably won't enjoy writing in this genre, because mysteries *per se* are escapist fiction for a mass audience, and they are read for entertainment only. Your readers want to be intrigued, scared, or puzzled; they want to match wits with your protagonist on an equal footing, and they will *not* tolerate being bored. Readers don't mind if a "serious" book gets tedious—Improving the Mind is supposed to be work—but mysteries are for pleasure, and you can't turn them into pulpits. To quote a Hollywood producer, "If you want to send a message, use Western Union."

This is especially true in a short story of ten to twenty-five typewritten pages. There simply isn't enough physical space to do more than lightly sketch in your settings and characters, because plot development *must* take precedence. And because you have to play fair with your readers and give them enough clues to work with, you learn to make descriptions do double duty.

Although I don't prepare an outline before I start writing, I do have to decide if the tone of my story's going to be light and frothy, or dead serious. Also, whose viewpoint will I use? Suspense develops from *how* the murder is committed and whether or not the murderer will be caught. If it's to be a straight "Whodunit-and-why?" then my detective (male or female, professional or amateur) becomes the protagonist who sifts through the clues, discarding red herrings as they swim past.

In my story, "To Hide a Tree" (*Alfred Hitchcock's Mystery Magazine*), for example, I show a small city experiencing a riot on a warm evening in April. At the fringe of the riot area, in a rundown street of deserted tenements and boarded-up warehouses, what appears to be a killing by a random sniper takes place. A man and his wife are riding along in their car when the window is shattered by a rifle bullet, and the wife is instantly killed. Or at least that's how it looks to the driver of the car behind and to the others who appear on the scene immediately after.

Setting this scene has taken 400 words of tight action. Now I slow the pace, step back, and describe the characters. The witnesses themselves are not important, and they are quickly tagged: young man in a VW, an elderly couple in a Ford sedan. But the dead woman's husband *is* important, so I write:

> Just under six feet, Watson was a thin man in his late forties. He wore lightweight gray slacks and his sports shirt was drenched

with perspiration and clung to his body, revealing a slight middle-age bulge at his waist.

If the reader were alert, he would now suspect something fishy about Watson, because I slipped a clue into that description. Remember, I'd already shown a very warm evening and that the killer's bullet had splintered the car window. Instead of being diverted by Watson's little pot belly, an experienced reader might well say, "Aha! If it's so warm and Watson is sweating so profusely, why were the car windows rolled up?"

And naturally, this is one of the questions I'll have my detective come up with when he's working out the solution at the end. If I've been successful, my reader will think, "Of course! Why didn't I notice that?"

The bones of your story

Anything that makes you think "what if—?" can be your starting point. "To Hide a Tree" was a variation of Poe's "Purloined Letter," my title taken from that old riddle, "Where does the wise man hide a tree?" Answer: "In a forest." I thought about all the cases of random killing connected with the riots this country has seen in the past ten years. What if one of those sniper killings hadn't been completely random? What if someone knew his city was ripe for an explosion and used that riot to camouflage a private murder?

I began to perceive the bones of a story: Watson, a middle-aged man, conservative, fed up with the protest movement, coupled with a wife whose radical philosophies infuriated him and who was beginning to influence the thinking of their only child. I'd let his wife's calculated rudeness to his boss keep him from an important promotion; and I'd rule out the simple expedient of divorce by having him fear that his teen-age daughter, whom he truly loves, would choose to live with the wife. For further motive, I'd let him decide that if he can make his wife's death look like the work of a freaked-out sniper, he would gain three things: removal of her hated presence and influence on their daughter; enough money from double-indemnity insurance to put his daughter into a private school; and—almost as important to him—the delicious irony of placing the blame on the element of society that he despises so fiercely.

How did it happen?

In this particular story, the most suspenseful aspect was not who did it or why, but rather *how* the murder was actually committed. If I stayed behind the husband's eyes and played fair with the reader, all my impact would be lost. I needed a detective to solve the mystery, and there were only two who would logically care enough to ferret out the facts: the daughter or the police. (If I have one absolute belief, it's that my characters must act logically. I can't manipulate them into doing stupid things just because I haven't held up my end and made a better job of plotting.)

The daughter is eliminated as "detective" because of her lack of technical knowledge and mobility, and that leaves a police detective. Two detectives, actually, so that their dialogue can *show* action instead of my having to tell it.

With these points clear in my mind, I'm ready to begin. Of course, I may get carried away with my own lyricism and waste two pages on the warm spring evening with nature's reaffirmation of life in the midst of man's violent denial. I indulge myself at this point and positively wallow in adjectives as I work my way into the story, because I know all that poetic sensitivity's going to get cut to one short paragraph in my final draft. (Mystery editors are notoriously prejudiced against poetic writing that doesn't advance the story line!)

Next, I show a young man in his VW driving along the edge of the riot area at about 7:30 p.m., when the car ahead slams on brakes and the man in it jumps out and starts yelling that his wife's just been shot by a sniper. The only reason for creating the VW driver is that I need an outside witness who can state that the husband had no chance to dispose of any trick weapon from the moment he jumped out of the car until my detective arrives on the scene. At that point, we can start watching the action through the detective's eyes, and he sees the clues I've already mentioned: the husband's sweat-drenched shirt, the closed car windows, the warm evening.

The game of cat-and-mouse

Now I can begin playing cat-and-mouse with both the reader and my detectives. I introduce the VW driver who thinks he was present when the wife was killed, but who didn't actually hear the shot because of all the police and fire sirens in the area. I have the medical examiner and lab reports say, yes, the time of death was around 7:30; and yes, the holes in the car window and dead woman's right temple came from an M-1 rifle fired from a distance of fifty feet at an elevation of twenty feet—all confirming Watson's story.

Yet, while my detectives are no geniuses, they aren't dummies either, and they've been policemen long enough to know that more wives are killed by their husbands than by anonymous snipers. By page ten, their investigations uncover enough about Watson's personality and motives to make him the chief suspect.

But for every two steps I let them advance, I set them back one to intensify the mystery: I let them learn that Watson used an M-1 in Korea, twenty years earlier, but no one's ever seen a rifle in his house. I give them the condemned tenement from which the fatal shot could have been fired, but I break all the windows on the second floor and leave them no fingerprints. I give them a bum who'd seen Watson in that tenement a week before, as he was figuring out the angle of trajectory, and I even let the bum identify Watson's picture—but only after he's been just as positive in identifying several other mug shots, thus making him an unreliable witness.

And all the time, I have them baffled by the question, "How could he've shot her from fifty feet away if he was sitting in the car with her at the same time?"

Suddenly, I ask myself how Watson knew he was going to be driving by this particular building with his wife. That means going back and establishing earlier in the story that they drove this route every Friday night to play bridge at her sister's house. This, in turn, becomes another clue for my detective, who badgers Watson by saying:

> "Neighborhood gossip had you two figured for a divorce. Except for that standing bridge date at her sister's, you two'd quit going out together. You say you hate bridge and can't stand your inlaws, so why'd you keep going if not to have an excuse to drive through an area everyone knew was ripe for a riot?"

Unlike Perry Mason's villains, who stand up and start blabbing a confession as soon as the finger of suspicion is pointed in their direction, *my* murderer is shrewd enough to sit tight, knowing there's no concrete evidence against him.

Clues and solutions

Meanwhile, as a sort of faint theme song in the background, I've alluded to springtime and nature throughout the story. When the detectives first go to Watson's house, they find him doing some yard work—cleaning gutters, cutting dead limbs from a tall maple tree—getting ready for spring. I've also kept the temperature bouncing up and down as it does in a northern April; and again, there's a dual purpose in both. Letting my detectives interview Watson in his yard shows them his twenty-foot extension ladder. Later, when the detectives have admitted defeat and are returning Watson's impounded car, the chilly weather shows them how Watson actually committed the murder without having the discovery seem to be a coincidence. As another writer has said, "I planted the hook in the first part of the story and now I'm ready to hang a climax· on it."

Do you have the solution? No? Hang on then!

While driving Watson's car, my detective notices something. Returning to headquarters, he re-examines photos taken at the death scene, which confirm his hypothesis; and now that he has a workable theory of how Watson could have done it, his boss will give him the search warrant he's been previously denied.

I deliberately hold back on *what* he noticed because revealing the *how* climaxes my story, and I want it to come in a dialogue of confrontation between the detective and the murdering husband so that the story can end almost immediately.

Warrants in hand, the detective explains that while returning the car, he noticed how powerful the heater was—only *he* hadn't turned it on. Yet photographs of the death scene do show the heater set at full blast. The closed windows and powerful heater have combined to throw the medical examiner's time of death off by a half-hour. Watson shot his wife in their own backyard from one of his maple trees and then staged a random sniper killing from the tenement a half-hour away.

As the detective concludes the short exposition, the search party find the hidden M-1 rifle. Then, and only then, does Watson's composure slip. Now that he's found out, I can allow him a little more humanity, can let his shoulders slump, and let him say:

> "All these past months, my daughter—she's been so quick to understand and make excuses for every no-good, lazy malcontent in the country." He looked at them despairingly. "I wonder if she can understand all this—or me?"

And that was the end. Or at least that was the end of my final draft. The first was thirty-seven pages long; the last was twenty-four. When it was as lean and spare and taut as I could make it, I sent it off to *Alfred Hitchcock's Mystery Magazine* and they bought it the following week—the best possible ending to any mystery plot!

18 BIRTH OF A SLEUTH

by *Ngaio Marsh*

HE WAS BORN with the rank of Detective-Inspector, C.I.D., on a very wet Saturday afternoon in a basement flat off Sloane Square, in London. The year was 1931.

All day, rain splashed up from the feet of passersby going to and fro, at eye-level, outside my water-streaked windows. It fanned out from under the tires of cars, cascaded down the steps to my door and flooded the area. "Remorseless" was the word for it and its sound was, beyond all expression, dreary. In view of what was about to take place, the setting was, in fact, almost too good to be true.

I read a detective story borrowed from a dim little lending-library in a stationer's shop across the way. Either a Christie or a Sayers, I think it was. By four o'clock, when the afternoon was already darkening, I had finished it, and still the rain came down. I remember that I made up the London coal-fire of those days and looked down at it, idly wondering if I had it in me to write something in the genre. That was the season, in England, when the Murder Game was popular at weekend parties. Someone was slipped a card saying he or she was the "murderer." He or she then chose a moment to select a "victim," and there was a subsequent "trial." I thought it might be an idea for a whodunit—they were already called that—if a real corpse was found instead of a phony one. Luckily for

123

me, as it turned out, I wasn't aware until much later that a French practitioner had been struck with the same notion.

I played about with this idea. I tinkered with the fire and with an emergent character who might have been engendered in its sulky entrails: a solver of crimes.

The room had grown quite dark when I pulled on a mackintosh, took an umbrella, plunged up the basement steps and beat my way through rain-fractured lamplight to the stationer's shop. It smelt of damp newsprint, cheap magazines, and wet people. I bought six exercise books, a pencil and pencil sharpener and splashed back to the flat.

Then with an odd sensation of giving myself some sort of treat, I thought more specifically about the character who already had begun to take shape.

Celebrated eccentrics

In the crime fiction of that time, the solver was often a person of more-or-less eccentric habit with a collection of easily identifiable mannerisms. This, of course, was in the tradition of Sherlock Holmes. Agatha Christie's splendid M. Poirot had his moustaches, his passion for orderly arrangements, his frequent references to "grey cells." Dorothy L. Sayers's Lord Peter Wimsey could be, as I now am inclined to think, excruciatingly facetious. Nice Reggie Fortune said—and author H. C. Bailey had him say it very often—"My dear chap! Oh, my dear chap!" and across the Atlantic there was Philo Vance who spoke a strange language that his author, S. S. Van Dine, had the nerve to attribute, in part, to Balliol College, Oxford.

Faced with this assembly of celebrated eccentrics, I decided, on that long-distant wet afternoon, that my best chance lay in comparative normality: in the invention of a man with a background resembling that of the friends I had made in England, and that I had better not tie mannerisms, like labels, round his neck. (I can see now that with my earlier books I did not altogether succeed in this respect.)

I thought that my detective would be a professional police-man but, in some ways, atypical: an attractive, civilized man with whom it would be pleasant to talk but much less pleasant to fall out.

He began to solidify.

From the beginning I discovered that I knew quite a lot about him. Indeed, I rather think that, even if I had not fallen so casually into the practice of crime-writing and had taken to a more serious form, he would still have arrived and found himself in an altogether different setting.

He was tall and thin with an accidental elegance about him and fastidious enough to make one wonder at his choice of profession. He was a compassionate man. He had a cockeyed sense of humor, dependent largely upon understatement, but for all his unemphatic, rather apologetic ways, he could be a formidable person of considerable authority. As for his back-ground, that settled itself there and then: he was a younger son of a Buckinghamshire family and had his schooling at Eton. His elder brother, whom he regarded as a bit of an ass, was a diplomatist, and his mother, whom he liked, a lady of character.

I remember how pleased I was, early in his career, when one of the reviews called him "that nice chap, Alleyn," because that was how I liked to think of him: a nice chap with more edge to him than met the eye—a good deal more, as I hope it has turned out. The popular press of his early days would refer to him as "the handsome inspector," a practice that caused him acute embarrassment.

On this day of his inception I fiddled about with the idea of writing a tale that would explain why he left the Diplomatic Service for the Police Force, but somehow the idea has never jelled.

His age? Here I must digress. His age would defy the investigation of an Einstein, and he is not alone in this respect. Hercule Poirot, I have been told, was, by ordinary reckoning, going on 122 when he died. Truth to tell, fictional investigations move in an exclusive space-time continuum where Mr. Bucket* in *Bleak House* may be seen going about his police investigations cheek-by-jowl with the most recent fledglings. It is enough to say that on the afternoon of my detective's arrival, I did not concern myself with his age, and I am still of the same mind in that respect.

His arrival had been unexpected and occurred, you might say, out of nothing. One of the questions writers are most often asked about characters in their books is whether they are based upon people in the workaday world—"real people." Some of mine certainly are, but they have gone through various mutations and in doing so have moved away from their original begetters. But not this one. He, as far as I can tell, had no begetter apart from his author. He came in without introduction, and if, for this reason, there is an element of unreality about him, I can only say that for me, at least, he was and is very real indeed.

Author-character relationships

Dorothy L. Sayers has been castigated, with some justification perhaps, for falling in love with her Wimsey. To have done so may have been an error in taste and judgment, though her ardent fans would never have admitted as much. I can't say I have ever succumbed in this way to my own investigator, but I have grown to like him as an old friend. I even dare to

---

* Mr. Bucket was created by Charles Dickens for the novel *Bleak House* (1852). He was the first important detective in English literature and became the prototype of the undramatic, colorless but honest, competent, and hardworking (as well as inevitably successful) police detective found in hundreds of novels since.—*Ed.*

think he has developed third-dimensionally in my company. We have traveled widely: in a night express through the North Island of New Zealand, and among the geysers, boiling mud and snow-clad mountains of that country. We have cruised along English canals and walked through the streets and monuments of Rome. His duties have taken us to an island off the coast of Normandy and to the backstage regions of several theatres. He has sailed with a psychopathic homicide from Tilbury to Cape Town and has made arrests in at least three country houses, one hospital, a church, a canal boat and a pub. Small wonder, perhaps, that we have both broadened our outlook under the pressure of these undertakings, none of which was anticipated on that wet afternoon in London.

At his first appearance he was a bachelor and, although responsive to the opposite sex, did not bounce in and out of irresponsible beds when going about his job. Or, if he did, I knew nothing about it. He was, to all intents and purposes, fancy-free and would remain so until, sailing out of Suva in Fiji, he came across Agatha Troy, painting in oils, on the boat-deck of a liner. And that was still some half-dozen books in the future.

There would be consternation shown by editors and publishers when, after another couple of jobs, the lady accepted him. The acceptance would be a *fait accompli,* and from then on I would be dealing with a married investigator, his celebrated wife, and later on, their son.

By a series of coincidences and much against his inclination, it would come about that these two would occasionally get themselves embroiled in his professional duties, but generally speaking he would keep his job out of his family life. He would set about his cases with his regular associate who is one of his closest friends; Inspector Fox, massive, calm, and plain-thinking, would tramp sedately in. They have been working together for a considerable time, and still allow me to accompany them.

But "on the afternoon in question," all this, as lady crime novelists used to say, "lay in the future." The fire had burnt clear and sent leaping patterns up the walls of my London flat when I turned on the light, opened an exercise book, sharpened my pencil, and began to write. There he was, waiting quietly in the background ready to make his entrance at Chapter IV, page 58, in the first edition.

I had company. It became necessary to give my visitor a name.

Earlier in that week I had visited Dulwich College. This is an English public school, which in any other country would mean a private school. It was founded and very richly endowed by a famous actor in the days of the first Elizabeth. It possesses a splendid picture gallery and a fabulous collection of relics from the Shakespearian-Marlovian theatre: enthralling to me who has a passion for that scene.

My father was an old boy of Dulwich College—an "old Alleynian," as it is called, the name of the Elizabethan actor being Alleyn.

Detective-Inspector Alleyn, C.I.D.? Yes.

His first name was in doubt for some time but another visit, this time to friends in the Highlands of Scotland, had familiarized me with some resoundingly-christened characters, among them one Roderick (or Rory) MacDonald.

Roderick Alleyn, Detective-Inspector, C.I.D.?

Yes.

The name, by the way, is pronounced "Allen."

19 NOTES ON THE SUSPENSE NOVEL

by *Harold Q. Masur*

As I WRITE this piece, with the *New York Times Book Review* in front of me, I note that six of the ten fiction titles on the Best Seller List are in the suspense category.

This is not an entirely new phenomenon. For several years now, crime and suspense novels have monopolized the list. Whatever its significance, at long last the virtue of solid, suspenseful storytelling is being handsomely, indeed lavishly, rewarded with cold, hard cash. What with paperback guarantees occasionally running to half a million dollars or more, even the one-shot author who hits the jackpot can retire to Acapulco to live out his days in baronial splendor. Especially since the major book clubs are now regularly including suspense novels among their selections. And with that kind of built-in audience, the movie companies too begin their bidding; so you see, we are getting into a very rarefied bracket.

Even so, after carefully analyzing most of the big ones, I cannot help but conclude that a large part of their success lies in the fact that the central plot core is not only unusual, but brashly inventive. A real whopper. Like an assassination attempt on General Charles de Gaulle; the hijacking of a New York subway train, holding the passengers for a million-dollar ransom; burglarizing the world's great diamond center; a marauding shark that threatens the economy of a resort community on Long Island; an uncontrollable flash fire of volcanic proportions in a skyscraper that traps prominent celebrants in the tower.

These ideas generate their own excitement. Tension and suspense are inherent in the very notions themselves. To pin them down, the writer must exercise his imagination. He cannot be afraid to tackle the big theme, and then to develop it so that its outcome seems not only logical but inevitable. Such a novel will sell. Vivid prose, solid characterization, colorful atmosphere will make it a critical success too.

The writer's springboard

Where do you start? Every writer has his own springboard. The mental alchemy that turns an idea into a final plot stems from your subconscious background and some plain hard thinking.

Here is how it works. Let us assume that the germinating seed for one author is some situation that captures his imagination. A girl starting her vacation cruise opens her trunk and finds a dead body. This idea is developed by asking questions. Who was the corpse? Her boss? Her ex-husband? A rich uncle? An unknown man? The decision is made; the author is launched on a new inquiry: What does the girl do with the body? Throw it overboard? Suppose she does and someone sees her. Will he stop the ship? Will he attempt blackmail? The author keeps up this type of inquiry until the foundation is strong enough to support a whole plot.

A second writer may evolve plot from character. Suppose he starts with a married couple and he decides that the husband is going to kill his wife. Our writer begins digging into their backgrounds. This naturally draws in other characters, and with them new ideas. Maybe the wife was unfaithful. Maybe the husband didn't kill her after all. The murderer is someone else. The husband is accused and must solve the crime in order to save his neck. Why is he under suspicion? Did he recently take out an insurance policy on his wife? Is he in love with another woman? Has his wife refused him a divorce? Does he need the insurance money because of business troubles? Was the wife involved in some nefarious deal the husband knew nothing about?

It is exactly this type of inquiry that will make your plot grow.

One more example. The jumping-off point for a third writer may be some theme that appeals to him. He reads about some new organization dedicated to bigotry and intolerance. He believes, perhaps, that someone is trying to keep the idea of Fascism alive. His theme is the desire for power. He considers this and develops ideas. Maybe there is a symbol that represents authority to certain underground groups. Perhaps the hero has unwittingly come into possession of this symbol. Menacing events occur as the villain and his henchmen try to regain its possession.

There comes a time in a writer's life when the well seems to have run dry. You rack your brains, you stare at the ceiling, you pace the room . . . nothing. Your mind is a blank. But the working writer cannot just sit and wait for inspiration. He must produce his allotment every day. So here is a gimmick I myself have used on occasion with some degree of success.

Read a published novel. Then about one-half or three-quarters of the way through, stop, close the book, set it aside. Now try to guess the identity of the villain. After having made your choice, figure out his motive.

If the author has concocted a decent yarn with any degree of ingenuity, chances are you'll be wrong on both counts. There is no cause here for gloom. See what you've accomplished. You have finally sent your imagination winging and you've come up with two of the most important elements in plotting a mystery novel that are entirely your own: 1) A new villain; 2) A fresh motive.

Both are unrelated to those of the original author. These two elements must inevitably lead you to additional characters and incidents. On the premise that few individuals live in a total vacuum, other members of the cast will naturally evolve: relatives, business associates, lovers, confederates, police, a host of individuals connected with the villain and the victim and the mechanics of the motive itself.

I can name a score of novels that spring from almost identical plot cores, and yet in the finished story bear no resemblance to each other. The unique qualities of each author, his personality, his style, his background, his way of thinking—all must of necessity produce a development that is different from that of any other writer.

Observation and awareness

Develop an awareness of the potential in news reports and fragments of conversation. Keep a notebook handy. Whenever you see or hear an item that seizes your curiosity, write it down.

Let me give you an example. In glancing through the *Wall Street Journal* one day, I ran across a piece about a group of wealthy entrepreneurs who formed a private syndicate for the purpose of advancing money to residual beneficiaries of wills and trusts in exchange for their legacies. More simply, it worked something like this: Suppose a man dies leaving an estate of one million dollars, providing in his will that the income should go to his widow, with the principal to his nephew on her death. But the widow is young. She might live for thirty years or more, and by that time the nephew would be an old man. He does not care to wait. So he might sell his million-dollar legacy to the syndicate for one hundred thousand dollars cash in hand.

Now, here is a situation fraught with opportunities for skulduggery and violence. It appealed to me. It had potential.

And ultimately it resulted in my novel, *The Legacy Lenders* (published by Random House and in paperback by Bantam Books).

In another case, I remember sitting with a group of people one evening discussing a particularly odious homicide that had been in the papers all week. Someone said, "How can any lawyer defend such a detestable murderer? Look at the evidence. He must know the man is guilty."

"That's not the point," I said. "The accused is entitled to his day in court. There is a presumption of innocence. He's not guilty until a jury says he's guilty."

A general debate followed, most of the participants arguing against me. The man was guilty when he committed the crime, not months later when some jury returned a verdict. I took the position that it was not within the lawyer's province to make any judgment as to guilt or innocence, that he would be usurping the jury's obligation and not fulfilling his own.

"What is his obligation?" they asked.

"To make the state prove its case," I said. "To give the defendant the best available defense."

Later that night, lying awake in bed, I kept wondering about the dilemma of a decent, honorable lawyer who comes across incontrovertible evidence during the course of a trial that his client is not only guilty, but that he's a psychopath, and that by winning an acquittal, he himself would be responsible for returning to society a man with homicidal tendencies.

It occurred to me that here was a valid, indeed a compelling, theme for a novel. I wanted to explore within the framework of a dramatic courtroom trial the moral imperatives of such a lawyer. I suggested it to my publisher; he liked it, and that led to my novel, *The Attorney* (published by Random House, with subsidiary rights acquired by Bantam Books, Playboy Book Club, and Universal Pictures for a feature film).

The point I am trying to make is that story ideas abound. A writer must train himself to recognize them. Get them down in that little notebook and let them simmer a while in your subconscious. You'll be surprised at the results.

Fine, you say. I've had a splendid idea for some time now, but I don't really know how to develop it, how to flesh it out with characters, background, incidents, complications. Well, I'm not going to tell you it's easy. Nothing worth doing well is easy.

Read. Read voluminously. When you find a story that holds your interest, read it again. Analyze it. Search out the central plot idea. Observe what the author did with it, how he expanded it. A good novel can be a very helpful textbook.

The nature of the crime

Your crime must be a serious one. Nothing less than murder will do. Life, no matter how mean its existence, is man's most precious possession. Once taken from him, it can never be restored. Murder is irrevocable. Hence there can be no compromise, and society has decreed that in most cases the murderer must be punished. Your villain must be provided with a motive strong enough for him to incur this risk. In real life a hoodlum may kill a man for the silver in his pocket, but your fictional killer must be more soundly motivated.

Roughly, motives may be divided into two main groups. These are the ones most often used:

1. GAIN
   (a) Financial—through insurance, inheritance, etc.
   (b) Political
   (c) Business
   (d) Valuable property—jewelry, inventions, etc.
   (e) Love—by the elimination of a rival
2. FEAR
   (a) Exposure of a previously committed crime—malpractice, embezzlement, car theft, etc.

(b) Exposure of illicit love

(c) Fear of danger to a loved one

(d) Fear of a rival—such as a businessman intent on ruining the murderer

(e) The necessity of keeping any secret vital to the safety of the villain

The above listing is by no means exhaustive, and it certainly overlaps, but it should help to point the way.

As a general rule, your murder method should not be bizarre or complicated. Be true to life and stick to the conventional methods. Use a knife, a gun, a blunt instrument, poison. For originality you can have the victim found under unusual circumstances. One novel I read had the corpse hidden in a spoiled case of spaghetti being hauled to an incinerator plant for disposal.

Clues and red herrings

Originality can be exercised when it comes to clues. A good clue is anything that actually points to the villain but is presented in a way that causes the reader to miss its significance. Almost anything under the sky may be a clue. There are two kinds: tangible clues, such as a glove found at the scene of the crime; and intangible clues, which are more difficult to define.

Here is an example: let us suppose that the victim is deaf, but can read lips and hold a conversation. The murderer is unaware of this fact. He waits until the victim is home alone, turns on the radio to cover the noise of his approach, and then shoots him. When the victim's family return, they know that he, being deaf, would not have put the set in operation. From this fact, the hero may deduce the killer's identity because everyone else was acquainted with the victim's affliction and would not have turned on the radio.

There are time-tested tricks in handling your clues. One of them is to present the clue followed by a bit of violent action so that the reader does not have time to digest it. Another is to include the clue with a group of other items, such as the contents of a purse, so that its significance is lost among them.

If you're not good at this, don't kill yourself. Clues are important, but not more important than having a good story to tell and telling it engagingly. Many British mysteries will bore you for 300 pages and then belt you silly with an astounding climax. It is my belief that the average reader would prefer to be entertained for 300 pages and not so surprised at the end.

We come now to the matter of red herrings. Every mystery novel has several good ones strewn about. A red herring is a device by means of which the reader's suspicions are distracted from the actual culprit and directed at one or more innocent persons.

Here is how it works. Suppose the heroine is guiltless, but we want the reader to suspect her. We begin by making the hero or viewpoint character begin to doubt her innocence. Seemingly, she blocks his path at every turn. She conceals information from the police. At one point the hero spies her throwing something into a pool of water. When he fishes it out it proves to be the murder weapon. At another point she makes violent love to him so that he will miss an appointment with a man who can supply vital information. Later she is seen leaving this man's room just before he is found dead.

Not only are these satisfactory red herrings, but they serve to make up many of the story's incidents and complications. At the end it may be explained that the girl was merely acting to protect her brother whom she mistakenly thought guilty.

About this business of violent love—well, sex is a part of life and may legitimately be a part of any novel, but not dragged in simply to titillate the reader. A sex crime of this sort should certainly not be the basic motivation. Some hard-boiled types gallop around despoiling gorgeous blondes, brunettes and redheads on every page merely to satisfy an overactive libido. If your characters get involved, let it be an integral part of the story complication itself.

In the denouement of your novel, all loose ends must be neatly tied together and explained. Briefly and succinctly. It is wise, technically, not to save your entire explanation for the end of the story and then throw it at your readers in one huge mass of deductions and conclusions. Feed it to them piecemeal. There are many items that may be revealed along the way without exposing the solution.

And now that he stands accused, your villain will not abandon hope and jump out the window. Not unless he's sure he's licked. For he must not be an imbecile or a weakling. In order to maintain suspense and uncertainty of outcome, he should be fearless, resourceful, crafty, and ruthless—a lesser scoundrel will not do. And a lunkhead would make enough errors to be nailed in the second chapter. So if he makes a break, let him do so because he realizes the futility of submitting to a trial.

If he fails to yank a vial of poison from his armpit, be certain the evidence against him will stand up in a court of law. The District Attorney must have more than a pretty set of theories to win a conviction. If the evidence is circumstantial, it should be overwhelming enough to leave no doubt in the minds of a jury. You can discuss these problems with a friendly lawyer.

Vital ingredient

A vital ingredient in any piece of fiction is suspense. If your story or novel fails to hold the readers' interest, they can reach over and turn on television, which can whip up the readers' emotions with "live" characters. All you have is words.

How can suspense be induced and then intensified to make readers keep turning the pages, so immersed in your story that they are oblivious to everything around them? It's a challenge, isn't it? I believe the movies offer a clue. Here is a fragment you have seen many times, and will probably see many times again. It embodies the very essence of suspense.

Our hero and his lady are on the run, trying to escape from a mortal enemy. The pursuer and his henchmen are closing in fast. They come within shooting range. The protagonists scramble into a waiting car. The hero turns the ignition key, but the engine only grinds and fails to start. Bullets spang against metal, window glass shatters. The battery is losing power. Now the enemy is only yards away. Tension in the audience mounts, becomes almost unbearable. All seems lost; the odds are too great. Breathing is suspended, everybody is on the edge of the seat. And then, at the last possible moment, the engine roars into life, and they're off.

Basic. Elementary. But it seems to work every time. What has the director contrived? What lesson can we learn? A rather important one, I think. When you come to a moment of crisis in your story, do not pass over it casually. Hold it. Milk it. Squeeze out the full potential of drama, excitement, suspense. After all, you have expended considerable effort reaching this point; exploit it. Remember how the film director focused his camera on the face of the girl and showed you her expression of panic and rising despair. Then shifting to the hero, his hand frantically twisting the ignition key, jaws clenched in desperation. And finally the pursuers, grim, inflexible, ruthless, merciless. So, too, must the writer suspend action while he concentrates on the expressions and emotions of his characters. If he has done his job, if the readers have identified at all, they will experience those same emotions. And that is what fiction is all about: feelings, emotion, identification, readers living the scene as it occurs.

As a reader, I relish every moment of a good story. Most of us live rather monotonous lives. The world of fiction offers vicarious adventure, excitement, even enlightenment, and at its finest sometimes rare and valuable insights.

Among other devices used to heighten suspense are the following:

1. As the protagonist approaches a solution, his new-found knowledge puts him in greater peril. He now poses a serious threat to the malefactors and must be neutralized or perhaps liquidated.

2. Seemingly insurmountable obstacles keep arising to prevent the accomplishment of his mission. Storms, a fallen bridge, an automobile accident, a blundering confederate, misinformation, spiriting away or death of a prospective informer, or anything else that your imagination might invent.

3. The hero (and the reader with him) is left hanging while something must be done—a serum analyzed, a negative developed, a ballistics test made—and constant obstacles delay their accomplishment.

4. Important evidence lost, concealed, or destroyed.

5. Kidnapping or threatening the life of another character in order to intimidate the hero.

All of these devices can still be profitably employed by handling them with freshness and genuine emotion.

I have found in the actual writing that it is helpful to keep notes of everything that needs to be explained or disposed of. Invaluable too is a list of all items to be mentioned several times: hotels, addresses, car models, thumbnail descriptions, anything in fact that may save you the tedious chore of riffling back through many pages to find something that eludes your memory.

There is one added satisfaction in writing a good suspense novel these days—you may find that what has been considered essentially a literary entertainment is now being treated as a work of mainstream importance.

20

MYSTERIES WITHIN MYSTERIES

by *Patricia Moyes*

AS A WRITER of mystery stories, the compliment I treasure most is when somebody says to me, "The characters in your books are so alive. They are just like real people." I find that this is often said on a note of faint surprise, as if the personages in a detective novel had no right to be anything more than cardboard puppets, dancing through the intricacies of the plot.

I have to admit that this surprise is sometimes justified. Some mystery authors seem content to sacrifice credibility of character to the speed and thrill of the action. Others—a more distinguished group—tend to create one splendidly rounded character in the person of their detective, who recurs in book after book, but they bother very little with the personalities of the supporting cast. For me, the reality of my people is tremendously important, and I like to think that my concern for them enhances the enjoyment of my readers.

"But," you may say, "a mystery novel should be fast-moving, baffling and exciting. Who wants to take time out for in-depth character studies and long descriptions of individual characters?"

Bringing characters to life

You are quite right. A long description will never bring a character to life in the mind of the reader. So, how is it to be done?

First, by what I can only call love and concern on the author's part. You have to take the time to think about your characters, until you know them like old friends. You should explore and discover far more about them than you will ever need to use in the book. Decide not only how they look, but how they dress, what they like to eat, what books they read, what their hobbies are. Above all, listen to them until you hear their voices in your mind.

This brings me to my second point. However well you may come to know your characters, it will do no good unless you have developed a technique for communicating your knowledge to your reader through the medium of the printed page. In my view, this is best achieved by dialogue.

Many excellent prose writers go all to pieces when they try their hands at dialogue. I think this comes about because writing dialogue takes a special discipline which they have never taken the time to study. There is a world of difference between words intended to be read, and words intended to be spoken, and, whether in a play or a book, all dialogue falls into the latter class. The writing of it is a technique, and it must be learned.

I wish I could simply recommend that every writer have the good luck I had—the chance to spend years working in the theater before I ever came to novel writing. Of course, that's not possible, but there is a lot you can do.

See as much professional theater as you possibly can. Don't just sit there and enjoy yourself; bring out your analytical faculties. Read the play both before and after you see it. Learn to distinguish among the various contributions which go to make up the production—those of the writer, the actor and the director. Remember that as a novelist your job will be even tougher than the dramatist's, for you will not have the benefit of a talented interpreter—a really good actor can make magic and touch his audience with the most banal of lines. Your dialogue will have to be good enough and punchy enough to make direct contact with your readers. If possible, join an amateur dramatic group and start looking at lines from the actor's viewpoint. You will very soon discover that there is a world of difference between dialogue that reads impressively, and dialogue that plays well. A critic once said about *The Taming of the Shrew,* "It's really a terrible play. The trouble is that it plays so superbly." Read your Shakespeare again, not as great literature, but as an actor's script. *He* knew all about dialogue.

Listen to people. Listen to everyone you meet, and take time to analyze your reactions. You will find that a great many of the opinions you form of people speaking are based not on what they say, but on how they say it.

For instance, that man in the railway train the other day. You classified him at once as fussy, self-centered, and a bit of an old woman. Why? He wanted the window closed. Well, there was nothing so strange about that; you were thinking of closing it yourself. All right, think back. He was reading a newspaper, and you noticed that instead of flapping the pages around like most people, he had folded it neatly into quarters in order to read his chosen piece. Then, he was already on his feet and closing the window before he spoke, and he certainly did not request your opinion. He said, "You don't mind if we have the window closed? I'm extremely prone to chills at this time of year."

One mannerism, one short sentence—and you had made up your mind as to the sort of man he was. You'll notice that it is not necessary to describe his appearance at all. Your readers will fill in the blanks for themselves.

How very different was that woman at the cocktail party.

"I'm Amanda Bickersteth. I've been *dying* to meet you. I've read *all* your books."

"I'm so—"

"Now, you must tell me exactly how you think up all those *marvelous* plots."

"Well, as a matter of—"

"That one set on the tropical island . . . you must know the Caribbean *inside out.* Come on now, do tell—which island was it really?"

"I don't—"

"Dwight and I go to St. Thomas every winter. Oh, I know *just* what you're going to say—it *is* crowded, but we just love it. Oh, dear, there's Dwight now. I'm afraid I must rush. It's been *so* interesting talking to you, I really feel I've learned *a lot* about writing . . . ."

You get the idea? One day, both those people will find a niche in one of your books.

"Creating" a work of fiction

This is not to say that you ever can or should take a real person and "put him into a book." Unless you are writing the story of his life, he will not fit conveniently into the mold of your plot. What's more, if you have a real-life model to draw from, you will always be asking yourself, "What would my friend do in these circumstances?" rather than, "What will my imaginary character do next?"

A work of fiction is a creation, and the people in it are, literally, your creatures. The man in the train and the woman at the party are no more than raw material, jottings in a notebook. (I don't keep one myself, except mentally, but many writers do and find it very useful.) One day, when you need a social chatterbox or an egocentric hypochondriac for your story or novel, a gesture or a phrase will emerge from your memory, digested and ready for use.

To return to the subject of dialogue. I advised you to listen until in your mind you could "hear" your people talking, and this is vitally important. Speak the lines of dialogue aloud— or else imagine them spoken by your character, in his or her voice and intonation. You will very soon find yourself thinking, "No, she wouldn't put it like that. She'd come straight to the point," or, "He wouldn't be able to resist being a bit long-winded over a thing like that." This may sound too easy, but I firmly believe that if every author followed those simple rules, a lot of books would be a great deal easier to read—and a lot of good novels could be transferred to the stage or the screen without the necessity for rewriting a lot of literally unspeakable dialogue.

"Defending" your plots

When I talk about getting to know your characters, I don't mean that you should hesitate to put pen to paper until you have mentally created at least half a dozen living, credible human beings. If you tried to do that, you would probably never start to write the book at all. It is here that we come close to the heart of what will always remain a mystery to me, and, I suspect, to many other writers. Does the writing create the character, or the character the writing? At what point is a fictional personality born? When does he or she become truly alive? All I can tell you is my own experience. My books start with a background—the place, the activity, the social ambience that forms the backdrop of the story. Secondly, I have to work out the plot like a problem in logic or mathematics.

At this stage, I freely admit, the characters are very shadowy indeed—a bloodless collection labeled "rich businessman," "social climber hostess," "ambitious young journalist," and so on. A stereotyped lot, to be sure, but most of us are stereotypes to strangers, who see us only from a distance. The closer we get to other people, the more their personalities begin to emerge from behind the convenient labels.

It is the same with fictional characters. As you write, listening all the time for those voices, remembering quirks of speech or behavior from real life, you will find your people stepping out of the shadows, revealing themselves in their own true personalities. If this sounds like a sort of miracle, I can only agree that it is just that. What is more, some of the stronger-minded characters are quite capable of taking your plot and twisting it to suit their own ideas. So far, I have managed to defend my basic plot structure—the murderer, the victim, the method, the motive, and the means of discovery—against all comers, but it has not always been easy. Designated murderers have developed such charm that they have nearly succeeded in talking themselves out of just retribution; victims can turn out to be so entertaining that I can hardly bear to part with their company early in the book.

With key characters like those, the author must either harden his heart or scrap the book and start again. Once you depart from your plot structure, you are lost, and your characters will fall with you. When it comes to the minor people in the story, however, it is a different matter. They grow from chapter to chapter like ivy up a wall. They become headstrong, stubborn, talkative, and possessive. They often behave in quite unexpected ways.

In my own novel writing I have had a young woman who simply refused to marry the eminently suitable young man I'd selected for her; a harsh, unsympathetic, middle-aged husband who turned out to be deeply and movingly in love with his young wife, although he could not find the way to tell her so; a serious-minded young bureaucrat who turned out to have a wickedly mischievous sense of humor that almost wrecked my plot (I should have been warned about him, because I had met his brother in an earlier book; frivolity obviously ran in the family).

As the author, of course, I could have simply forced all these characters to behave as I had originally intended them to do. This might have made my job somewhat easier—but it would have destroyed all my satisfaction in the work, because it would have withdrawn from my creatures the fragile breath of life which I had offered them, and which they had accepted. And, for sure, nobody would ever have paid me that nice compliment, "They are just like real people."

21 VERISIMILITUDE IN THE CRIME STORY

by *Albert F. Nussbaum*

I WAS SITTING at one of the four-place tables in the mess hall of the U.S. Penitentiary, Leavenworth, Kansas. My two companions were serving sentences for violations of narcotics control laws. Throughout the meal, they talked about places they had been, drugs they had used, and times they had been arrested or had somehow avoided it. Then, as we were getting up to leave, one casually asked the other: "By the way, who was your connection in St. Louis?"

The second man set his tray back on the table and glared angrily. It looked as though there might be a taboo against asking the name of a drug supplier. "Who was my connection in St. Louis?" he asked, as though trying to make sense of an idiot's babbling. *"Who* was my connection? In St. Louis—" he pounded his chest once "—*I* was the connection!"

Besides illustrating the fact that no one, regardless of his situation, wants to be put on the bottom, this incident has another point to make: prisons *are not* full of men claiming to be innocent. Though movies, TV, books and magazines are always depicting convicts as men who fervently deny any wrongdoing, just the opposite is true. Prison, like every society, has a social structure, a pecking order, but its values are reversed. At the top of the prison social ladder are the big-time swindlers and bank robbers; at the bottom are the petty thieves and sexual deviates. A man who claimed to be innocent would find he had no standing at all.

I'm sure most convicts play down their offenses when talking to officials and outsiders, but they seldom do so among themselves. I've heard hundreds of prisoners brag about what they got away with, but I've never heard one claim that the police had arrested the wrong man. In fact, it's not uncommon for a car thief or check passer to pretend he's a bank robber in an effort to gain more acceptance.

Realistic details and facts

This is just one example of how the verisimilitude, the illusion of reality a writer creates by carefully weaving realistic details and interesting facts into his work, is often flawed in crime stories. Almost every writer tries his hand at a crime story sooner or later, but few seem to give much thought to the special hazards they face. As a result, many writers have unknowingly included inaccurate details or completely false "facts."

Since few writers have firsthand knowledge of police procedures and criminal operations, they must depend upon research for details. One writer's error can find its way into print so many times that it becomes generally accepted as true. That's how the prison-is-full-of-innocent-men cliché came into being, and that's how many others are being perpetuated. Unfortunately, it takes only one small error, if detected by the reader, to destroy an otherwise perfect illusion of reality.

Once this danger is recognized, the solution becomes obvious: a crime story should be researched in exactly the same way as any other piece of fiction. A writer should not use fiction as a source of "facts" for a crime story any more than *Lost Horizon* would be used as a source of facts about the Himalayas, or the Doctor Kildare books as a source of medical data. The best place to go for information is always to an expert who has the answers you want or to a non-fiction book on the subject. And, if a writer is ever tempted to use something he has read about in a fictional piece, or seen on TV or in the movies, he should check it carefully first. Anything that can't be confirmed shouldn't be used.

Striking a balance

The goal of the crime story is the same as for all other commercial fiction—to entertain. It accomplishes this goal, or fails to, in the same way all commercial fiction does—by the various balances it maintains, or fails to maintain. The writer uses bits of reality to build an illusion of reality. He must balance his cold facts with skillful plotting and believable characters. Just as it is important to attain a balance between too much dialogue and not enough, and too much exposition and not enough, it is important, in crime fiction especially, to find a balance between too much detail and not enough.

The crime writer *is not* trying to teach anyone anything, least of all how to commit a crime. In fact, since the theme of crime fiction is most often *Crime Does Not Pay,* any effort of the writer toward Fagin-like teaching would be self-defeating. Instead, just as he must find and hold the balance between too much detail as a whole and not enough, he should give only that amount of criminous detail necessary to establish verisimilitude, without seeming to be instructive.

This last is easier to accomplish than it sounds; for once every effort has been made to include only factual detail, no reader, no matter how knowledgeable, can find blunders that will shatter the illusion and his faith in the writer's expertise. After that, a minimum of criminous detail is all that is needed.

The greatest threat to a crime writer's verisimilitude is his own memory. Crime fiction is written by people who like to read it. Consequently, many writers have a storehouse of "facts" that simply aren't so. And, just as we will continually misspell some words until the error is pointed out, the writer will repeat these facts until he has some reason to doubt their accuracy.

Repeating errors

I've seen some errors many times. For instance, we have all read or heard about wax impressions. I can't count all the times I have read about someone jamming soft wax into a lock and removing a perfect likeness of the lock's key. Sometimes, through the miracle of movies and TV, I've even seen it done. Unfortunately, it's impossible. If it weren't, all locks would have been replaced by armed guards long ago. This story probably got its start around the turn of the century. At that time, one of the most common locks had a huge weakness. It was discovered that if a blank key were dipped in hot wax to give it a thin coating, and then inserted into the lock, the wax would pick up impressions of the lock's wards, showing where to file to make a key. Because of this lack of security, these warded locks have long since been replaced by Yale-type pin-tumbler locks in most cases, but crime fiction inherited the wax impression.

Speaking of locks and keys, writers often make a couple of other errors. It takes two hands to pick a lock. If a character does it while holding a flashlight, he'll have to hold the light with his teeth. Also, "skeleton" keys are not used in pin-tumbler locks. "Master" keys, "pass" keys, "try" keys, yes, but not "skeleton." Like the man who says "hep" instead of "hip," the author who writes about "skeleton" keys dates himself.

Another thing we've all read about or seen in movies is safe manipulation. The burglar or detective, hero or villain, presses his ear to the door of a safe, gives the combination dial a few turns, and *presto!* the door swings silently open. Although it is possible to manipulate some combination locks quite easily, none of the descriptions of it that I've seen come close to the reality. For one thing, the tumblers of a safe are flat, disc-shaped pieces, each with a notch along its outer edge. As the dial is turned, these tumblers are rotated. When they are lined up properly, the safe can be opened. The tumblers of a safe do not drop or fall anywhere; therefore, hearing plays no part in manipulation. Keen eyesight and a sensitive touch are necessary, however, so it's unlikely anyone would attempt manipulation with a flashlight as the only source of illumination, or while wearing gloves. And, contrary to every description I've seen, it's the *last* number of the combination that is discovered first, followed by the next-to-last number, and so on.

I suppose someone might say the details of safe manipulation were probably distorted on purpose some time in the past to keep knowledge out of the wrong hands, but I doubt that is the reason. Everything I've just written is as accurate as I can make it, but no one could hope to open a safe with only the information I've given. Most writers pride themselves on their realism. I believe that false facts and inaccurate details are usually the result of misinformation and faulty research, not an intentional act of the writer.

Of course, the examples I have given aren't likely to be noticed by the average reader—both prison life and locksmithing are fairly esoteric subjects. That probably explains why these errors have gone unchallenged as long as they have.

The facts of firearms

On the other hand, the United States is one of the more gun-conscious countries, and even those who don't own firearms and haven't handled them, know how they operate—everyone, it seems, except crime writers. As in the case of locks and safes, crime writers' knowledge of handguns is often tied to a fifty-year-old technology, or else a nonexistent one.

Automatic pistols and revolvers are both handguns, but that is about the only similarity between them. A revolver has a cylinder that swings out for loading and unloading. As the trigger is pulled or the hammer cocked, the cylinder rotates, lining up a new firing chamber with the barrel. An automatic on the other hand is much flatter than a revolver and is usually made ready for firing by inserting a loaded magazine (*not* a clip!) into the hollow handgrip. Although most automatic pistols have one or more safety catches, revolvers do not. There is no well-known revolver equipped with a manual safety. What appears in photographs to be a safety catch on the left side of many revolvers is actually the cylinder release. Also, the practice of leaving an empty chamber under the hammer of a revolver went out with Jesse James, or very nearly so. Modern revolvers have safety features incorporated into their designs that make this precaution unnecessary.

There is one other difference between automatics and revolvers that crime writers seem unaware of—despite the special effects produced by TV and movies, revolvers cannot be silenced effectively. Hiram Maxim patented the first firearm silencer back about the time he perfected smokeless powder, and there have been many new and improved designs since then, but none of them will work on a revolver. All firearm silencers operate by reducing the sound of the weapon's report which is caused by the rapid release of powder gases. Revolvers have a slight space between the cartridge cylinder and the barrel. Noise-producing gas is able to escape at this point, and so, revolvers cannot be silenced effectively. Here again, accuracy does not require that a writer give the construction details of a silencer, any more than it was necessary to give a graphic description of manipulation. If anything, the use of only accurate details should allow the writer to produce the desired effect with a minimum number of them.

Stories for entertainment

Other than through carelessness, there is one other way that crime writers sometimes flaw their stories—they sometimes forget their goal is entertainment and try to hit their readers over the head with a club-like message. In one of his last books, Raymond Chandler introduced a character whose sole purpose seemed to be to voice the author's personal opinions, and the story came to an abrupt halt while he did it. I've always seen this as an example of one time a master of the crime genre made a mistake; but in recent years I've read short stories that by comparison make Chandler's puppet character seem a very subtle device.

After the Supreme Court handed down its *Miranda* v. *Arizona, Escobedo* v. *Illinois,* and other decisions in the areas of representation and procedure, newspapers and magazines carried numerous articles both pro and con. Soon after that, there were many stories published that were complete distortions of the legal process. The actual effect of these decisions was far less than either supporters or detractors had expected. Most recent decisions in these areas have not been ruled retroactive; a man in prison cannot use them to effect his release. And in only two cases was the Court's decision instrumental in the release of the man who had brought the original action. The Court reaffirmed existing law that had been ignored; but, except for setting guidelines for the future, a favorable decision resulted only in a new trial for a man, not freedom.

In the case of the stories that showed blood-stained murderers being released on technicalities, I think the authors' propagandizing hurt the stories more than any simple inaccuracy might have done. If a writer has a gripe, if something is bothering him, if he feels the urge to climb upon a soapbox, he should write an article.

22 SUSPENSE FICTION AND A SENSE OF PLACE

by *Elisabeth Ogilvie*

OF ALL THE suspense and Gothic writers I admire, the best ones are those who can create an atmosphere that makes me hold my breath. They can soak a scene with menace. This requires eyes and ears for external details and knowing how much to use without slowing the pace of the story. This demands that a writer think herself into the scene, so that *she* is hearing the uncanny silence or the tiny giveaway sound; *she* glimpses the familiar face in the crowd; *her* heart beats hard and *her* throat dries because of what may be around the turn in the corridor or the road.

This effect is worth working for; a novel is nothing without it. In my efforts to attain it, I use a great deal of description to create an atmosphere that is physically vivid and real. When my own ears are twitching and my hands cold with apprehension, the action evolves naturally. Later on, I cut away anything that impedes the flow of the novel.

Characters and their environment

All of my novels depend strongly on environment: My people are creatures of their environment, except for the strangers who must come to terms with that background or be defeated by it. Therefore, the "people of the place" must be believable

153

and easy in their frame of reference, and their movements natural to the setting.

Ideas? They should come to you from everywhere: a face, a voice, a remark, a news item, a building, an empty road, a deserted street, someone hurrying, a dog barking in the night. The important thing is to *begin,* no matter how, even if you don't use that original beginning in your second draft—or ever. I still begin without any planning at all for the first scene. I *plunge.* Then after I get something down on paper, I am committed, and I can take the time to outline. I have always found that too much detailed planning before I write even the first line can use up the impetus.

The process is continuous. At two in the morning, out walking with the dog, I forget my annoyance, and my imagination takes over. "As she stood shivering on the lawn waiting for Jill to stop eating grass, clouds blew across the face of the moon, and in the sudden dark she heard—" Or "saw—" *what?* Bolting for the house, dragging the dog, I knew afterwards it was probably a deer out there, but for story purposes, it's someone on a surreptitious errand. Looking over old books in a deserted house is a natural stimulant; I came right home that day and started a story.

And how long could a fugitive manage to hide out in that locked-up cottage on the point? (I always look in when I go by, just in case, but so far only squirrels.) Visiting in the city, I wonder why the man next door always walks alone at midnight. In real life he just likes to walk before he goes to bed. In the story inspired by his footsteps, as he starts out on his solitary stroll around the block, he will be transformed into a man who will some day be found dead, with his wife missing; or it will be the other way around; or maybe they'll *both* be missing, with the coffee cups still warm on the table, as in the *Marie Celeste* mystery. And the innocent insomniac heroine who knew about his midnight habits has probably Seen Something Else which she doesn't know is important, and she gives it away to the friendly young man who comes poking around the house, and *he*—

And that's how the fascinating process goes on. Your mind darts in all directions at once, trying to catch hold of every bright firefly of possibility. You consider art or jewelry theft; espionage (reports hidden in the sugar tin); drugs; pure passion; blackmail; hidden insanity. You have a whole glorious assortment to choose from; you have all kinds of exciting openings and angles. You can have royalty in exile or a desperate housewife who belongs to the PTA, though that's not why she's desperate, at least for the purposes of your story. You can have a man planning murder or one who fears he may have done murder. You can have a frightened girl who doesn't know where to turn, or one with nerves of iron and a brain like a computer.

Suspense tales can be set anywhere. You can use the city or the country, the west or the east, mountains or seashore; ships, airplanes, trains; exotic backgrounds or humble ones. Suspense happens anywhere, provided you know your locale thoroughly.

Settings for Gothics

Gothics are more or less limited. There are only so many reasons for placing an undefended young female in mysterious and isolated surroundings, preferably ancient mansions with lots of room in them, though the mansion ploy is not *de rigueur*. The narrow form presents a challenge because of its very narrowness; a good Gothic must be solid from the ground up, like the solid old buildings in which much of the action takes place. A suburban housewife finds terror in an ordinary, well-lighted art gallery; a young woman falls in love in the fresh air and sunshine of the seacoast, amid the wild strawberries, and doesn't guess her salty lover is a killer. Another woman stumbles into a murder case and later feels bereft when she realizes a friend is a dangerous psychopath, because they had enjoyed each other's company so much and had so much in common. None of these woman is in the idiot-heroine tradition: I have no patience with females who know by the pricking of their thumbs that something wicked this way comes, and then insist on barging into places where a self-respecting cat would have the common sense not to go.

In my novel *The Face of Innocence,* the heroine is a "Band Mother," a PTA member, and her husband owns a hardware store. Within a quiet suburban setting, she meets her private horror face-to-face. She lives a nightmare, while attempting to keep up with the rhythms of daily life, and when the trouble is over, very few people in the town know that she's been involved in anything.

In *Weep and Know Why,* the action takes place on a nature preserve. Because of its isolation, it is possible for two people to disappear and their bodies be hidden. Because the place attracts geologists, ornithologists, botanists, and marine biologists, nobody in the area questions the credentials of two supposed archaeologists searching for traces of a prehistoric people. And because wildlife refuges attract poachers, this leads to still another murder.

Image of a Lover confines all the action to what is possible and appropriate in an island community in the year 1896. The daily business of the place, its events and amusements, all belong to that era. The characters are not people of the 1970's dressed up in period costumes, thinking and behaving like people of today. They are 1896-people, strongly influenced by the mores of that time, even when they are in rebellion.

Begin in the middle

One classic method of tossing the reader straight into the middle of things is to begin with a scene from late in the story, one of those taut moments when everyone seems to be drawing a long breath just before the grand cataclysm. Then the story flashes back to the actual beginning of events, to tell what happened to bring things to this pass. I used the flashback in my novel *Bellwood,* but in my other stories a straightforward beginning has done just as well, as long as the action starts to build up almost at once. This needn't be physical, but can be accomplished by foreshadowing. Extremes work here. The heroine may be in a restless, unhappy mood that takes her from safe surroundings into dangerous ones, or she may be completely happy and at peace with herself. In either case, the reader should at once think, "Something's going to happen to *her.*" A man is the type who attracts trouble as a magnet attracts iron filings; he calls for careful watching, as he may a) turn out to be killed, b) turn out to be really quite nice, c) turn out to be nasty. And what about the extremely kind and pleasant person who may be hiding a fiend's nature behind his smile?

Of course, since the reader knows this is a suspense story, it's obvious that *something* is going to happen before long. The goal is to give as fresh and original a treatment as possible to basically familiar situations.

Whether your protagonist is running his own show, trying to escape or to control circumstances, or whether he doesn't know what is happening or why but is both threatened and challenged by the mysterious goings-on, all scenes must move the action inexorably toward the climax. At the same time, you should use every opportunity for subtle and nerve-racking suspense. It's all right, in fact it's necessary, for the principal to go off on false trails now and then, as long as his reasons for doing so are logical and the reader can believe in them as well. If there's no secret about who the evil-doer is, the suspense lies in wondering if he'll escape or how he'll be finally trapped. He must almost make it often enough so that the reader won't know until the end whether or not the villain will get away.

All the time I was working on *Where the Lost Aprils Are,* I was thinking of it simply as a love story. But readers reacted to it as a suspense story, so I've been analyzing it as objectively as possible (I keep wanting to rewrite or delete)—to try to see how I plaited three strands into one tight braid of suspense.

The three strands are these:

1. Miriam's parents' story, which exists even if she doesn't know what it is. All that she'd known of it was her mother's very brief statement, and some old snapshot albums showing her mother as a girl among strangers in a nameless place. Some of the strangers are identified by first names or nicknames, some are as anonymous as the setting. She knows only that it is somewhere in Maine.

2. Miriam's own story, the change in her life from the moment of the headlong escape through the looking glass, not only into another world but another dimension.

3. The town of Parmenter, the new dimension—not only a theater for events but, as always with my work, a major character without whom the others would have no existence.

I came to the conclusion that *Where the Lost Aprils Are* is a suspense story after all, because Miriam is in suspense all the way through the book. She has been in suspense ever since her mother told her that she was illegitimate but not who her father was. And when Miriam finally does know the truth, she is still in suspense, because her life is left hanging in a kind of limbo until she can come to terms with the ghosts of her past.

I could have started the novel with the prosaic first paragraph of Chapter Three. Well, maybe it's not prosaic, but it is quiet. However, I like to plunge into a situation and then find out why it's happening. So we begin with Miriam's dread of April, wishing she could go back to her twenty-fourth April and "make it come out differently." For the past three years, she has all but wept her way through that month. And *why?*

She cannot—or will not—explain to Mike, the man who loves her and whom she thinks she can't love back.

A few pages later, in Chapter Two, the playing of a tape she discovered in a box of odds and ends sends her into a spasm of grief and horror which she can't hide from Mike. And because he forces her to face what is haunting her, she goes back in time to that April of three years ago. Her narrative begins in Chapter Three with that maybe-not-so-prosaic paragraph—the simple statement that when she was twelve years old she found out that she was illegitimate. She covers twelve years in this chapter, ending with the moment when she finds, by accident, the name of the place in the old snapshots: *Parmenter*.

The name dominates and obsesses her, as the identity of her unknown father has for years. (Her mother died without telling her any more.) She finds the town on the map and rearranges her work so she can go there. Her entry into this quiet farming community among the hills is what I have described as a through-the-looking-glass experience because she is walking into her mother's past. She moves in its ambience, yet she knows nothing of it. She is tuned to the place as if through an array of psychic devices, the very hills seem to cry out to her, and yet she can't decipher or translate any of these impressions. The people themselves, though friendly to the stranger, don't react to her name.

She strains to see resemblances in the faces around her, at least in those of persons her mother's age, who might as youngsters be in the photographs. She rents a cottage from Mrs. Barstow of Fourleaf Farm and is tempted to question her, but a natural reticence keeps her from doing so. She doesn't want to attract curiosity. And, because of her unknown father, she might step very painfully on certain toes.

There are the normal informational resources of a small town, and she explores them one by one, offering innocuous and credible reasons. She mentions remote Maine ancestors, but neither the tax collector nor the town clerk can find her surname in their records, recent or old.

More suspense for Miriam. Until now she has believed she carried her mother's actual surname, and now she knows it is a false one. Finally, she invents an excuse to study back issues of high school yearbooks in the school library, and discovers her mother's picture with her real name beneath it. It sets off fireworks in her head. She has already heard that name—the surname—in a conversation somewhere.

She wants to rush out of the library and say to someone—anyone—"I have roots here. I'm not just anybody, I'm somebody. You knew my mother. You must have known my father."

But after that first impulse, she doesn't really want to shout it. It is too personal. "Finding her name, finding *her,* was finding myself. Being born."

She looks through the boys' pictures for some phantom resemblance to herself, but doesn't find it. Then she goes to find the family farm, which she had heard mentioned in an argument between Mrs. Barstow and a neighbor. They are both interested in acquiring the property, which is to be sold at auction by the town. The place has been deserted for years, and as far as anyone knows, all the heirs are dead.

In the April silence, Miriam finds the ruins of a burned house and barn. Her mother's life here speaks to her in the wind blowing through the pines on the hill, and from the new iris choked in the grass by a granite doorstep.

Two strands have now come together, that of Parmenter and that of her mother's existence in Parmenter. The third strand is about to touch. Mrs. Barstow's son has followed her and finds her crouched, weeping by the iris. Until now, she has seen him as spoiled, his mother's darling, smugly certain of his good looks and his charm and his talent. Now she is glad of some sympathy from someone her own age, and while it's nothing so pat as instant love, it is friendship, which counts for a good deal.

Painfully and sometimes reluctantly, yet unable to give up, Miriam works towards the truth. Sensitized by everything, she sees distress in the lives that brush hers, while Parmenter seems to be serenity itself in the early spring light. Mrs. Barstow worries about her son; Rory is under some great strain of his own. Pretty, wholesome Eunice, daughter of the town's founding family, is unhappily enmeshed in Barstow affairs. Miriam, by her chance discovery of the town's name, has landed in the midst of a situation which might have gone on for some time at the just-short-of-intolerable stage. Miriam's presence accelerates its destructive force.

After a good hard fight against it, Miriam falls in love with Rory, and now the three strands are woven closely together. To destroy one is to destroy the whole.

Life in Parmenter goes on. Lambs and calves are born, fields ploughed, birds are returning, the tree frogs sing in the swamps, the brooks are swollen. The days are broken by the arrival of the egg truck, the milk truck, the bulk feed truck, the vet to see a sick cow. Occasionally, Apollo the bull breaks through a fence and holds up traffic. There are Grange Hall dances, the volunteer firemen's poker nights, choir practice and church, the selectmen's and assessors' meetings. People drive to the shire town for shopping and the movies. Most of them are living on several levels, like Miriam, and most, like her, have a secret.

Rory is pushing her to claim the family land. She feels its pull; it has already claimed *her*. But she dreads what might happen when her identity is known to the people in the town. Who in Parmenter is going to resent, fear, or be driven to despair by the appearance of her mother's daughter?

She wants to cut free from Parmenter with Rory, to leave it for good, as her mother had. But that wasn't really a clean cut, because her mother held onto the albums and the few letters which gave Miriam the clue to her past. And when Miriam goes alone to the farm to take a last farewell, she is as desolate at giving it up as she would have been if she had just found her father and couldn't keep him.

When she finally does leave Parmenter, it is not as she had expected to go, but in shock, which stays with her through three Aprils of relentless nightmares and ceaseless weeping. Yet, like her mother, she couldn't cut the last tie. She has not given up the farm, but has numbly paid the taxes on it every year. She knows now who her father is; she knew before she left Parmenter, but in the end it hadn't mattered that much, because by then she had become a whole person with her own loves and wars, nobody else's.

And when all those loves are gone and the wars won or lost, it is the *place* that remains. She doesn't want to see it again, but she can't bear to part with it.

Mike Andric makes her go back and admit that she is a part of Parmenter and that Parmenter is a part of her, and no separation is possible.

Except for Miriam, and now Mike, those who knew the whole tragedy of Fourleaf Farm are dead. A few half-guessed it, but they'll never say so. For two centuries, Parmenter has absorbed all the memories of good and evil done among these hills and streams. When Miriam goes back with Mike, the new lambs still bleat in the spring air, and the peepers are in the swamps. Time and place display their healing indifference to the affairs of men.

Unique atmosphere

A city block, a suburban street, a school, a theater, a library, a factory or a farm—any place, anywhere, can provide a luxuriant setting for suspense, incredibly rich with color and detail. It's all there if you look for it. The *feel* of the place must be so strong that readers are captured and imprisoned in its scents and sounds and the special atmosphere peculiar and private to it. They should be able to watch the characters do their work, whether in the fields, on the ocean, in a laboratory, running a household, teaching school, or managing a business. They should see what the characters see, hear what they hear, as they go about their lives. When they have finished the novel, readers should think, consciously or unconsciously, "This story could not have taken place anywhere else but where it did, and I was *right there* when it happened."

23 TO A WOULD-BE DETECTIVE STORY WRITER

by *Joyce Porter*

MY DEAR RUPERT:

Your letter, which I received a few days ago, indicates that after many years of drifting about, you intend to earn your living by writing detective stories. I gather that you wish me to give you the benefit of my experience and advise you how to succeed in what appears to be your chosen career. I undertake this with considerable reluctance, for write detective stories you may; live off the proceeds you certainly won't!

If I had any surefire tips on how to become a world-famous writer of murder mysteries, I would have taken them years ago and made a fortune.

I started writing at the age of thirty-six. It had always struck me that writing would be a nice, cushy job, a pleasant way of earning money without actually working for it—but I must stress that I had no burning ambition to be an author. It was just one of those vague daydreams that nobody has any intention of doing anything about. I would equally well have liked to be a millionaire, or even a prima ballerina.

Still, being a writer looked a slightly less potty idea than any of the others so, in my spare time, I wrote a book. It was a detective story, because that was practically the only type of fiction I ever read. My favorite writer was (and still is) Georges Simenon, and my first fifty pages were devoted to a vain effort to produce an English Maigret. On the fifty-first page, two lights dawned. I wasn't any Simenon, and my detective wasn't a bit like any of the coppers I actually knew. Eventually, I don't quite know how, I found myself landed with a detective who couldn't detect, and I felt much happier with him. Personally, I wouldn't read a funny detective story if you paid me, and I just don't understand how it is that I came to write the dratted things. I'd really like to write those huge complicated novels about the achievement and exercise of power, but I can't.

Consistency of experience

The first thing every budding detective story writer has to decide is whether he or she is going to do things the hard way or the easy way. I will just tell you briefly what the hard way is on the off chance that you might care to follow it.

The hard way to write detective stories is to treat every book you write as a separate entity in the way that an ordinary novelist usually does. Charles Dickens, for example, didn't link all his books together by giving them a similar format or by repeating the main characters. Nor did Charlotte Brontë or Ernest Hemingway. Now, some people (very few) write mystery stories like this and they are to be congratulated on their powers of imagination and penchant for hard work. They are not to be imitated, though—at least not by the likes of you and me. For us there is, thank God, a much less strenuous technique.

What we are aiming at is to keep on writing the same detective story—for a lifetime if necessary—and publish it under different titles. Well, not *exactly* the same detective story, but as near to the same as we think we can get away with, because readers of detective stories actually want to keep reading the same novel! They are, you see, addicts. If they were in search of new and exciting experiences, they wouldn't keep reading one of the most stereotyped forms of literature we have. But they aren't just hooked on detective stories in general: often they're addicted to particular types of detective fiction and sometimes to the work of particular writers. In extreme cases, you'll find a real fanatic whose peculiar craving can be satisfied only by the works of one author. But what detective fiction readers insist upon is consistency of experience.

What I mean by "consistency of experience" is that if detective story readers pull a Dick Francis book off the shelf, they expect it to be about horse racing. And, unless Dick Francis has suddenly taken leave of his senses, about horse racing it will be. This applies to all the great names in the mystery writing genre. Agatha Christie: English upper middle-class with the dead body on the hearth rug in front of the library fire; Ed McBain: tough, realistic, "smile when you say that, buddy!" New York cops; Emma Lathen: business backgrounds with an urbane banker as detective. . . . One could go on forever.

To be a successful detective story writer, all you have to do is get as large a readership as possible habituated to you.

And how you achieve this laudable ambition is dead easy, too—at least in theory. You have to invent a really gripping, interesting, strongly drawn, everlasting detective, around whom all your books will be centered. Once you have a detective, the rest is kid stuff. Not only will his presence give your novels the consistency that your fans are looking for, but he will—if he's good enough—allow you to get away with murder in other directions as well. Your plots, for instance, don't have to be as clever, because your readers will be interested not so much in how the murder mystery is solved as in how your hero-sleuth solves it. A good detective can paper over a multitude of sins, especially those of omission.

You would doubtless appreciate a few tips on how to create your own detective. Of course, you'll want to invent someone original, and this is where you might find that the going gets a trifle sticky. You see, it's all been done before. We've had black detectives and yellow detectives, blind detectives, asthmatic detectives, crippled detectives. We've had women detectives, child detectives, lecherous ones, and homosexuals. We've even, if my memory serves me correctly, had a midget. As far as physical characteristics go, I'm very much afraid that we've run the gamut, though I'm sure you'll be able to accept the challenge and come up with something new. I don't remember reading about a dope-sniffing, bead-wearing, teen-age, police-baiting detective, but I just may have missed him.

Actually, before you get to the stage of endowing your sleuth with some unforgettable quirk or trait, you have to make up your mind about a couple of other details. For example, are you going to plump for an amateur or a professional detective?

There's a lot to be said for making your detective a proper policeman. For one thing, it's more realistic. The number of real-life murders solved by amateurs in the last hundred years wouldn't, I imagine, use up the fingers of one hand. But, there are snags. It's very hard to make your fictionalized policeman-detective distinct from all the other fictionalized detectives who have preceded him. By their very nature, police forces tend to shun admitting the extremes of eccentricity into their ranks. Then again, one is also likely to make some pretty terrible mistakes with police procedure, and this can lose you friends and make you enemies, although the conventions of the detective story do allow the ignorant author a fair amount of latitude.

Credible amateurs

The odds are that you'll settle on an amateur or private detective and, if you do, there's nothing to be ashamed of. After all, what else was Sherlock Holmes? A private detective certainly allows you more elbow room when it comes to personal characteristics—a bigamous alcoholic with a stutter, perhaps?—but there are snags here, too.

Tracking down a cunning murderer takes time and money. From where does your fellow get these essential commodities? See what I mean? You've got to provide your investigator either with an ample private income or some sort of a job which furnishes him with lots of both leisure and lolly. Favorite professions for amateur detectives in the past have been doctors, lawyers and clergymen of all denominations. You could, of course, make him a private detective—but that's not a wildly original idea, either, is it? I expect you'll come up with something really new if you just put your mind to it. University teacher? It's been done!

Not that a credible job for your detective is going to solve all your problems. There are lots of others. How, for instance, are you going to explain why Mr. Ordinary Citizen is forever tripping over dead bodies? I've been knocking around for some considerable time now (and it feels like much, much longer), but I've been remotely connected with only two murders, neither of which was either mysterious or interesting.

And why, if there has been a homicide, doesn't somebody call in the police and let them handle it? Well, either you can set your slaying in some isolated spot where, for the moment, the cops can't go—in a submarine under the North Pole, or where floods have swept away the only bridge—or you can have the police investigating the murder in parallel with your paragon sleuth. This, too, is a ploy which has frequently been used before, and generally it has been to the detriment of the police, who are not only outsmarted but often patronized into the bargain. One can only suppose that the authors of these works were not car drivers.

If there is a foolproof formula, I'm as greedy to have it as anybody else. People talk happily about plot construction and character motivation; I just get an idea for a book, sit down, and write it. The only thing I can think of that I do deliberately is to reduce description to the bare minimum. This is simply because, whenever in my reading I come to two-page word pictures of the view from the study window or three hundred lines on the beauty of the heroine, I skip. In big jumps.

The mechanics of writing

About the mechanics of writing, though, I am very fussy. I write by hand with a very sharp pencil, and I always buy folio-sized books which are meant to be used with carbons and have very thin, crackly paper. I find these books with their numbered pages ideal for my purpose. I reckon that a chapter is about fourteen pages in my handwriting, so I always mark the page round about which the chapter should end. I also know now that the complete novel should be one whole foolscap book in length, plus an extra forty pages or so.

I write the whole book straight off. I always start with working notes listing the names and ages of the characters, their family relationships if these are important, and plans of rooms or streets when I have to be careful about the geography. I'd like these preliminary notes to be very clear and concise, but they rarely are. As I have gained more experience I find that these notes get sketchier and sketchier. Nowadays I prefer not to have every last detail planned in advance as this tends to make the actual writing rather boring. Much to my amazement, boredom has proved to be my main occupational hazard, and so it is important to me to have to think up something new once the book is under way.

When I've finished the manuscript, I type it out. I correct spelling and grammatical mistakes as I type and generally polish it up. The final appearance of the typescript is very important to me, and I make it as attractive as I can.

I have one virtue as a writer and one claim to some sort of professionalism. Once I've started a book, I finish it. Always. No matter how fed up and dissatisfied I get, I struggle on to the bitter end. I think this is something you might do well to emulate. It is in my opinion what separates the professionals from the dabblers. Half a novel is a sheer waste of good paper.

Now I come to think of it, this is the only advice I can give you: The only way to become a writer is to write. Writing for publication isn't a hobby. It's a job, and very few people are lucky enough to enjoy their jobs. I certainly don't. I'd sooner read a book about how to write a novel than sit there and write one. I'd sooner do almost anything than shut myself up all alone every day and get on with it. The only pleasure I get out of it is the excitement of thinking about the next novel and the blessed relief of finishing the current one. The part in between is hell, and nobody and nothing can help you with that.

When you get right down to it, whether or not you can write anything worthwhile is a matter strictly between you and the publisher. Everything else is totally extraneous to the issue. And the publisher can't do a thing until he has your effort, whatever it is, in front of him. With the best will in the world he can only judge on what you have actually written—not on what you've thought about writing or learned about writing.

Rejection slips are depressing. Dog-eared manuscripts thudding home to roost on the doormat are depressing. But, by the time the tenth rebuff of your little masterpiece smacks you in the teeth, you ought to be past caring. You'll be halfway through your next novel by then, won't you? If you've that much self-confidence, pigheadedness, and simple cheek, you may make it one day. If you haven't, you certainly won't.

All the best.

Yours,

J.P.

24 THE ELEMENTS OF SUSPENSE

by *Bill Pronzini*

ONE OF THE happiest developments in publishing in recent years has been the growth in stature of the suspense novel. There was a time when suspense fiction was considered "category," and those of us who wrote it or hoped to write it could expect little more than modest sales and a modest reputation. Now, however, a high percentage of fiction best sellers are suspense novels of one type or another, and the demand for fresh new work is greater than ever—not only by publishers and readers, but by Hollywood for theatrical and television films. The future of the suspense story is very bright indeed.

I've been reading, writing and admiring this type of fiction for a number of years, and yet when I'm asked just what it is that makes a successful suspense novel, I've always been at somewhat of a loss to offer a comprehensive explanation. Suspense is contingent upon a great many factors, such as subject matter, style, theme, and the individual author's vision and interpretation. It took me a long while to learn how to handle the more subtle aspects of suspense—and I'm still learning.

I do think there are certain basic elements, or foundations, of suspense which can be found in any successful work. I keep these elements in mind whenever I plot, and whenever I write a novel or a story.

Subject matter

The *subject matter* of today's suspense novel must be unique, interesting, and as momentous to the principal characters as possible. Several of the recent suspense best sellers, for example, dealt with "can't-miss" topics—ideas at once containing built-in suspense factors and offering the reader fascinating information on subjects about which he probably knew little. Novels that come immediately to mind are: *Jaws* (sharks and the hunting of a killer shark), *The Billion Dollar Sure Thing* (international high finance), *The Taking of Pelham One Two Three* (the New York City subway system), *The Tower* and *The Glass Inferno* (holocaust in high-rise buildings).

A suspense novel need not always deal, of course, with great disasters or fantastic extortion ploys or national and international activities. Plots can be simple as well as complex, and there can be dozens of characters or only a few; the important thing is that the subject matter be innovative in terms of handling and development. My own two most successful books, *Panic!* and *Snowbound,* were as unalike as two suspense novels can be. *Panic!* dealt with a man named Jack Lennox, who witnessed a murder by professional assassins in a roadside oasis in the Southwest, and fled into the desert to escape the killers: a simple plot, peopled with a total of five characters. *Snowbound,* on the other hand, dealt with a much more complex situation and a multitude of characters. It is the story of what happens when three desperate criminals take refuge in a tiny mountain valley in the Sierra Nevada; the valley is then cut off from the outside world by an avalanche a few days before Christmas, and the psychotic leader of the criminals decides to take over the seventy-five inhabitants and loot the valley, building by building.

There is a wealth of subject matter on which a writer can draw for a suspense novel. No subject is too bizarre or too improbable. Excellent books have been written on everything from reincarnation to computer thievery to the actual physical theft of a bank. And yet, writers to date have only scratched the surface of possible story ideas. There are thousands more just waiting for someone like you or me to use.

Setting and background

The *setting* of a suspense story, like its subject matter, is a vital element of suspense. It, too, should be as unique and interesting as possible.

Large and small American cities have always made good settings, but even more fascinating to readers are foreign locales and wilderness areas such as mountains and oceans, deserts and jungles and polar ice caps. The theory which states that "a writer should *always* write what he knows" is not necessarily valid. Careful research can compensate for any lack of personal knowledge. As a case in point, I've published two pseudonymous suspense novels set in Singapore and Malaysia without ever having been there. Your research must be extensive, however; the better you know your locale, the better you'll be able to write about it—and the less likely you'll be to make mistakes. Never be content with superficial research and superficial facts.

I firmly believe that background should play a vital role in the story, that it should not be insignificant or incidental. Ideally, in fact, it should become a major character directly affecting the plight of the protagonist or protagonists (as was the case in both *Panic!* and *Snowbound*). This helps to create and maintain suspense.

You should, as well, establish the background as a consequential factor as early as possible, as dramatically as possible; give the reader an immediate idea of how prominent in the overall suspense the setting will be. I opened both *Panic!* and *Snowbound* with descriptive passages for just that reason:

Panic!:

The desert surrounded the moving bus like an earthly vision of hell.

Heat shimmered in liquid waves on the polished black ribbon of the highway, in thick tendrils across the arid wastes extending eastward to the horizon, westward to a low stretch of reddish foothills. The noonday sun, in a charred cobalt sky, was a fiery yellow-orange ball . . . Nothing moved beyond the dust-streaked windows except the heat; the only sign of life was a carrion bird, a black speck that seemed to lie motionless above something dead or dying in the distance.

Snowbound:

Mantled with a smooth sheen of snow, decorated with tinsel and giant plastic candy canes and strings of colored lights, the tiny mountain village looked both idyllic and vaguely fraudulent, like a movie set carefully erected for a remake of *White Christmas*. The dark, winter-afternoon sky was pregnant with more snow. . . . On the steep valley slopes to the west, south and east, the red fir and lodgepole pine forests were shadowed, white-garbed, and as oddly unreal as the village itself.

Mood and tone

Another extremely important element for the writer to consider is what the *mood and tone* of his story will be: brooding horror, understated horror, straightforward narrative out of which tension builds inexorably, even tongue-in-cheek humor or comedy. It depends, of course, on the subject matter. It would have been a mistake for me to have told *Panic!* or *Snowbound* in any but a grimly straightforward style, because the plots of both books were too deadly serious to approach in any other way. The suspense novels of Donald Westlake, on the other hand—and they *are* suspense novels—work so beautifully because of Westlake's perfect feel for comedy.

Once you have settled on the proper mood and tone for your story, you must maintain it throughout. Nothing shatters suspense faster than fluctuation—brooding horror on one page, whimsy on another. Beginning writers should be especially chary of injecting humor (or "comic relief") into any but a basically lighthearted story line. Some established professionals can do this and get away with it, but for the most part it tends to strain credulity. When you are tempted to have a character joke or make a wisecrack in a life-and-death suspense novel, you should place yourself in the role of the character. Would *you* be able to joke if *you* were the individual involved? Most likely, your answer will be no; most likely as well, the humor will be better left unwritten. The converse is also true: if the tone of your book is whimsical, it would be a mistake to have the characters think or speak in deeply philosophical or metaphysical monologues.

Menace

Without *menace*, of course, there is no suspense, and thus any suspense novel must fairly crackle with it. But menace can take many forms, can be simple or complex, physical or psychological. The successful suspense tale utilizes a combination of menaces—obvious and subtle, primary and subordinate.

The obvious and primary menace is the basic story line: a man or woman or group of people in fear of their own lives, security, sanity, or the lives, security or sanity of others. This menace can come from other individuals, from authority or symbols of authority, from external factors such as fire or storm or other natural phenomena, or from within the mind. In any case, it must be strong, immediate, personal.

One of the subtler types of menace grows out of the characters themselves—their personalities, prejudices, weaknesses, etc. The protagonists in *Panic!* and *Snowbound* had basic flaws and weaknesses which lent additional menace to the situations in which they found themselves. In the former, Jack Lennox had been running away from crises all his life, and therefore from himself; and Jana Hennessey, the woman he encounters in the desert, had suffered an emotional trauma she couldn't come to terms with. In *Snowbound*, Zachary Cain had withdrawn from a world which he hated because he blamed it for the death of his entire family; and Rebecca Hughes allowed self-pity to govern her life because of a faithless husband and an inability to cope with her problems. All of these characters were, in effect, menacing *themselves*.

The setting can also effectively establish and enhance the subordinate type of menace. A few additional examples from *Panic!*:

> The sun is fire above, and the rocks are fire below. The heat drains moisture from the tissues of Lennox's body, drying him out like a strip of old leather, swelling his tongue, causing his breathing to fluctuate. It is almost three o'clock now, and the floor of the desert wavers with heat and mirage; midafternoon is the hottest part of the day out here, temperatures soaring to 150 degrees and above . . .

> [Jana and Lennox are] running now through a sea of cactus —barrel, agave, saguaro, prickly pear, cholla, beavertail. Thorns like tiny needles, like slender jade daggers, like gleaming stilettos rip at their skin, at their clothing, inflicting painful but half-noticed scratches and punctures that bleed for a moment and then dry up almost immediately.

And from *Snowbound:*

> The blizzard continued to gather strength as the night progressed, dumping huge quantities of snow on Hidden Valley and on the high, steep cliffs through which the country road passed down into the valley . . . Drifts built higher and higher along the cornice at the near, lee side of the western cliff crown . . .
> And the entire cornice gave way.
> Billowing snowclouds choked the air like white smoke, and a massive tidal wave of snow and ice and rock flooded downward with a thunderous vibratory roar that was as loud as a bomb

blast in the early-morning stillness. Granite outcroppings were ripped loose as though they were no more than chunks of soft shale; trees were buried, uprooted, or snapped like matchsticks and carried along. And in a matter of seconds, the plunging mass filled a section of the pass the way a child would fill an excavation in the sand . . .

Cain bunched the collar of his coat tighter against his throat . . . His feet were so achingly chilled now that he had almost no feeling in his toes; he lifted first one leg and then the other, like a man doing calisthenics in slow motion, to keep the blood circulating. The movement of time seemed to have slowed down to an inert crawl, as if the bitterly cold night had managed to wrap it, too, in a cloak of ice—

Characterization and motivation

One of my most strictly adhered-to writing axioms is: *If the characters aren't believable, flesh-and-blood people, the reader won't care what happens to them no matter how suspenseful the subject matter or background.*

The days when fiction writers could get by on plot alone, with cardboard characters, are long gone. Today's reader wants to know why characters think the way they do, why they act the way they do; wants to know their idiosyncrasies, their hang-ups, their passions—everything about them. And the more the reader knows, the more completely involved in their plight he or she becomes.

If the protagonists are facing some sort of internal as well as external crisis, as were the characters in *Panic!* and *Snowbound,* suspense is heightened because the reader is wondering: Will he or she come to terms with that internal crisis? If so, how? Protagonists who are strong characters from the beginning should not only be placed against seemingly insurmountable odds, but made to question their own strength in overcoming those odds. In short, there must be conflict *within* characters in addition to conflict *between* characters.

Superhero types with no weaknesses and no uncertainties about themselves are also unacceptable in today's suspense novel. The reader has to be able to identify with someone imperiled, someone facing a deadly predicament, and it isn't easy for most of us to identify with a person who is fearless and utterly in control of every situation. Also, protagonists must never be detached—i.e., merely observers with nothing at stake personally.

Pace and action

Pace is perhaps the most important of all elements of suspense. No matter how interesting the subject, setting, and character, a novel can fail if the pace is poorly handled.

There must always be forward movement in fiction and particularly in suspense fiction: plot twists, new characters, fresh menaces. These should be introduced consistently from beginning to end, never in uneven lumps and particularly never in lumps early in the book. The anticipation of something new taking place on the very next page is what keeps readers reading, and is what pace is all about.

A corollary to the above is that a writer must never halt forward movement with pages of superfluous facts: long narrative or dialogue sections concerning the background of characters, descriptions of places and things, encyclopedic information on, for instance, diamond-cutting, should that happen to be the basic subject of the book. When large amounts of information are necessary to the plot, sprinkle it throughout in small doses. Facts not relevant to the plot, but relevant to character motivation or menace, should be as briefly presented as possible.

When there is continuous forward movement, suspense builds naturally and progressively from the opening pages through various crises to its climax at the end. For the denouement must always come at the high point of a suspense novel

—if the writer reaches the climax too early, readers will feel let down by the time they get to the final page.

A few words about *action:*

Some types of suspense novels require little or no action, but other types—such as *Panic!* and *Snowbound*—need much larger amounts. If your book falls into this category, you must be careful neither to underwrite nor overwrite. Underextension causes the reader to feel he has been cheated, because too much has happened too quickly; overextension leads to repetition, and can cause the reader to become either irritated or bored, hence destroying suspense.

Unnecessary violence, and improbable, contrived or clichéd chase and fight scenes should never be used; the handling of action sequences must be completely original and natural. Also there should be crisis points within action scenes, which simply means that the reader should never be sure of exactly what is going to happen. An example of an unacceptable action sequence is a hero systematically tracking down a villain, for there is little suspense to be found in methodology. Another pitfall to be avoided is action that continues too long without something new happening—e.g., new dangers, a different level of desperation, a change of immediate scenery (such as in a chase which begins in a forest and then moves into a town).

These, then, are the basic elements, the foundations of suspense. The writer whose book has a solid foundation has half the battle won, for the structure he or she builds on it should be fundamentally sound. And with careful attention, hard work, and a little insight into the more subtle aspects of suspense, that structure could be something very fine indeed.

25 CREATING HEROINES FOR GOTHIC NOVELS

by *Willo Davis Roberts*

THE GOTHIC NOVEL is currently one of the most popular forms of fiction. Its readers range from teeny-boppers to grannies, with a surprising number of male readers thrown in. As both a writer and an avid reader of Gothics, I'm at once gratified and disappointed by the boom.

Gratified, because this means there are more books of this type around to read and I can sell what I like to write; disappointed by the quality of many of the books currently appearing on the stands.

Like most devotees of genre fiction, the Gothic readers are insatiable. They'll comb the library shelves and the paperback racks, looking for new stories. There are usually plenty of them, but increasingly the reader is let down when she discovers that the heroine is such a ding-bat that she probably deserves whatever fate she meets in the spooky old castle.

For quite a number of years, the best-selling authors of Gothics were a small and select group of women writers who turned out top-notch, well-written, entertaining novels. But half a dozen authors couldn't turn out enough Gothics to satisfy the fan who wants to read three, four, five or more books a week. Most Gothic writers manage to write only one or two books a year.

In the meantime, the demand has grown so furiously that

those who used to write only westerns and science fiction are turning to the Gothic because there's a ready market for it in paperback, and the pay is good. According to an authority in the field, approximately half the Gothics being published in this country today are written by men. Because publishers believe that women will not read Gothics written by men, most of these male writers use pseudonyms.

Of the men I know who have inched over into the Gothic field because of the profits to be made there, not one really seems to enjoy writing this kind of story. It's very much a format type of thing, and always deals with a young woman in danger in mysterious surroundings. Perhaps men can't quite manage to get into this character, which is why so often their books sound as if the writers didn't enjoy writing them. Unfortunately, when that is the case, the reader doesn't particularly enjoy them either.

I don't mean to suggest that the poorer Gothics are written exclusively by men. (But when I compare the westerns and the science fiction written by the men who write mediocre Gothics, the difference in quality is most revealing, for they write very well indeed in the categories they most enjoy.) However, I do think the Gothics which turn out to be disappointing often are that way because of one primary factor: The heroine is incredibly stupid. She gets into situations where her life is in danger, and if she had half a brain in her head, she would run screaming in the opposite direction. Instead of that, she goes bungling along, being lured into ambushes and traps that are apparent at once to the reader. But she doesn't catch on, no matter how often these things happen; she trembles and cries a lot, but she never has the good sense simply to pick up her belongings and go home.

It is for the would-be Gothic writer that I therefore offer my very strong opinion that the heroine of a Gothic novel *doesn't have to be an idiot.*

Not only that, *she shouldn't be.* If she is, the writer is too lazy to deserve to sell his or her manuscript. In the over forty novels I have sold, most of them Gothics, not one heroine stayed in a dangerous situation because she was too stupid to see that she was going to get killed if she stuck around. She stayed . . . and the story existed . . . because even though she was reasonably intelligent, it took her a while to find a way out.

Unlikely but credible

How do you keep this girl in the gloomy old mansion after she's begun to realize that someone is dropping stone urns on her head or shooting at her with broadhead arrows out on the private archery range?

There are several ways to do this. You can put the girl in physical surroundings that preclude escape, such as behind a wall with a locked gate or on an island. (Don't forget to disable the boats!) In *Sing a Dark Song,* Dauna is trapped in a once elegant but now decrepit mansion from which there is no escape, except over or through a stream swollen to flood stage, and the only bridge is destroyed by the murderer.

In my *Key Witness,* Brenna St. John is lured into action she would not otherwise have undertaken by her concern for her beloved dog. And a storm of hurricane force traps her in an old inn, making it difficult to leave either by car or on foot. An isolated setting for the story, such as the barren Mendocino Coast of California in *Cape of Black Sands,* may be sufficient in itself to prevent a sensible girl from running, when telephone lines are cut and she doesn't have the keys for the vehicles.

Historical and period Gothics

A special word must be said about the historical Gothic, as opposed to the contemporary ones we have been considering. Many readers prefer the period story, and this opens a new avenue of thought, simply because seventy or a hundred years ago, women had much less freedom and were far more dependent upon the men in their lives for financial support. In *White Jade,* set in 1885, I have Cecelia Cummings, a spirited and non-fainting type, more or less captive in her grandfather's mansion because she has no money, no means of earning a living, and she is responsible for a younger crippled brother.

In *The Jaubert Ring,* my heroine Saunielle Hunter is at first unaware that her life is threatened, and then is held in a dangerous house by her concern for a missing father and her responsibility for three other women, one of them an elderly, senile aunt. It is realistic for a girl to undertake actions on behalf of people she loves when she would back hastily away if her only concern was for herself. If the person is a child who cannot be removed from the danger area, as in my *Becca's Child,* the heroine may be entirely sensible yet unselfish enough to risk her own life—if she believes the child's is at stake.

A word of caution here: Many situations that could have been considered plausible in the 1800's would not pass today (penniless nurse, governess, relative unable to flee because she has no means of taking care of herself), but don't fall into the trap of depriving your historical heroine of her natural common sense, and don't have her swooning at every turn. In spite of tight lacings, genuine fainting wasn't all that common. Editors are beginning to demand more realism. As one recently stated, "We want heroines who can tie their own shoes." And, as in any story, the protagonist is supposed to get out of her predicament by her own wits and actions; she mustn't be the type who sits and waits to be rescued by the handsome hero. Make her struggle, mentally and physically, when it's logical to do so.

New traps, new escapes

In any case, you must make the action and plot sound *real.* Gothics are written for fun; the reader is willing to suspend disbelief at some of the strange circumstances in which the heroine finds herself. But chances are the reader *isn't* going to swallow any story in which the girl will stay in a house where someone has just tried to poison her (she gave her milk to the cat, which immediately died in convulsions), if all she has to do is walk out the door and get on a bus. Your heroine *has to make a realistic and intelligent attempt to escape.* Part of the challenge (and the fun) of writing Gothics is to come up with some new trap for the poor heroine just when she's figured a way out.

The reader is looking for thrills and adventure, and that's what you have to offer her. But here again, make it reasonably believable. If the heroine has to do something so terrifying you know *you* couldn't do it, give her a compelling and convincing reason for trying it. In my *The Watchers,* Joan Gwayne must choose between sitting and waiting to drown in a subterranean cave, and attempting to get out through the channel filling with sea water. She isn't a strong swimmer and has little hope of doing that, but she has her small daughter with her; she will try anything to save the child.

Here, then, are the principal factors that determine the heroine's actions: She is given no choice because of the physical surroundings or situation, and she acts to protect either her own life or that of someone she cares about a great deal.

I have given specific examples of the ways in which a writer can produce exciting and action-packed stories without leaving the reader indignant at the heroine's stupidity. There are many more in the novels of Naomi A. Hintze, Madeleine Brent, Barbara Michaels, and Velda Johnston, as well as the newer writers coming up.

It's worth the effort to write a good story, about believable people who are at least as intelligent as the reader. If the *reader* can clearly see that the young woman has a way out and should take it, the heroine must also see it.

Write about a heroine we can identify with, and care about, and cheer for through 250 pages, and chances are we'll be reading *your* name on the cover of a new Gothic very soon now.

26 WHAT WILL HAPPEN— AND WHEN?

by *Richard Martin Stern*

WHAT IS there to say about suspense in fiction? That it belongs in whodunits and the cliff-hangers of adventure tales, and has no place in "straight, serious" fiction? Poppycock.

Suspense in its broadest form is the stuff of which all fiction is, or ought to be made. It is suspense that catches the reader's interest, carries him along with you, makes him turn the page and read on instead of putting the book down for—maybe— another time. Think about it.

Would you go back into the theatre for the last act of, say, *Hamlet,* if the author had not with conscious craft led you to the point where you simply had to know what was going to happen and how? And isn't that what suspense is all about?

I have read that people lined the wharf in New York waiting for the mail packet from England to dock so they could read the latest installment of Dickens's *Old Curiosity Shop* to find out if Little Nell did indeed die. If that is not suspense, I don't know the meaning of the word.

But how does the writer manage to achieve it?

Ah, there we get to the heart of the matter. I do not pretend that I have any formula for instant success, but there are certain guidelines that can be set forth.

Guidelines

First and foremost, the reader must care. That sounds obvious; unfortunately too many writers forget it. The reader must care, and that means that he must have an interest in the characters. Plot alone will not do it.

People are born, fall in love, grow sick and die every day, but you don't know them and so what happens to them is not really important to you. But when these things happen to someone close, someone you care about, then these events are drama, and you await their outcome in a mood that can only be called suspenseful.

How many stories or books have you and I started to read and then tossed aside because we didn't give a damn what happened to the names that appeared on the pages? All manner of weird and wonderful things could be going on, but unless the writer had given us characters with whom we could identify and about whom we cared, there was no urge to turn the page; there was no quality of suspense.

In remarks he made at West Point, William Faulkner kept returning to a single phrase: "the human heart in conflict." Another way to put it is with the question my agent used to ask too often about stories of mine: "Where is the love versus duty?" A phrase and a question that go directly to character, which is where it all begins.

That is not to say that plot is unimportant in the building of suspense. Plot is very important, obviously, because without it nothing happens—as is the case in what I refer to as "navel novels," where everyone sits around cross-legged contemplating his identity crisis—and what is suspenseful about that?

And so characters there must be about whom the reader cares, and plot to provide action and to demonstrate the human heart in conflict—and quite probably love versus duty. Now you have the tools with which to build suspense. How do you go about it?

Well, one way you do *not* go about it is by trickery. Dishonesty will out and become in the current jargon "counterproductive." As a writer friend of mine puts it, if your character opens a can of beans, somebody has to eat them. You can do all manner of things to misdirect your reader, as a magician onstage misdirects your attention, but the rabbit you eventually pull out of the hat has to be a real rabbit, not a mouse you sneaked in at the last moment as a substitute. Level with your reader, and he will go along; cheat him and you have lost your audience. So much for the *do nots.*

A sense of time

In many, if not most, stories, a sense of time is important, and this can be a powerful tool with which to build suspense. The minutes, the hours, the days are ticking away, and will whatever is going to happen take place in time? Turn the pages and see. In my long novel, *The Tower,* the entire action takes place in less than twelve hours, and the major action in a little over four. For purposes of plot (suspense) it was mandatory that the ticking minutes be emphasized. I used the simple device, by no means original, of heading each chapter with its time span, thereby making time itself a part of the story. Thus: 9:00 a.m.—9:33 a.m.; 11:10 a.m.—12:14 p.m.; etc. The final paragraph reads: "The time was 8:41. It had been four hours and eighteen minutes since the explosion." I have been told that the device was successful.

Sequence is another factor that is important in the building of suspense. Again, that ought to be obvious, but I am afraid it not always is. How many books or stories have you and I read in which the writer has shot the works halfway through his tale, and from that point on it is plodding downhill? Where then has suspense gone?

Sometimes I like to think of a story as a kind of hill climb. You start at the bottom and work your way up. There are dips and rises, but always you are working toward the top of the hill. When you arrive at the top, which is the story's climax, you face a steep drop-off, and you get to the bottom just as quickly as you can. Why? Because you have used up your suspense, you have shot the works, you have sung your big aria, and, to continue to mix the figures of speech, you want to get offstage while the audience is still applauding.

Pace and climax

A writer friend of mine once asked, "Where do you go when you've started your story on high C?" Good question, and I think the answer is that you drop an octave or two as fast as you can and then start climbing again. You want your story to build, its pace to quicken, its excitement to grow— then you are building the suspense and pulling the reader along with you.

Do not mistake me. The growth can be quiet, understated, low-key; C. P. Snow's novels come to mind, or Marquand's. But the growth, the quickening pace, the climb to the top of the hill ought to be there, and in Snow's and Marquand's novels it is; and so is suspense. C. P. Snow speaks of the "narrative art," and when he is asked what he means, he says that it is the art of making the reader turn the page. Is that not precisely what we are talking about?

In the heyday of the great national magazines, the "slicks," the craft of serial writing reached a high state of expertise. Basically, the serial was a single story running through, let us say, three installments of thirty pages each. (There could be as few as two installments, or as many as eight, but the technical problems remained the same.) Each installment had to carry on the main story, but it also had to have a smaller story of its own, a subplot, if you will, or at least a large problem presented but not completely solved, thereby whetting the reader's appetite for the next issue in which problem number one would be solved, and problem number two presented. And so it went, the story rising in pitch to the final installment in which everything was solved and the story quickly ended.

It is, I think, not a bad format to keep in mind. Probably because I served my apprenticeship in the slicks, I find it ingrained in my subconscious. Always the story must rise—but not too fast. As with a pot that must not be allowed to boil over, the heat must be reduced, slowed down, to let the reader take a few easy breaths and maybe go out to the refrigerator for a fresh beer. Then start at him again, making the story rise, quicken, so that tension mounts. This is the essence, and whether you are writing mystery, adventure, romance, "straight, serious" fiction, or whatever, juveniles or adults, hardcover or soft, this is the way to C. P. Snow's "narrative art," the art of making the reader turn the page. This is suspense.

27 SETTING AND BACKGROUND IN THE NOVEL

by *Mary Stewart*

ALTHOUGH I must confess that I have my doubts whether one writer can tell another how to write anything at all, or even describe adequately how he does it himself, I know that there is something heartening and helpful about the very community of experience. Every writer started somewhere, and no writer worth his salt ever had it easy, or ever will; so it is possible that a brief attempt to summarize the way I tackle certain phases of writing may be of interest to others.

Place makes plot

Almost without my realizing it, I have come to have the reputation of setting my suspense stories exotically—Avignon, Skye, Savoy, Corfu—and of using these settings not just as background color, but dynamically, almost as a "first character" of the book. I do, in fact, start with the setting. I used to think it was chance that led me into this way of writing. When I wrote my first book, *Madam, Will You Talk?*, I had never written a story before, and it seemed natural, in that icy winter when the impulsion to write finally outweighed even my diffidence in starting, to choose the most exciting—and the hottest—place I had then been to. I found, in the writing of the book, that the tough, strange, romantic setting exactly suited the kind of thing I wanted to write; that it did, in fact, dictate its own kind of plot; and that to allow it to permeate every corner of the story could do nothing but enrich that story.

This was obviously the kind of thing that suited me, so, book by book, from this kind of start I formed my own personal work map. A place which had had a powerful impact on my senses and imagination would suggest a story line and an atmosphere into which I could put my characters, and let their reactions to the setting, and to each other in that setting, work themselves out into a plot. The fact that I chose a different setting for each of my books made (I think) for variety in treatment and atmosphere, even though the basic ingredients of the "suspense novel" must to some extent stay the same.

Of course I did not discover this working method by chance, as, in fact, each writer's way of working must come out of deep-rooted patterns of thought and behavior which at some point find their own way of expression. I can see now where my own method came from. I am country bred, with a deep interest in natural history, over which is grafted my profession of English Literature, and a passion for ancient history and folk-lore. So I find that my type of imagination quickens most readily in beautiful places where legend and history add an extra light of excitement to the kind of life that is lived there today.

This work map, like all writers' methods, is an intensely personal thing, and, while it suits me, it would possibly suit nobody else; but my own use of setting as a take-off point, and thereafter as an integral part of the novel, has suggested to me one or two general observations which may possibly be of interest or use.

Dynamic and static uses of place

I suppose there are two main uses of setting, the dynamic and the static. Probably the best example of the former—

where the place is as vivid as the people—is Emily Brontë's *Wuthering Heights*. In this, the prototype of the romantic novel, the characters grow out of the place, and so does the action; the story would be unthinkable in any other setting. Wuthering Heights itself is the hero, not Heathcliff, who is in a way only a humanization of the stormy moorland and is most "real" when he is a voice in the wind.

What I have called static setting is more common; that is, the use of setting merely as a background for human action, the giving of a local habitation and a name to a story which could have happened almost anywhere.

Whichever way the setting is used, it is of paramount importance. I have, in the past, come across novels with scanty or token settings, in which the people moved and talked against no vividly defined background. Of these novels I can now remember nothing except the growing exasperation and difficulty of reading, which I at length traced to its cause. On the other hand, novels which were trivial apart from their vivid settings, for example, the stories of Gene Stratton Porter, have remained in my mind ever since my teens when I read them.

Any attempt to set a novel vividly and dynamically must involve descriptive writing. This is a real danger point, and should be done with care, and sparely. The "set piece" describing a place is by its nature static, and should be used only where action needs to be temporarily suspended, like the pause in music. It should never be used for its own sake, and it should not be used at length. But the periodic interruption of the action by brief descriptive passages can be a powerful weapon in the writer's hand. These can work like the curtain in the theatre—to open a scene, or act as changeover points for emphasis and direction either of action or emotion. They can break up a long dialogue or action sequence and provide points of rest; they can be emotive; they can also allow the writer to slip essential information in among semi-relevant or purely atmospheric detail.

Sensation by action

Most important of all, perhaps, is the power that a vivid setting gives you, the writer, over your reader: the way it lets you catapult him bodily into the action. Nothing takes a reader more immediately into the being of a fictional character than the swift recognition of some common experience: "Yes, it does feel like that . . . or smell like that . . . or look like that." By exploiting the simple sensation, the writer can transport his reader into the character's skin, transcending barriers of personality, even of sex. The quickest and most vivid way is the concrete one, that is, not the abstract description of sensation, but the illustration of sensation by action. Once the action has suggested the sensation to the reader, once you can get him vividly to share the physical responses of the character, he is also free to enter that character's mind.

To take a random example from a book of mine, *My Brother Michael*: There is a point where the heroine, herself in considerable danger, is forced to be a silent witness to a particularly unpleasant murder.

> I shut my eyes. I turned my head away so that my cheek, like my hands, pressed against the cool rock. It smelt fresh, like rain. I remember that under my left hand there was a little knob of stone the shape of a limpet shell.

Later:

> I was shaking, and covered with sweat, and hot as though the chilly cleft were an oven. Under the fingers of my left hand the stone limpet had broken away, and it was embedded in the flesh, hurting me. . . .

Two things have been done here. The feel and smell of damp rock, which everyone recognizes, have taken the reader inside the girl's skin and therefore right into her predicament; and her unconscious action in breaking off the bit of stone should suggest stress of mind more vividly than any direct statement. It is a fact that in moments of severe stress, one's mind often fastens on some small physical irrelevancy which may remain in the memory more vividly even than the agony itself.

(I would suggest here in passing that the dynamic use of setting is a weapon that no historical novelist can afford to ignore. To describe scenes, dresses, ways of life of a different age, may make the story move like a pageant in front of us; but to take us alive into another period of time, the senses must be invoked in the way described above. This was the challenge that I took up when I wrote my first historical novel *The Crystal Cave*. It was not deliberate choice that gave me as my setting the most obscure period of British history, the "dark age." It might be argued that this freed the imagination more than a better-known period, but it did involve building a "real" and plausible world out of something unknown and unmapped and, moreover, obscured further beneath a veil of implausible tradition. I used the same resources and techniques as in my suspense novels: community of experience laid over careful research. People think differently in different times, but their bodies feel and react as they always did. The animal is older than the human spirit.)

Vivid close-ups

As for the actual techniques of description and setting, here, as everywhere, the basic rule is simplicity. The most vivid "atmospheric" setting is done, not with elaborate description which tires the reader's powers of mental build-up, but with the selection of one or two telling details. This is how Graham Greene, one of the masters of setting, does it. No long, drawn-out panning down the village street, just one short, vivid close-up of a vulture hunched on a corrugated iron roof in tropical rain, and you have all the torrid squalor of Africa in a sentence. And this same detail occurs again. The repetition is effective and cumulative, but needs a practiced hand, or the device edges toward symbolism, which is a clumsy way of "getting through," and ineffective when the symbolism is the personal symbolism of the author, and not the real thing worn smooth with—literally—centuries of use. A good story should be carried alive into the heart of the reader, and this is only done by the writer's passion disciplined by the writer's skill in the techniques of communication.

Every writer finds his own techniques, but perhaps I could suggest one or two ideas which were starting points for me. In the description of a whole landscape, a wide-angle picture, it is probably best to start at the horizon and work in. Draw in from the large general effects of sky and atmosphere, till you get to the close-ups, the plants at the edge of the road where your observer is standing. Of course, there are times when you must do it the other way around, but choose which way to direct the observer's eye, and keep to it.

A physical setting should never be built up too elaborately. What a writer is doing is opening a gateway on *someone else's imagination.* You have to build your effects by using the reader's experience and terms of reference at the same time as your own. So don't force his imagination too hard into the shape of yours. Give him the main points, place them for him, and then let him fill in out of his own experience. He'll do this anyway, so there is no point in distorting his picture with yours. For example, nothing is worse than reading a detailed description of a room. Something of the size and style and color, and perhaps three telling details, are all that is necessary. If the reader furnishes the room with pieces he knows, it will be all the more vivid for him. I, myself, always found illustrated books very trying; they clashed with my own much more (to me) vivid picture.

And now let me finish with an apology. First of all, for using my own work as an illustration; but the only writer of whose motives you are almost sure is yourself, and motive, rather than result, was what concerned me. Second, for having certainly done, almost everywhere in my own writing, the exact opposite of what I have suggested here. But there are, I repeat, no rules. And I am well aware that no writer who is worth anything ever writes to anyone else's plan. All he does is to read what the other fellow says, raise an eyebrow, mutter "I couldn't work like that," and go his own way.

28 PLOTS IN CRIME FICTION

by *Michael Underwood*

WHETHER you call them mysteries, thrillers, detective stories, or, more trendily, novels of suspense, the best examples contain elements implicit in each of these descriptive terms. Moreover, in a world of rapidly changing tastes and fashions, the crime novel (to give the species an embracing name) endures, primarily because of its basic ingredients. These will obviously appear in varying proportions according to the type of book you are writing. For example, the old-fashioned detective story which was in vogue in the 1920's and 1930's emphasized detection and mystification more than thrills and suspense, though it usually had all these elements. Similarly, the spy story had its accent on thrills and suspense and was less concerned with the other two ingredients. In using the past tense, I do not mean to imply that either of these types of book is dead, though it is certainly true that both would now seem to have yielded to other forms, at least temporarily. To be sure, the great detective story writers of the pre-World War II years —Dorothy Sayers and Agatha Christie, for example—are still widely read and in demand, but today's aspiring crime fiction writer will probably find it much more difficult to persuade a publisher to take on an old-style detective story as a first novel, however great its other merits, than, for example, a police procedural or a suspense novel with an interesting background.

So much by way of introduction. Though what it introduces

I am not quite sure. However, it enables me to get on with telling you something about my own writing.

I began writing crime novels for the best possible reason, namely that I enjoyed reading them. I became addicted as a schoolboy, which was a long time ago, and determined then that one day I would write one myself. At that time, authorship struck me as about the most interesting, fascinating and glamorous pursuit anyone could follow. Almost half a century later, I may have become rather less starry-eyed about the glamour part, but I still regard writing as the most satisfying and self-fulfilling aspect of my life. And I speak as one whose writing is confined to evenings and weekends. My qualification for preaching to you is that I have written over two dozen books, all crime novels and all a bit different, I hope.

Plots that satisfy

Whatever sort of crime story you choose to write, remember that the plot is of paramount importance. Plots come more easily to some than others. I am one of those writers who finds the construction of a plot akin to chipping away at solid rock with a toothpick. I look with envy—and also with a certain measure of suspicion—at fellow writers who tell me they have so many plots in their heads that they will never live long enough to use them.

However substantial your other writing skills, I venture to say that, unless you have a sound plot, you will not write a good crime story. You may feel you can get by with an absorbing background and interesting characters, but if the plot is deficient, this will eventually become apparent; the reader will experience a sense of letdown by the time he reaches the end of your book. Indeed, the greater the writer's *other* skills, the greater the reader's sense of letdown if the plot is weak, as the reader will have been carried forward, expecting a satisfying denouement, and then be deprived of this at the very last moment. I always know when I have a good plot, i.e. a natural plot, and I am ruefully aware when I have a contrived plot.

And the book with the contrived or artificial plot is a much harder one to write.

For me, a contrived plot relies on coincidence and fortuitous happenings. A natural one is one in which nothing jars or stretches credulity but leaves the reader utterly satisfied at the end. It all fits together like a well-made jigsaw; nothing has to be forced into place.

Working out the plot takes me almost as long as writing the book, and by plot, I mean the whole skeleton of the story. Often friends say to a writer, "I have a wonderful idea for a book," and then proceed to describe an opening scene. "Yes, go on," you say, encouragingly. "That's it. That's the plot," they retort. But it's not a plot at all. It's no more than an idea. I'm not belittling ideas, as they are the seeds from which plots grow, but an idea shouldn't be confused with the plot itself. Almost everyone has an idea for a book, but very few nurture that idea until it becomes a plot. And until you do have a plot, you cannot write a crime novel.

A man murders his wife/mistress in a fit of temper and dashes off to tell the police what he has done. When they go to his house, the body has vanished.

Here is an idea, but it is certainly not a plot. On the other hand, it is not too hard to see the various directions in which the idea could be developed into a plot. Has he told the police the truth? If not, why not? Who would want to remove the body and why? Answer those questions and you're on your way to devising a plot. Each answer will pose another question which will require an answer and so on until you have a fully shaped plot.

You neglect the plot at your peril—the peril being a book that falls apart at the end, whatever its excellences on the way.

Starting points

Looking back over my own list of published books, I often find it difficult to recall how the plots came to be conceived. Obviously, there was an idea at the beginning of each, but such is the developing and tortuous process of plotting a crime story that the original idea is frequently lost from sight by the end. Some people start with a character, others with a situation, often these two in conjunction, and build from there. This is certainly my own most frequent starting point, rather like the grain of sand in the oyster shell, though let me quickly add that in no sense do my plots bear any resemblance to pearls. In the days of the classical detective story, in which characters were less important than the mechanism of the plot, most of the protagonists would start with some fiendishly ingenious way of committing undetectable murder or with an apparently unbreakable alibi. The intellectual puzzle was what readers wanted and were given. Tastes have now changed and become more sophisticated, and the crime novel is no longer regarded as a poor relation of so-called straight fiction.

Today's readers demand more than a mere puzzle. Having constructed your plot, you must not allow yourself to be deflected from it. In a crime novel, nothing should happen which is not relevant to the plot. You may be brilliant at baking bread and long to share your expertise with your readers. You should do so, however, only if the loaf you have lovingly described baking in chapter 4 is going to poison the victim in chapter 7, or become the conveyor of a time bomb to be placed on his breakfast table in chapter 10. Nothing, repeat, nothing, should appear in your book which does not further the plot. The plot is everything. You may be able to get away with a deficiency of plot in other forms of fiction, but not in a crime novel.

The characters—who must not be cardboard pieces—often present themselves once you have your plot. Because I happen to be a criminal lawyer, I set many of my books against a legal background, and inevitably lawyers and police figure among my characters. Obviously, one tries to make one's characters interesting people and not just types. At the same time, one has to avoid making them so way-out that they become

simply tiresome to the reader. Each of us is an individual with
certain characteristics, some delightful, others rather less so,
and I have personally not found it too hard to give a touch
of individuality to the characters in my stories, even to those
who have little more than a walk-on part. I like to think that
I've become reasonably successful at this. I also believe an
author should show detachment toward his characters. At any
rate, that he should not appear to be in love with any of them.
To me, one of the most enjoyable parts of writing is finding
names for my characters. Not only should the names you
choose help to delineate the characters but they should fit
them like a well-made suit of clothes. One should avoid having
Tom and Tim in the same book, or Mrs. Elm and Mrs. Tree.
This only leads to confusion, and makes the reader have to
turn back in the book to clear his mind as to which is which.

New, authentic backgrounds

Background is much more important than it used to be.
Because readers are more sophisticated, they want stories set
against new and interesting backgrounds, so you have crime
novels with authentic backgrounds: mountain climbing, horse
racing, banking, tribal reserves, art galleries, law courts,
mining and numerous other fields of activity. Successful crime
authors using such backgrounds include Emma Lathen (Wall
Street banking); Dick Francis (horse racing); H. R. F. Keat-
ing (Indian background with Indian detective, Inspector
Ghote); and Peter Lovesey (Victorian sporting backgrounds).

I employ my knowledge of criminal courts and police procedure as part of the fabric of many of my books, but I have
only once used a real-life case and translated it into a work
of fiction. On the other hand, I may use a real incident,
suitably adapted, for a bit of color. But on the whole I do not
devise plots out of my working life. You may have no firsthand
experience of any of these backgrounds, but don't feel frus-

trated. The odds are that you have firsthand knowledge of some aspect of life which can be made interesting. Speaking for myself as a reader, I regard it as a bonus if, in the course of enjoying a good crime novel, I also learn something about some aspect of living of which I previously knew nothing. But it is only a bonus. I do not read crime books in order to learn how to catch trout or to make wine. Indeed, I have on occasion been put off reading a book because its background held no interest for me. And, anyway, remember that the background must always be subordinate to the plot. It must not be allowed to obtrude so that it finally submerges the plot and becomes an indigestible digression. This can happen when a writer is unwilling to discard any of the points of his research. Perhaps he has lived in a plastic bubble at the bottom of the ocean or camped in an asbestos tent inside a volcano and is determined that the reader shall have every last detail of his experience. Fine! But not in a crime novel.

I am a great admirer of the novels of Julian Symons. He is a splendid craftsman and an immensely literate (not literary) writer. Obviously, some of his plots are better than others, but he has never done other than provide me with delicious enjoyment. If I have to pick one favorite, it is Symons. I also remain a great admirer of Raymond Chandler. Apart from his plots, I found myself completely hooked by his Southern California settings. I never visit California now without trying to recapture some of the magnetism he created for me.

Improving the craft

Plot, characters, background. What else? Simple, effective English to weld the lot together and keep the reader turning the pages. I say no more than that because everyone has his own literary style. I am merely stating my own preference as a reader. I shall never be capable of writing deathless prose, and I invariably excise the purple passages which I find have crept into a first draft of a book. I choose to believe that my writing has improved since my early books—and so it should have done. For writing crime novels is a craft and, therefore, subject to improvement as a result of practice. To me, simple, effective English means, primarily, the avoidance of clichés, of opacity of meaning, and of inelegant sentences.

Crime stories have a record of durability. Every generation produces its new authors and, most happily, its new readers too. If you are minded to write one, be encouraged by the fact that though the market is dominated by American and British writers, the readership is far wider. Indeed, worldwide.

29

SPRINGBOARD TO SUSPENSE FICTION

by *Phyllis A. Whitney*

THERE IS ONE question that is always asked of the writer by the non-writer and it comes so often that those of us who write develop an automatic wince when we hear it. The question, of course, is, "Where do you get your ideas?" It's not that it isn't a legitimate question, but that the answer seems both so obvious and so complicated that it is hard to answer.

The simple, obvious answer is, "Everywhere," and it sends the questioner away as mystified as ever. Since non-writers never have any ideas for stories, there seems a magic in the way a complicated novel starts from nothing—and appears as a whole in a printed book.

It is the complicated part of that answer that I would like to deal with here. Because, of course, there are many, many times when the writer has no ideas at all, when we start from scratch and often without inspiration. We then do need a springboard to launch us into that first idea, to which other ideas will keep attaching themselves until hundreds of manuscript pages have been filled and we have that completed book.

The non-writer doesn't understand that a plot is not something that appears full-blown, miraculously, from nowhere. It is something that grows painstakingly, a bit at a time, often through periods of despair and drought. Yet there *are* moments when miracles do happen and something comes clear in an instant—though not as a rule the whole thing.

Pleasure in places

My own springboard, from which I take off in the beginning, is usually a new setting. I have a strong feeling toward places, and when I am entranced by a setting, I can take pleasure in writing about it as a background for my story. A real setting furnishes endless ideas for story scenes, and even gives me an introduction to people who may be helpful in working out my characters. I don't like to transfer real people into my stories, because they would never behave as I want them to. But the ideas expressed by those I talk with in a special setting give me the knowledge to make my own characters in such a setting true to life.

While the background must always come early in the development of a story for me, it is not necessarily the first springboard. A year or so ago, I had a strange dream. I don't usually remember dreams, but I woke up with this one vividly in mind. I had been wandering on a hillside, perhaps a mountainside, with woods all around. Set down in the middle of this wooded area was what appeared to be a huge, circular barn. The door was locked, but I went in anyway, as one does in dreams, to behold the strangest of scenes: a bullring, with a larger-than-life-size stone bull standing in the center of it. Mystery, with no answer, because I woke up immediately and with just one thought in mind: *What a wonderful title for a book*.

I lost the barn in the course of writing the novel, but *The Stone Bull* became the title of my next book, and I now know all about that bull on the mountainside. My setting came second in the development of this story—when I had to choose my mountain. Since the Catskills are not too far from where I live, I found a suitable area and went there to stay for a week.

Once I am in the place of my choice, I work hard every minute. I fill a notebook with random description and set down any plot ideas that may come to me, inspired by the place. I take several rolls of color film, turning my camera on anything that might be useful to me when I get home. I take advantage of everything the place offers that might give me story material—hiking trails, rowing a boat, riding in a truck —or whatever. I collect maps of the region, colored postcards, brochures, books. Sometimes my collection grows so heavy that I have to send it home separately. But I am seldom able to spend more than a week to ten days in any place I visit. Because of my "outsider's" view, I always write from the viewpoint of a stranger new to the area.

One of the most interesting and rewarding setting searches I've made was on a trip to Norway. It came about by chance. While working on one book, I always have an eye open for anything that may lead me into the next one. A friend had just returned from a trip to Scandinavia, and she spoke with enthusiasm of the colorful city of Bergen. I went to the library and looked up Bergen, and my compass direction was set for Norway.

I try, if possible, to prepare for my arrival on the new scene by writing letters ahead of time. Even when my books were not well known, I wrote to librarians before I arrived and usually found a warm welcome. I go to travel agencies, and send letters to consulates, explaining that I mean to write about a certain locality, and I am often given introductions and offers of help. Doors may sometimes be slammed suspiciously in my face, but no writer ever takes "no" for an answer, and I keep insisting that I must get off the beaten track, find out how people live, see the inside of a few homes. The tourist things are fine, but I want more than that.

On location

Once on location, I choose carefully those things to do that will be most useful to me. Bergen is a small place geographically, and was easy to cover. When I was writing about Istanbul, I had a more difficult problem. I couldn't possibly come in as a stranger and learn all about that exotic city in a short time. But I had done my homework by reading and knew that I would visit one famous mosque, a fortress on the Bosporus, one covered bazaar, a village on the water, and other sights. To these I would return more than once, so that I could come to know them well. Of course, once you are in a place, there will be things to see and do that you couldn't dream of ahead of time. The unexpected is always happening, and you will fit it into your schedule if it seems to offer possibilities.

As a suspense writer, I am always alert for two things in particular: A likely means of murder that fits the setting, and the right place for the "chase" scene of my climax. It is sometimes disconcerting to residents when I exclaim with delight that some spot of beauty or historic significance is a lovely place for a murder!

In Bergen I discovered my climax setting when we drove out to visit one of the few remaining wooden churches that date back to the beginnings of Christianity in Norway, and which have been marvelously preserved. This one was a museum piece a little way out of Bergen, and its setting was an eerie park of gnarled roots and forbidding pines. I took a dozen pictures right there, and when I came to my climax scene, I had details to use that I could never have captured fully in notes alone. The pictures were so real that I could even invoke my mood, my feelings about the place.

A character and the search

Once my setting has been chosen, there is another means of launching me into my story that I must immediately seek. I must develop a main character faced by a problem, and I must find a means to get her to the setting of my choice.

In the case of *Listen for the Whisperer,* a romantic suspense novel set in Bergen, I started out with the idea of a young woman who had been abandoned as a child by her famous actress mother and raised by the father she adores. She has grown up resenting the entire legend of her mother, a woman who is now living in Norway, and whom she hasn't seen since birth. Her father in dying has left word that he wants her to seek out her mother. She goes there against her will, with an obligation to fulfill. Thus we are launched into a psychological situation filled with opportunities for emotion, conflict—and, of course, mystery.

Before writing *The Golden Unicorn,* I wasn't able to travel abroad, and had to choose a setting closer to hand. The village of East Hampton on Long Island was suggested to me by a writer friend, and I went out to spend a few days there. When a setting is not as foreign and exotic as I like, I must especially seek out small things. I must walk the hard sand of a beach near the water's edge, with all the summer people gone, and with a feeling of loneliness, of sadness, because winter lies ahead and the empty houses are shuttered. I must *experience* this. My own emotions must be examined for every nuance. I take snapshots of the old beach houses peering down from their high dunes. I note the scraps of broken shell, the dark seaweed cast upon empty sand, a line of footprints where the sand is damp. I am aware of the long straight line of shore, stretching toward Montauk, and I feel the wind at my back, I listen to the ocean and the gulls, I see the smoke trail of a freighter on the Atlantic. Of just such small things is emotion composed, and I will use them all later. When my heroine walks that particular beach, it will be as real for her as it was for me. Such impressions cannot always be photographed, and they go down in my notebook.

In this case the springboard of the human situation was a girl who had been adopted and whose adoptive parents had died. She must start out on what those who have been adopted call The Search. It is a search for her own being and heritage.

I had to do a great deal of research on adoption for this book, and much conjuring of ways in which to lead my heroine to East Hampton.

All the things I've been describing are done deliberately on the road to creating a story from empty white paper. But there is something else that enters in from time to time along the way. And this is the thing that is most difficult to explain to that non-writer. Yes, my dear Virginia, there *is* a Santa Claus. There *are* miracles.

One of them happened to me in an especially impressive way when I was working on *The Golden Unicorn*. Because the East Hampton scene is not all that exotic, I had to cast around in doing my research for any extras that might be useful. So I drove out to Montauk at the eastern tip of Long Island, saw the windswept little town, and the lighthouse on the point. I even arranged to visit the New York Ocean Science Laboratory before I came home. But how on earth was I to get any of this into my story?

I saw the problem coming while I was still in the plotting stage, and it had not cleared up by the time I was writing. It would be necessary to take five characters out to Montauk in order to use that setting. I needed that much more wordage in the story, I needed a gap when these characters would be away from East Hampton, and I wanted to use Montauk as a break from the East Hampton scenes. But how was I to do this? In a story, no moves can be made that have nothing to do with the plot. Travelogues are tiresome. There must be a reason to go, and something interesting must happen that will affect the story, affect the main problems that face the heroine. Only I couldn't think of a thing that would answer these conditions. Nothing.

From long experience I have learned that the most difficult of problems can be solved, that there is always a way. But I was getting very close to the Montauk scene in my writing, and I still hadn't the faintest idea of how I could use it. Finally, I gave up forward writing and went back to read the whole manuscript through from the beginning.

Harnessing the subconscious

On the day before I *had* to solve the problem, I lay down in the afternoon for a nap, and began idly to think about what I might do. And in that relaxed state, suddenly, without warning, I saw it, all there in my mind: A good scene, a dramatic and necessary scene, with a new character introduced whom I'd known nothing about moments before. No nap. I got right up and wrote it all down before it could escape, and the next day, I went to my typewriter and turned out one of the good, dramatic scenes in the book.

Call it the subconscious, call it Santa Claus, call it what you like, there is something there that goes to work on creative problems without conscious effort on the writer's part, and works out all the details when you're not even looking.

This wasn't the only time that happened to me. For the subconscious is something I use constantly in my writing, and it never fails me when I need it badly. In the case of *The Golden Unicorn,* it worked a little more spectacularly than usual. Nevertheless, I had taken all the right steps to bring about the solution. There are three: 1. Think about the problem and feed it into your mind. 2. Leave it alone and turn to other things. 3. After an interval, take it out and look at it. Usually, the answer will be there. If not, repeat the process.

The most interesting thing to me in this particular instance was the fact that everything in the solution was already buried in the body of what I had written. The setting of a particular house had been mentioned and the extra character planted, but never used. I hadn't been able to see the solution consciously, but when it all came to me in a flash, it was absolutely right. The new happenings grew out of everything that went before, and they led into what was to come. I now needed to go back and pull what was embedded to the surface, so that I could move the story along naturally to future happenings. But it took very little revision to do this.

On certain rare occasions when no trip at all was possible, I have done an entire background without visiting the scene. This was true of *Spindrift*. I had planned to visit Newport, Rhode Island, but illness and other difficulties intervened, so that I couldn't travel. The Newport Public Library helped me with lists of books I could read. The Newport Chamber of Commerce (another good source of information) sent me a packet of maps and brochures. My publisher sent me a marvelous book of photographs, and before I was through, I had walked all around Newport in my imagination. I also had the generous assistance of a library board member who lived in Newport and could keep me from making mistakes. The houses I used in the story were invented out of bits and pieces of reality, as the houses in my stories usually are.

There are still other springboards that can be used to give us any amount of story material when we are in that searching process. An interesting vocation will do it. Jobs, professions, exotic businesses are full of story material. So is almost any unusual human condition.

In one of my books for young people, *Secret of the Emerald Star*, setting isn't awfully important. The story could have been placed almost anywhere. I happened to use Staten Island, because that was where I was living at the time. My springboard was the subject of blindness. I wanted to write about a child who was blind. She wouldn't be my heroine, but would be a girl in whom the heroine became interested.

Through emotion to essence

Knowing nothing about blindness, I began first of all to read. But factual research is never enough. It is necessary to find a way to experience with your own emotions whatever it is you mean to write about. My first step was to visit a school in Manhattan where blind and sighted young people came together. The blind had their own homeroom, but they mingled with the others in moving about the school. Both groups got to know and accept each other.

I spent some time in that homeroom and talked with a number of blind children. One young girl was particularly outgoing, and it was she who introduced me to the world of the blind. I walked with her on the street, I went home with her and learned how she kept the possessions in her room so that she could easily identify colors, and distinguish whatever else she needed to know. But more than anything else, this girl gave me something I could feel and experience. Her own courage and lively interest in everything around her came through, and with her help I was made a rich enough person emotionally to write about a world I had known nothing about before.

The *essence* of a place, a person, a situation, is always what we must search for as writers. I remember sitting on a ruined wall in Camirus on the island of Rhodes in Greece—a town that Homer once knew. The ancient stones were as warm in the sun for me as for all those who had come before, and the pillars of the ruined temple as golden-white under the intensely blue sky of the Grecian isles. The distant sea was there as so many centuries had seen it before me; as I sat upon my wall, a small green lizard came out on the stones beside me. Only the lizard and I belonged to *now*. All this was *essence* that would later go into the books I set in Greece.

Where do ideas for stories come from? Where do they *not* come from? And how very enriching our search for these stories can be.

30
WRITING AND SELLING THE POLICE PROCEDURAL NOVEL

by *Collin Wilcox*

WHAT ARE THE ingredients of the police procedural novel, and of the series that can follow a successful first book?

First of all, a police procedural novel must hold up a mirror to the squad room. But the mirror must be contoured to selective refraction. The real-life homicide detective's work is essentially dull. For one thing, the police usually know "whodunit." It's usually the husband, drunk on Saturday night and arguing with his wife. One drink too many—one too many epithets— and homicide gets the call. Until a few years ago, when heroin-related street crime began blighting our cities, eighty per cent of the murder victims had close ties with their murderers. Sixty-five per cent of the victims and their murderers were blood relatives. Alcohol was a factor in seventy-five per cent of all murders, not to mention cheap, readily available handguns, the so-called Saturday night specials. And, most unsatisfying of all to the mystery fan, most "all in the family" murderers don't even try to escape. Many of them simply sit beside the body of their victims, alcoholically blubbering. Many more, worse yet, from the reader's point of view, call the police. Heroin-related robbery and murder are just as senselessly capricious, just as horribly wasteful as their alcohol-induced counterparts. In either case, someone dies for no rational reason.

Obviously, these aren't the murder cases that will titillate the average mystery reader. In suspense fiction, murder must be diabolical. Nor are readers interested in homicide detectives who aren't constantly involved in shoot-outs and hot pursuits, despite the fact that in reality, investigating the typical homicide is a long, tedious process, much of which is accomplished on the phone.

Research—plus imagination

I've been told that my novels have a realistic flavor, and people are constantly asking how much time I spend in research. I reply that I once worked as a law enforcement officer. (I taught reading and writing in a New Jersey prison for a few months, and I *did* retrieve a couple of escapees, one of whom got as far as New Orleans.) And, yes, I've spent a little time at the San Francisco Homicide Bureau—two hours, I think. For the rest of it, I occasionally watch *Kojak, The Blue Knight, Policewoman, Streets of San Francisco, Baretta, Barney Miller, Police Story* (offbeat and humorous), and, in past years, *Lineup* (the best of the television lot, I think). When I describe my casual research habits, some people feel vaguely cheated. Others writers lecture me on the importance of research. I reply that it's often easy to become confused by the facts. I also paraphrase Barbara Tuchman, commenting that research is endlessly beguiling, but writing is hard work. Writing is also an exercise in imagination. Most editors would never buy a work of fiction that exactly reflects the average homicide investigation.

To the publishers—and therefore to the writer—mystery/suspense novels can be happy exceptions to mainstream fiction's red ink problems. Prudently edited and merchandised, the average hardback mystery novel will at least break even. With the original investment recovered, hardback publishers can relax and enjoy their 50% share of the book's domestic softcover sale and the book club sale, if any. (Writers receive 100% on foreign sales.) These subsidiary sales figures are usually modest, but they're generally steady and fairly predictable. One suspense book a year will (almost!) produce a reasonable living. Two books a year—preferably two series running concurrently and published by two different publishers —will usually provide writers with a few luxuries. In time, if their books become popular and are regularly reissued by the paperback publishers, the writers could even become rich (especially if Hollywood beckons—another case where the writer gets 100% as a rule)! With very few exceptions, though, suspense writers never become rich until they've published at least ten books (that is, books with identifiable market appeal, like mysteries, science fiction, Gothics, etc.). Genre books are usually limited to about 65,000 words. Because they are aimed at a ready market, genre suspense novels are generally restricted to plots that have been proven salable. Editors are constantly looking for innovative plots—but not *too* innovative.

Rules—to be followed or broken

Based on their knowledge of the marketplace, editors have certain rules of content for their mystery/suspense list. Sometimes these rules are relaxed or broken, often with spectacular sales results. Usually, though, the editor stays with the rules, thus assuring his employer that vital return on his investment. Here are some of the rules:

1. Length should be 55,000 to 65,000 words, so that price can be competitive. All of my Dodd, Mead and Random House books were 60,000 words. A few began longer, but were edited down to that length. However, *The Faceless Man* is about 90,000 words. I broke a rule, and the editors went along. Length can make people pay attention, provided the story isn't dull.

2. There should be a murder early in the story. This convention is almost universal. There should be another murder, related to the first, later in the story.

3. Action should occupy a limited time—a few days, at the most (despite the fact that most homicide investigations take weeks).

4. The crime's solution must represent a triumph of good over evil and should demonstrate that the detective is smarter than the murderer, or more virtuous, or quicker, or braver. However, police procedural novels don't normally rely on the classic Agatha Christie "hidden clue" device. Modern police procedural novels often substitute shoot-outs for Poirot-style deduction. In fact, it's my feeling that the mystery/suspense genre is moving away from the classical whodunit, toward a form modeled on television programming. In many TV crime shows, we know who is guilty before the credits are rolled. Similarly, in publishing, suspense (what happens to the victim or the villain next) may be replacing mystery (whodunit? how? why?).

5. The murder must be premeditated and should have an interesting, complex motive. For the crime writer—or at least for me—it's difficult to concoct a motive for murder that seems believable. Drunkenness or madness or drug addiction aren't acceptable, at least not to most editors. In the end, most of us opt for murder for gain, or murder to conceal some terrible secret. Lately, however, our society condemns so little that it seems silly to have the villain commit murder to conceal, say, an extra-marital affair, or an inconvenient pregnancy. On the other hand, the profit motive continues to rage unabated. If an extra-marital affair means that the husband could be financially disadvantaged in divorce court—if he could save himself a few hundred thousand by murdering his paramour to keep her quiet—then we have a believable motive.

6. Despite the enormous success of some authors who write mystery/suspense in the first person, many editors distrust the "I" narrative. They often feel that the first-person narrative can become too introverted and the action line therefore blurred. I would tend to agree. Additionally, the third-person narrative gives the writer more flexibility to experiment with multiple viewpoints and perhaps more dramatic plots, less limited by strict reality.

7. In every successful novel, there is an element of suspense, or narrative drive. If the reader doesn't want to turn the page, the story isn't successful. If the writer isn't deeply involved in his story, neither is the reader. This sense of involvement—this most essential single ingredient of all good writing—is one that can never be taught in a classroom, or learned over a few drinks or even analyzed. Some writers simply engage their readers more compellingly than others, for reasons that are as obscure as differences in earlobes, signatures or success with the opposite sex.

The professional approach

There is little that I can add to the conventional wisdom a published writer seeks to pass on to someone still unpublished. The magic phrase, of course, is "never give up." As long as you're still trying—still turning out a given number of pages each day—there's always the possibility of success, provided your life is organized for a long, discouraging, impecunious wait. You must first survive the "printed rejection" period. We all went through it, and it's terrible. You spend months of your life working on a book that's rejected with a form letter, printed by the thousands and usually unsigned. Soon, though —in another year or so, if you're really working—you'll begin getting personal letters of rejection from editors, especially if you've tried two or three different submissions to the same house—and if the submissions show both promise and progress.

Editors are only interested in tough, tenacious, productive writers. They don't make money on softies or dilettantes. If you get rejection letters—personal letters, signed by editors—you're getting closer. Not close, maybe, but closer. If the editors criticize your work, or make suggestions for improvement, consider yourself fortunate. Editors are very busy people. If they didn't think it was possible that someday they could make a profit on one of your books, they wouldn't spend valuable time criticizing your work. So pay close attention to the criticism of editors and agents and published writers. If you do, you'll learn—and eventually succeed. You'll be a published author. When that miracle finally comes to pass, some will call you lucky. People envy the stereotyped writer his free and easy life style. To the layman, the writer doesn't work, not really. But you—and every other professional writer —will know better.

INNOVATORS AND CRITICS

31 DETECTIVE FICTION: ORIGINS AND DEVELOPMENT

by *Dorothy L. Sayers*

THE ART of self-tormenting is an ancient one, with a long and honourable literary tradition. Man, not satisfied with the mental confusion and unhappiness to be derived from contemplating the cruelties of life and the riddle of the universe, delights to occupy his leisure moments with puzzles and bugaboos. The pages of every magazine and newspaper swarm with cross-words, mathematical tricks, puzzle-pictures, enigmas, acrostics, and detective-stories, as also with stories of the kind called "powerful" (which means unpleasant), and those which make him afraid to go to bed. It may be that in them he finds a sort of catharsis or purging of his fears and self-questionings. These mysteries made only to be solved, these horrors which he knows to be mere figments of the creative brain, comfort him by subtly persuading that life is a mystery which death will solve, and whose horrors will pass away as a tale that is told. Or it may be merely that his animal faculties of fear and inquisitiveness demand more exercise than the daily round affords. Or it may be pure perversity. The fact remains that if you search the second-hand bookstalls for his cast-off literature, you will find fewer mystery stories than any other kind of book. Theology and poetry, philosophy and numismatics, love-stories and biography, he discards as easily as old razorblades, but Sherlock Holmes and Wilkie Collins are cherished and read and re-read, till their covers fall off and their pages crumble to fragments.

Both the detective-story proper and the pure tale of horror are very ancient in origin. All native folk-lore has its ghost tales, while the first four detective-stories in this book* hail respectively from the Jewish Apocrypha, Herodotus, and the Æneid. But, whereas the tale of horror has flourished in practically every age and country, the detective-story has had a spasmodic history, appearing here and there in faint, tentative sketches and episodes, until it suddenly burst into magnificent flower in the middle of the last century.

Early History of Detective Fiction

Between 1840 and 1845 the wayward genius of Edgar Allan Poe (himself a past-master of the horrible) produced five tales, in which the general principles of the detective-story were laid down for ever. In *The Murders in the Rue Morgue* and, with a certain repulsive facetiousness, in *Thou Art the Man* he achieved the fusion of the two distinct genres and created what we may call the story of mystery, as distinct from pure detection on the one hand and pure horror on the other. In this fused genre, the reader's blood is first curdled by some horrible and apparently inexplicable murder or portent; the machinery of detection is then brought in to solve the mystery and punish the murderer. Since Poe's time all three branches—detection, mystery, and horror—have flourished. We have such pleasant little puzzles as Conan Doyle's *Case of Identity,* in which there is nothing to shock or horrify; we have mere fantasies of blood and terror—human, as in Conan Doyle's *The Case of Lady Sannox,*[1] or supernatural, as in Marion Crawford's *The Upper Berth;*[2] most satisfactory of all, perhaps, we have such fusions as *The Speckled Band,*[3] or

---

* The book referred to here and in several places throughout this article is "The Omnibus of Crime" edited by Dorothy L. Sayers (Harcourt, Brace & Co.) in which this chapter originally appeared as the Introduction.—*The Editor*

[1] Conan Doyle: *Round the Red Lamp.*

[2] Marion Crawford: *Uncanny Tales.*

[3] Conan Doyle: *Adventures of Sherlock Holmes.*

The Hammer of God,[4] in which the ghostly terror is invoked only to be dispelled.

It is rather puzzling that the detective-story should have had to wait so long to find a serious exponent. Having started so well, why did it not develop earlier? The Oriental races, with their keen appreciation of intellectual subtlety, should surely have evolved it. The germ was there. "Why do you not come to pay your respects to me?" says Æsop's lion to the fox. "I beg your Majesty's pardon," says the fox, "but I noticed the track of the animals that have already come to you; and, while I see many hoof-marks going in, I see none coming out. Till the animals that have entered your cave come out again, I prefer to remain in the open air." Sherlock Holmes could not have reasoned more lucidly from the premises.

Cacus the robber, be it noted, was apparently the first criminal to use the device of forged footprints to mislead the pursuer, though it is a long development from his primitive methods to the horses shod with cow-shoes in Conan Doyle's *Adventure of the Priory School*.[5] Hercules's methods of investigation, too, were rather of the rough and ready sort, though the reader will not fail to observe that this early detective was accorded divine honours by his grateful clients.

The Jews, with their strongly moral preoccupation, were, as our two Apocryphal stories show, peculiarly fitted to produce the *roman policier*.[6] The Romans, logical and given to law-making, might have been expected to do something with it, but they did not. In one of the folk-tales collected by the Grimms, twelve maidens disguised as men are set to walk across a floor strewn with peas, in the hope that their shuffling feminine tread will betray them; the maidens are, however,

---

[4] G. K. Chesterton: *The Innocence of Father Brown.*

[5] Conan Doyle: *Return of Sherlock Holmes.*

[6] In *Bel and the Dragon* the science of deduction from material clues, in the popular Scotland Yard manner, is reduced to its simplest expression. *Susanna,* on the other hand, may be taken as foreshadowing the Gallic method of eliciting the truth by the confrontation of witnesses.

warned, and baffle the detectives by treading firmly. In an Indian folk-tale a similar ruse is more successful. Here a suitor is disguised as a woman, and has to be picked out from the women about him by the wise princess. The princess throws a lemon to each in turn, and the disguised man is detected by his instinctive action in clapping his knees together to catch the lemon, whereas the real women spread their knees to catch it in their skirts. Coming down to later European literature, we find the *Bel-and-the-Dragon* motif of the ashes spread on the floor reproduced in the story of Tristan. Here the king's spy spreads flour between Tristan's bed and that of Iseult; Tristan defeats the scheme by leaping from one bed to the other. The eighteenth century also contributed at least one outstanding example, in the famous detective chapter of Voltaire's *Zadig*.

It may be, as Mr. E. M. Wrong has suggested in a brilliant little study,[7] that throughout this early period "a faulty law of evidence was to blame, for detectives cannot flourish until the public has an idea of what constitutes proof, and while a common criminal procedure is arrest, torture, confession, and death." One may go further, and say that, though crime stories might, and did, flourish, the detective-story proper could not do so until public sympathy had veered round to the side of law and order. It will be noticed that, on the whole, the tendency in early crime-literature is to admire the cunning and astuteness of the criminal.[8] This must be so while the law is arbitrary, oppressive, and brutally administered.

We may note that, even to-day, the full blossoming of the detective-stories is found among the Anglo-Saxon races. It is notorious that an English crowd tends to side with the policeman in a row. The British legal code, with its tradition of

---

[7] Preface to *Tales of Crime and Detection*. World's Classics. (Oxford University Press, 1924.)

[8] e.g. *The Story of Rhampsinitus; Jacob and Esau; Reynard the Fox; Ballads of Robin Hood*, etc.

"sportsmanship" and "fair play for the criminal" is particularly favourable to the production of detective fiction, allowing, as it does, sufficient rope to the quarry to provide a ding-dong chase, rich in up-and-down incident. In France, also, though the street policeman is less honoured than in England, the detective-force is admirably organised and greatly looked up to. France has a good output of detective-stories, though considerably smaller than that of the English-speaking races. In the Southern States of Europe the law is less loved and the detective-story less frequent. We may not unreasonably trace a connection here.

Some further light is thrown on the question by a remark made by Herr Lion Feuchtwanger when broadcasting during his visit to London in 1927. Contrasting the tastes of the English, French, and German publics, he noted the great attention paid by the Englishman to the external details of men and things. The Englishman likes material exactness in the books he reads; the German and the Frenchman, in different degrees, care little for it in comparison with psychological truth. It is hardly surprising, then, that the detective-story, with its insistence on footprints, bloodstains, dates, times, and places, and its reduction of character-drawing to bold, flat outline, should appeal far more strongly to Anglo-Saxon taste than to that of France or Germany.

Taking these two factors together, we begin to see why the detective-story had to wait for its full development for the establishment of an effective police organisation in the Anglo-Saxon countries. This was achieved—in England, at any rate—during the early part of the nineteenth century,[9] and was fol-

---

[9] In a letter to W. Thornbury, dated February 18, 1862, Dickens says: "The Bow Street Runners ceased out of the land soon after the introduction of the new police. I remember them very well. . . . They kept company with thieves and such-like, much more than the detective police do. I don't know what their pay was, but I have no doubt their principal complements were got under the rose. It was a very slack institution, and its head-quarters were the Brown Bear, in Bow Street, a public house of more than doubtful reputation, opposite the police-office." The first "peelers" were established in 1829.

lowed about the middle of that century by the first outstanding examples of the detective-story as we know it to-day.[10]

To this argument we may add another. In the nineteenth century the vast, unexplored limits of the world began to shrink at an amazing and unprecedented rate. The electric telegraph circled the globe; railways brought remote villages into touch with civilisation; photographs made known to the stay-at-homes the marvels of foreign landscapes, customs, and animals; science reduced seeming miracles to mechanical marvels; popular education and improved policing made town and country safer for the common man than they had ever been. In place of the adventurer and the knight errant, popular imagination hailed the doctor, the scientist, and the policeman as saviours and protectors. But if one could no longer hunt the manticora, one could still hunt the murderer; if the armed escort had grown less necessary, yet one still needed the analyst to frustrate the wiles of the poisoner; from this point of view, the detective steps into his right place as the protector of the weak—the latest of the popular heroes, the true successor of Roland and Lancelot.

Edgar Allan Poe: Evolution of the Detective

Before tracing further the history of detective fiction, let us look a little more closely at those five tales of Poe's, in which so much of the future development is anticipated. Probably the first thing that strikes us is that Poe has struck out at a blow the formal outline on which a large section of detective fiction has been built up. In the three Dupin stories, one of which figures in the present collection, we have the formula of the eccentric and brilliant private detective whose doings are chronicled by an admiring and thick-headed friend. From

[10] The significance of footprints, and the necessity for scientific care in the checking of alibis, were understood at quite an early date, though, in the absence of an efficient detective police, investigations were usually carried out by private persons at the instigation of the coroner. A remarkable case, which reads like a Freeman Wills Crofts novel, was that of R. v. Thornton (1818).

Dupin and his unnamed chronicler springs a long and distin-guished line: Sherlock Holmes and his Watson; Martin Hewitt and his Brett; Raffles and his Bunny (on the criminal side of the business, but of the same breed); Thorndyke and his various Jardines, Ansteys, and Jervises; Hanaud and his Mr. Ricardo; Poirot and his Captain Hastings; Philo Vance and his Van Dine. It is not surprising that this formula should have been used so largely, for it is obviously a very convenient one for the writer. For one thing, the admiring satellite may utter expressions of eulogy which would be unbecoming in the mouth of the author, gaping at his own colossal intellect. Again, the reader, even if he is not, in R. L. Stevenson's phrase, "always a man of such vastly greater ingenuity than the writer," is usually a little more ingenious than Watson. He sees a little further through the brick walls; he pierces, to some extent, the cloud of mystification with which the detective envelops himself. "Aha!" he says to himself, "the average reader is supposed to see no further than Watson. But the author has not reckoned with me. I am one too many for him." He is deluded. It is all a device of the writer's for flattering him and putting him on good terms with himself. For though the reader likes to be mystified, he also likes to say, "I told you so," and "I spotted that." And this leads us to the third great advantage of the Holmes-Watson convention: by describ-ing the clues as presented to the dim eyes and bemused mind of Watson, the author is enabled to preserve a spurious appear-ance of frankness, while keeping to himself the special knowl-edge on which the interpretation of those clues depends. This is a question of paramount importance, involving the whole artistic ethic of the detective-story. We shall return to it later. For the moment, let us consider a few other interesting types and formulæ which make their first appearance in Poe.

The personality of Dupin is eccentric, and for several liter-ary generations eccentricity was highly fashionable among detective heroes. Dupin, we are informed, had a habit of living behind closed shutters, illumined by " a couple of tapers which, strongly perfumed, threw out only the ghastliest and feeblest of rays." From this stronghold he issued by night, to promenade the streets and enjoy the "infinity of mental excitement" afforded by quiet observation. He was also given to startling his friends by analysing their thought-processes, and he had a rooted contempt for the methods of the police.

· Sherlock Holmes modelled himself to a large extent upon Dupin, substituting cocaine for candlelight, with accompaniments of shag and fiddle-playing. He is a more human and endearing figure than Dupin, and has earned as his reward the supreme honour which literature has to bestow—the secular equivalent of canonisation. He has passed into the language. He also started a tradition of his own—the hawk-faced tradition, which for many years dominated detective fiction.

So strong, indeed, was this domination that subsequent notable eccentrics have displayed their eccentricities chiefly by escaping from it. "Nothing," we are told, "could have been less like the traditional detective than"—so-and-so. He may be elderly and decrepit, like Baroness Orczy's Old Man in the Corner, whose characteristic habit is the continual knotting of string. Or he may be round and innocent-looking, like Father Brown or Poirot. There is Sax Rohmer's Moris Klaw,[11] with his bald, scholarly forehead; he irrigates his wits with a verbena spray, and carries about with him an "odically-sterilised" cushion to promote psychic intuition. There is the great Dr. Thorndyke, probably the handsomest detective in fiction; he is outwardly bonhomous, but spiritually detached, and his emblem is the green research-case, filled with miniature microscopes and scientific implements. Max Carrados has the distinction of being blind; Old Ebbie wears a rabbit-skin waistcoat; Lord Peter Wimsey (if I may refer to him without immodesty) indulges in the buying of incunabula and has a

---

[11] Sax Rohmer: *The Dream Detective.*

pretty taste in wines and haberdashery. By a final twist of the tradition, which brings the wheel full circle, there is a strong modern tendency to produce detectives remarkable for their ordinariness; they may be well-bred walking gentlemen, like A. A. Milne's Anthony Gillingham, or journalists, like Gaston Leroux's Rouletabille, or they may even be policemen, like Freeman Wills Crofts's Inspector French, or the heroes of Mr. A. J. Rees's sound and well-planned stories.[12]

There have also been a few women detectives,[13] but on the whole, they have not been very successful. In order to justify their choice of sex, they are obliged to be so irritatingly intuitive as to destroy that quiet enjoyment of the logical which we look for in our detective reading. Or else they are active and courageous, and insist on walking into physical danger and hampering the men engaged on the job. Marriage, also, looms too large in their view of life; which is not surprising, for they are all young and beautiful. Why these charming creatures should be able to tackle abstruse problems at the age of twenty-one or thereabouts, while the male detectives are usually content to wait till their thirties or forties before setting up as experts, it is hard to say. Where do they pick up their worldly knowledge? Not from personal experience, for they are always immaculate as the driven snow. Presumably it is all intuition.

Better use has been made of women in books where the detecting is strictly amateur—done, that is, by members of the family or house-party themselves, and not by a private consultant. Evelyn Humblethorne[14] is a detective of this kind,

[12] A. J. Rees: *The Shrieking Pit; The Hand in the Dark;* (with J. R. Watson) *The Hampstead Mystery; The Mystery of the Downs,* etc. Messrs. Rees and Watson write of police affairs with the accuracy born of inside knowledge, but commendably avoid the dullness which is apt to result from a too-faithful description of correct official procedure.

[13] e.g. Anna Katherine Green: *The Golden Slipper;* Baroness Orczy: *Lady Molly of Scotland Yard;* G. R. Sims: *Dorcas Dene;* Valentine: *The Adjusters;* Richard Marsh: *Judith Lee;* Arthur B. Reeve: *Constance Dunlop;* etc.

[14] Lord Gorell: *In the Night.*

and so is Joan Cowper, in *The Brooklyn Murders*.[15] But the really brilliant woman detective has yet to be created.[16]

While on this subject, we must not forget the curious and interesting development of detective fiction which has produced the *Adventures of Sexton Blake,* and other allied cycles. This is the Holmes tradition, adapted for the reading of the board-school boy and crossed with the Buffalo Bill adventure type. The books are written by a syndicate of authors, each one of whom uses a set of characters of his own invention, grouped about a central and traditional group consisting of Sexton Blake and his boy assistant, Tinker, their comic landlady Mrs. Bardell, and their bulldog Pedro. As might be expected, the quality of the writing and the detective methods employed vary considerably from one author to another. The best specimens display extreme ingenuity, and an immense vigour and fertility in plot and incident. Nevertheless, the central types are pretty consistently preserved throughout the series. Blake and Tinker are less intuitive than Holmes, from whom, however, they are directly descended, as their address in Baker Street shows. They are more careless and reckless in their methods; more given to displays of personal heroism and pugilism; more simple and human in their emotions. The really interesting point about them is that they present the nearest modern approach to a national folk-lore, conceived as the centre for a cycle of loosely connected romances in the Arthurian manner. Their significance in popular literature and education would richly repay scientific investigation.

Edgar Allan Poe: Evolution of the Plot

As regards plot also, Poe laid down a number of sound keels for the use of later adventures. Putting aside his instructive excursion into the psychology of detection—instructive, be-

[15] G. D. H. & M. Cole.

[16] Wilkie Collins—who was curiously fascinated by the "strong-minded" woman—made two attempts at the woman detective in *No Name* and *The Law and the Lady.* The spirit of the time was, however, too powerful to allow these attempts to be altogether successful.

cause we can trace their influence in so many of Poe's successors down to the present day—putting these aside, and discounting that atmosphere of creepiness which Poe so successfully diffused about nearly all he wrote, we shall probably find that to us, sophisticated and trained on an intensive study of detective fiction, his plots are thin to transparency. But in Poe's day they represented a new technique. As a matter of fact, it is doubtful whether there are more than half a dozen deceptions in the mystery-monger's bag of tricks, and we shall find that Poe has got most of them, at any rate in embryo.

Take, first, the three Dupin stories. In *The Murders in the Rue Morgue*, an old woman and her daughter are found horribly murdered in an (apparently) hermetically sealed room. An innocent person is arrested by the police. Dupin proves that the police have failed to discover one mode of entrance to the room, and deduces from a number of observations that the "murder" was committed by a huge ape. Here is, then, a combination of three typical motifs: the wrongly suspected man, to whom all the superficial evidence (motive, access, etc.) points; the hermetically sealed death-chamber (still a favourite central theme); finally, the *solution by the unexpected means*. In addition, we have Dupin drawing deductions, which the police have overlooked, from the evidence of witnesses (superiority in inference), and discovering clues which the police have not thought of looking for owing to obsession by an *idée fixe* (superiority in observation based on inference). In this story also are enunciated for the first time those two great aphorisms of detective science: first, that when you have eliminated all the impossibilities, then, whatever remains, *however improbable*, must be the truth; and, secondly, that the more *outré* a case may appear, the easier it is to solve. Indeed, take it all round, *The Murders in the Rue Morgue* constitutes in itself almost a complete manual of detective theory and practice.

In *The Purloined Letter,* we have one of those stolen documents on whose recovery hangs the peace of mind of a distinguished personage. It is not, indeed, one of the sort whose publication would spread consternation among the Chancelleries of Europe, but it is important enough. The police suspect a certain minister of taking it. They ransack every corner of his house, in vain. Dupin, arguing from his knowledge of the minister's character, decides that subtlety must be met by subtlety. He calls on the minister and discovers the letter, turned inside out and stuck in a letter-rack in full view of the casual observer.

Here we have, besides the reiteration, in inverted form,[17] of aphorism No. 2 (above), the method of *psychological deduction* and the solution by the formula of the *most obvious place.* This trick is the forerunner of the diamond concealed in the tumbler of water, the man murdered in the midst of a battle, Chesterton's *Invisible Man* (the postman, so familiar a figure that his presence goes unnoticed),[18] and a whole line of similar ingenuities.

The third Dupin story, *The Mystery of Marie Rogêt,* has fewer imitators, but is the most interesting of all to the connoisseur. It consists entirely of a series of newspaper cuttings relative to the disappearance and murder of a shopgirl, with Dupin's comments thereon. The story contains no solution of the problem, and, indeed, no formal ending—and that for a very good reason. The disappearance was a genuine one, its actual heroine being one Mary Cecilia Rogers, and the actual

---

[17] "The business is very simple indeed, and I make no doubt that we can manage it sufficiently well ourselves; but then I thought Dupin would like to hear of it because it is so excessively *odd.*"

"Simple and odd," said Dupin.

"Why, yes; and not exactly that either. The fact is, we have all been a good deal puzzled because the affair *is* so simple, and yet baffles us altogether."

"Perhaps it is the very simplicity of the thing which puts you at fault," said Dupin.

The psychology of the matter is fully discussed in Poe's characteristic manner a few pages further on.

[18] G. K. Chesterton: *The Innocence of Father Brown.*

place New York. The newspaper cuttings, were also, *mutatis mutandis*, genuine. The paper which published Poe's article dared not publish his conclusion. Later on it was claimed that his argument was, in substance, correct; and though this claim has, I believe, been challenged of late years, Poe may, nevertheless, be ranked among the small band of mystery-writers who have put their skill in deduction to the acid test of a problem which they had not in the first place invented.[19]

Of the other Poe stories, one, *Thou Art the Man*, is very slight in theme and unpleasantly flippant in treatment. A man is murdered; a hearty person, named, with guileless cunning, Goodfellow, is very energetic in fixing the crime on a certain person. The narrator of the story makes a repulsive kind of jack-in-the-box out of the victim's corpse, and extorts a confession of guilt from—Goodfellow! Of course. Nevertheless, we have here two more leading motifs that have done overtime since Poe's day: the trail of false clues laid by the real murderer,[20] and the *solution by way of the most unlikely person*.

The fifth story is *The Gold Bug*. In this a man finds a cipher which leads him to the discovery of a hidden treasure. The cipher is of the very simple one-sign-one-letter type, and its solution, of the mark-where-the-shadow-falls-take-three-paces-to-the-east-and-dig variety. In technique this story is the exact opposite of *Marie Rogêt;* the narrator is astonished by the antics of his detective friend, and is kept in entire ignorance of what he is about until *after* the discovery of the treasure; only then is the cipher for the first time either mentioned or explained. Some people think that *The Gold Bug* is Poe's finest mystery-story.

Now, with *The Gold Bug* at the one extreme and *Marie Rogêt* at the other, and the other three stories occupying intermediate places, Poe stands at the parting of the ways for

[19] Sir Arthur Conan Doyle's successful efforts on behalf of George Edalji and Oscar Slater deserve special mention.

[20] See also *The Story of Susanna*.

detective fiction. From him go the two great lines of development—the Romantic and the Classic, or, to use terms less abraded by ill-usage, the purely Sensational and the purely Intellectual. In the former, thrill is piled on thrill and mystification on mystification; the reader is led on from bewilderment to bewilderment, till everything is explained in a lump in the last chapter. This school is strong in dramatic incident and atmosphere; its weakness is a tendency to confusion and a dropping of links—its explanations do not always explain; it is never dull, but it is sometimes nonsense. In the other—the purely Intellectual type—the action mostly takes place in the first chapter or so; the detective then follows up quietly from clue to clue till the problem is solved, the reader accompanying the great man in his search and being allowed to try his own teeth on the material provided. The strength of this school is its analytical ingenuity; its weakness is its liability to dullness and pomposity, its mouthing over the infinitely little, and its lack of movement and emotion.

Intellectual and Sensational Lines of Development

The purely Sensational thriller is not particularly rare—we may find plenty of examples in the work of William Le Queux, Edgar Wallace, and others. The purely Intellectual is rare indeed; few writers have consistently followed the *Marie Rogêt* formula of simply spreading the *whole* evidence before the reader and leaving him to deduce the detective's conclusion from it if he can.

M. P. Shiel, indeed, did so in his trilogy, *Prince Zaleski*, whose curious and elaborate beauty recaptures in every arabesque sentence the very accent of Edgar Allan Poe. Prince Zaleski, "victim of a too importunate, too unfortunate Love, which the fulgor of the throne itself could not abash," sits apart in his ruined tower in "the semi-darkness of the very faint greenish lustre radiated from an open censer-like *lampas* in the centre of the doomed encausted roof," surrounded by

Flemish sepulchral brasses, runic tablets, miniature paintings, winged bulls, Tamil scriptures on lacquered leaves of the talipot, mediæval reliquaries richly gemmed, Brahmin gods, and Egyptian mummies, and lulled by "the low, liquid tinkling of an invisible musical-box." Like Sherlock Holmes, he indulges in a drug—"the narcotic *cannabis sativa:* the base of the *bhang* of the Mohammedans." A friend brings to him the detective problems of the outside world, which he proceeds to solve from the data given and (except in the final story) without stirring from his couch. He adorns his solutions with philosophical discourses on the social progress of mankind, all delivered with the same melancholy grace and remote intellectual disdain. The reasoning is subtle and lucid, but the crimes themselves are fantastic and incredible—a fault which these tales have in common with those of G. K. Chesterton.

Another writer who uses the *Marie Rogêt* formula is Baroness Orczy. Her *Old Man in the Corner* series is constructed precisely on those lines, and I have seen a French edition in which, when the expository part of the story is done, the reader is exhorted to: "Pause a moment and see if you can arrive at the explanation yourself, before you read the Old Man's solution." This pure puzzle is a formula which obviously has its limitations. Nearest to this among modern writers comes Freeman Wills Crofts, whose painstaking sleuths always "play fair" and display their clues to the reader as soon as they have picked them up. The intellectually minded reader can hardly demand more than this. The aim of the writer of this type of detective-story is to make the reader say at the end, neither: "Oh well, I knew it must be that all along," nor yet: "Dash it all! I couldn't be expected to guess that"; but: "Oh, of course! What a fool I was not to see it! Right under my nose all the time!" Precious tribute! How often striven for! How rarely earned!

On the whole, however, the tendency is for the modern educated public to demand fair play from the writer, and for the Sensational and Intellectual branches of the story to move further apart.

Before going further with this important question, we must look back once more to the middle of the last century, and see what development took place to bridge the gap between Dupin and Sherlock Holmes.

Poe, like a restless child, played with his new toy for a little while, and then, for some reason, wearied of it. He turned his attention to other things, and his formula lay neglected for close on forty years. Meanwhile a somewhat different type of detective-story was developing independently in Europe. In 1848 the elder Dumas, always ready to try his hand at any novel and ingenious thing, suddenly inserted into the romantic body of the *Vicomte de Bragelonne* a passage of pure scientific deduction. This passage is quite unlike anything else in the Musketeer cycle, and looks like the direct outcome of Dumas' keen interest in actual crime.[21]

But there is another literary influence which, though the fact is not generally recognised, must have been powerfully exerted at this date upon writers of mystery fiction. Between 1820 and 1850 the novels of Fenimore Cooper began to enjoy their huge popularity, and were not only widely read in America and England, but translated into most European languages. In *The Pathfinder, The Deerslayer, The Last of the Mohicans,* and the rest of the series, Cooper revealed to the delighted youth of two hemispheres the Red Indian's patient skill in tracking his quarry by footprints, in interrogating a broken twig, a mossy trunk, a fallen leaf. The imagination of childhood was fired; every boy wanted to be an Uncas or a Chingachgook. Novelists, not content with following and imitating Cooper on his own ground, discovered a better way, by transferring the romance of the woodland tracker to the surroundings of their native country. In the 'sixties the generation who had read Fenimore Cooper in boyhood turned, as novelists and

[21] He published a great collection of famous crimes.

readers, to tracing the spoor of the criminal upon their own native heath. The enthusiasm for Cooper combined magnificently with that absorbing interest in crime and detection which better methods of communication and an improved police system had made possible. While, in France, Gaboriau and Fortuné du Biosgobey concentrated upon the police novel pure and simple, English writers, still permeated by the terror and mystery of the romantic movement, and influenced by the "Newgate novel" of Bulwer and Ainsworth, perfected a more varied and imaginative genre, in which the ingenuity of the detective problem allied itself with the sombre terrors of the weird and supernatural.

The Pre-Doyle Period

Of the host of writers who attempted this form of fiction in the 'sixties and 'seventies, three may be picked out for special mention.

That voluminous writer, Mrs. Henry Wood, represents, on the whole, the melodramatic and adventurous development of the crime-story as distinct from the detective problem proper. Through *East Lynne*, crude and sentimental as it is, she exercised an enormous influence on the rank and file of sensational novelists, and at her best, she is a most admirable spinner of plots. Whether her problem concerns a missing will, a vanished heir, a murder, or a family curse, the story spins along without flagging, and, though she is a little too fond of calling in Providence to cut the knot of intrigue with the sword of coincidence, the mystery is fully and properly unravelled, in a workmanlike manner and without any loose ends. She makes frequent use of supernatural thrills. Sometimes these are explained away: a "murdered" person is seen haunting the local churchyard, and turns out never to have been killed at all. Sometimes the supernatural remains supernatural, as, for instance, the coffin-shaped appearance in *The Shadow of Ashlydyat*. Her morality is perhaps a little oppressive, but she is by no means without humour, and at times can produce a shrewd piece of characterisation.

Melodramatic, but a writer of real literary attainment, and gifted with a sombre power which has seldom been equalled in painting the ghastly and the macabre, is Sheridan Le Fanu. Like Poe, he has the gift of investing the most mechanical of plots with an atmosphere of almost unbearable horror. Take, for example, that scene in *Wylder's Hand* where the aged Uncle Lorne appears—phantom or madman? we are not certain which—to confront the villainous Lake in the tapestried room.

 " 'Mark Wylder is in evil plight,' said he.

 " 'Is he?' said Lake with a sly scoff, though he seemed to me a good deal scared. 'We hear no complaints, however, and fancy he must be tolerably comfortable notwithstanding.'

 " 'You know where he is,' said Uncle Lorne.

 " 'Aye, in Italy; everyone knows that,' answered Lake.

 " 'In Italy,' said the old man reflectively, as if trying to gather up his ideas, 'Italy. . . . He has had a great tour to make. It is nearly accomplished now; when it is done, he will be like me, *humano major*. He has seen the places which you are yet to see.'

 " 'Nothing I should like better; particularly Italy,' said Lake.

 " 'Yes,' said Uncle Lorne, lifting up slowly a different finger at each name in his catalogue. 'First, Lucus Mortis; then Terra Tenebrosa; next, Tartarus; after that Terra Oblivionis; then Herebus; then Barathrum; then Gehenna, and then Stagnum Ignis.'

 " 'Of course,' acquiesced Lake, with an ugly sneer. . . .

 " 'Don't be frightened—but he's alive; I think they'll make him mad. It is a frightful plight. Two angels buried him alive in Vallombrosa by night; I saw it, standing among the lotus and hemlocks. A negro came to me, a black clergyman with white eyes, and remained beside me; and the angels imprisoned Mark; they put him on duty forty days and forty nights, with his ear to the river listening for voices;

and when it was over we blessed them; and the clergyman walked with me a long while, to-and-fro, to-and-fro upon the earth, telling me the wonders of the abyss.'

" 'And is it from the abyss, sir, he writes his letters?' enquired the Town Clerk, with a wink at Lake.

" 'Yes, yes, very diligent; it behoves him; and his hair is always standing straight on his head for fear. But he'll be sent up again, at last, a thousand, a hundred, ten and one, black marble steps, and then it will be the other one's turn. So it was prophesied by the black magician.' "

This chapter leads immediately to those in which Larkin, the crooked attorney, discovers, by means of a little sound detective work of a purely practical sort, that Mark Wylder's letters have indeed been written "from the abyss." Mark Wylder has, in fact, been murdered, and the letters are forgeries sent abroad to be despatched by Lake's confederate from various towns in Italy. From this point we gradually learn to expect the ghastly moment when he is "sent up again at last" from the grave, in the Blackberry Dell at Gylingden.

"In the meantime the dogs continued their unaccountable yelling close by.

" 'What the devil's that?' said Wealden.

" 'Something like a stunted, blackened branch was sticking out of the peat, ending in a set of short, thickish twigs. This is what it seemed. The dogs were barking at it. It was, really, a human hand and arm. . . .'"

In this book the detection is done by private persons, and the local police are only brought in at the end to secure the criminal. This is also the case in that extremely interesting book *Checkmate* (1870), in which the plot actually turns upon the complete alteration of the criminal's appearance by a miracle of plastic surgery. It seems amazing that more use has not been made of this device in post-war days, now that the reconstruction of faces has become comparatively common and, with the perfecting of aseptic surgery, infinitely easier than in Le Fanu's day. I can only call to mind two recent examples of this kind: one, Mr. Hopkins Moorhouse's *Gauntlet of Alceste;* the other, a short story called *The Losing of Jasper Virel,* by Beckles Willson.[22] In both stories the alterations include the tattooing of the criminal's eyes from blue to brown.

For sheer grimness and power, there is little in the literature of horror to compare with the trepanning scene in Le Fanu's *The House by the Churchyard.* Nobody who has ever read it could possibly forget that sick chamber, with the stricken man sunk in his deathly stupor; the terrified wife; the local doctor, kindly and absurd—and then the pealing of the bell, and the entry of the brilliant, brutal Dillon "in dingy splendours and a great draggled wig, with a gold-headed cane in his bony hand . . . diffusing a reek of whisky-punch, and with a case of instruments under his arm," to perform the operation. The whole scene is magnificently written, with the surgeon's muttered technicalities heard through the door, the footsteps—then the silence while the trepanning is proceeding, and the wounded Sturk's voice, which no one ever thought to hear again, raised as if from the grave to denounce his murderer. That chapter in itself would entitle Le Fanu to be called a master of mystery and horror.

Most important of all during this period we have Wilkie Collins. An extremely uneven writer, Collins is less appreciated to-day than his merits and influence deserve.[23] He will not bear comparison with Le Fanu in his treatment of the weird, though he was earnestly ambitious to succeed in this line. His style was too dry and inelastic, his mind too legal. Consider the famous dream in *Armadale,* divided into seventeen separate sections, each elaborately and successively fulfilled in laborious detail! In the curious semi-supernatural rhythm of *The Woman in White* he came nearer to genuine achievement, but, on the

---

[22] *Strand Magazine,* July 1909.

[23] In the British Museum catalogue only two critical studies of this celebrated English mystery-monger are listed: one is by an American, the other by a German.

whole, his eerieness is wiredrawn and unconvincing. But he greatly excels Le Fanu in humour, in the cunning of his rogues[24] in character-drawing, and especially in the architecture of his plots. Taking everything into consideration, *The Moonstone* is probably the very finest detective story ever written. By comparison with its wide scope, its dove-tailed completeness and the marvellous variety and soundness of its characterisation, modern mystery fiction looks thin and mechanical. Nothing human is perfect, but *The Moonstone* comes about as near perfection as anything of its kind can be.

In *The Moonstone* Collins used the convention of telling the story in a series of narratives from the pens of the various actors concerned. Modern realism—often too closely wedded to externals—is prejudiced against this device. It is true that, for example, Betteredge's narrative is not at all the kind of thing that a butler would be likely to write; nevertheless, it has an ideal truth—it is the kind of thing that Betteredge might think and feel, even if he could not write it. And, granted this convention of the various narratives, how admirably the characters are drawn! The pathetic figure of Rosanna Spearman, with her deformity and her warped devotion, is beautifully handled, with a freedom from sentimentality which is very remarkable. In Rachel Verinder, Collins has achieved one of the novelist's hardest tasks; he has depicted a girl who is virtuous, a gentlewoman, and really interesting, and that without the slightest exaggeration or deviation from naturalness and probability. From his preface to the book it is clear that he took especial pains with this character, and his success was so great as almost to defeat itself. Rachel is so little spectacular that we fail

---

[24] Collins made peculiarly his own the art of plot and counter-plot. Thus we have the magnificent duels of Marion Halcombe and Count Fosco in *The Woman in White;* Captain Wragge and Mrs. Lecount in *No Name;* the Pedgifts and Miss Gwilt in *Armadale.* Move answers to move as though on a chessboard (but very much more briskly), until the villain is manœuvred into the corner where a cunningly contrived legal checkmate has been quietly awaiting him from the beginning of the game.

to realise what a singularly fine and truthful piece of work she is.

The detective part of the story is well worth attention. The figure of Sergeant Cuff is drawn with a restraint and sobriety which makes him seem a little colourless beside Holmes and Thorndyke and Carrados, but he is a very living figure. One can believe that he made a success of his rose-growing when he retired; he genuinely loved roses, whereas one can never feel that the great Sherlock possessed quite the right feeling for his bees. Being an official detective, Sergeant Cuff is bound by the etiquette of his calling. He is never really given a free hand with Rachel, and the conclusion he comes to is a wrong one. But he puts in a good piece of detective work in the matter of Rosanna and the stained nightgown; and the scenes in which his shrewdness and knowledge of human nature are contrasted with the blundering stupidity of Superintendent Seagrave read like an essay in the manner of Poe.

It is, of course, a fact that the Dupin stories had been published fifteen years or so when *The Moonstone* appeared. But there is no need to seek in them for the original of Sergeant Cuff. He had his prototype in real life, and the whole nightgown incident was modelled, with some modifications, upon a famous case of the early 'sixties—the murder of little William Kent by his sixteen-year-old sister, Constance. Those who are interested in origins will find an excellent account of the "Road murder," as it is called, in Miss Tennyson Jesse's *Murder and its Motives*, or in Atkey's *Famous Trials of the Nineteenth Century*, and may compare the methods of Sergeant Cuff with those of the real Detective Whicher.

Wilkie Collins himself claimed that nearly all his plots were founded on fact; indeed, this was his invariable answer when the charge of improbability was preferred against him.

" 'I wish,' he cries angrily to a friend, 'before people make such assertions, they would think what they are writing or talking about. I know of very few instances in which fiction exceeds the probability of reality. I'll tell you where I got many of my plots from. I was in Paris, wandering about the streets with Charles Dickens, amusing ourselves by looking into the shops. We came to an old book stall—half-shop and half-store—and I found some dilapidated volumes and records of French crime—a sort of French Newgate Calendar. I said to Dickens "Here is a prize!" So it turned out to be. In them I found some of my best plots.' " [25]

Not that Collins was altogether disingenuous in his claim never to have o'erstepped the modesty of nature. While each one of his astonishing contrivances and coincidences might, taken separately, find its parallel in real life, it remains true that in cramming a whole series of such improbabilities into the course of a single story he does frequently end by staggering all belief. But even so, he was a master craftsman, whom many modern mystery-mongers might imitate to their profit. He never wastes an incident; he never leaves a loose end; no incident, however trivial on the one hand or sensational on the other, is ever introduced for the mere sake of amusement or sensation. Take, for example, the great "sensation-scene" in *No Name*, where for half an hour Magdalen sits, with the bottle of laudanum in her hand, counting the passing ships. "If, in that time, an even number passed her—the sign given should be a sign to live. If the uneven number prevailed, the end should be— death." Here, you would say, is pure sensationalism; it is a situation invented deliberately to wring tears and anguish from the heart of the reader. But you would be wrong. That bottle of laudanum is brought in because it will be wanted again, later on. In the next section of the story it is found in Magdalen's dressing-case, and this discovery, by leading her husband to suppose that she means to murder him, finally induces him to cut her out of his will, and so becomes one of the most important factors in the plot.

[25] Wybert Reeve: "Recollections of Wilkie Collins," *Chambers' Journal*, Vol. IX., p. 458.

In *The Moonstone,* which of all his books comes nearest to being a detective-story in the modern sense, Collins uses with great effect the formula of the most unlikely person[26] and the unexpected means in conjunction. Opium is the means in this case—a drug with whose effects we are tolerably familiar to-day, but which in Collins's time was still something of an unknown quantity, de Quincey notwithstanding. In the opium of *The Moonstone* and the plastic surgery of *Checkmate* we have the distinguished forebears of a long succession of medical and scientific mysteries which stretches down to the present day.

During the 'seventies and early 'eighties the long novel of marvel and mystery held the field, slowly unrolling its labyrinthine complexity through its three ample volumes crammed with incident and leisurely drawn characters.[27]

Sherlock Holmes and His Influence

In 1887 *A Study in Scarlet* was flung like a bombshell into the field of detective fiction, to be followed within a few short and brilliant years by the marvellous series of Sherlock Holmes short stories. The effect was electric. Conan Doyle took up the Poe formula and galvanised it into life and popularity. He cut out the elaborate psychological introductions, or restated them in crisp dialogue. He brought into prominence what Poe had only lightly touched upon—the deduction of staggering

[26] Franklin Blake—the actual, though unconscious thief. By an ingenious turn, this discovery does not end the story. The diamond is still missing, and a further chase leads to the really guilty party (Godfrey Ablewhite). The character of this gentleman is enough to betray his villainy to the modern reader, though it may have seemed less repulsive to the readers in the 'sixties. His motive, however, is made less obvious, although it quite honourably and fairly hinted at for the observant reader to guess.

[27] We must not leave this period without mentioning the stories of Anna Katherine Green, of which the long series begins with *The Leavenworth Case* in 1883, and extends right down to the present day. They are genuine detective-stories, often of considerable ingenuity, but marred by an uncritical sentimentality of style and treatment which makes them difficult reading for the modern student. They are, however, important by their volume and by their influence on other American writers.

conclusions from trifling indications in the Dumas-Cooper-
Gaboriau manner. He was sparkling, surprising, and short. It
was the triumph of the epigram.

A comparison of the Sherlock Holmes tales with the Dupin
tales shows clearly how much Doyle owed to Poe, and, at the
same time, how greatly he modified Poe's style and formula.
Read, for instance, the opening pages of *The Murders in the
Rue Morgue,* which introduce Dupin, and compare them with
the first chapter of *A Study in Scarlet.* Or merely set side by
side the two passages which follow and contrast the relations
between Dupin and his chronicler on the one hand, and between
Holmes and Watson on the other:

> "I was astonished, too, at the vast extent of his reading;
> and, above all, I felt my soul enkindled within me by the
> wild fervour, and the vivid freshness of his imagination.
> Seeking in Paris the objects I then sought, I felt that the
> society of such a man would be to me a treasure beyond
> price; and this feeling I frankly confided to him. It was at
> length arranged that we should live together . . . and as
> my worldly circumstances were somewhat less embarrassed
> than his own, I was permitted to be at the expense of renting,
> and furnishing in a style which suited the rather fantastic
> gloom of our common temper, a time-eaten and grotesque
> mansion . . . in a retired and desolate portion of the Fau-
> bourg Saint Germain . . . It was a freak of fancy in my
> friend (for what else shall I call it?) to be enamoured of the
> Night for her own sake; and into this *bizarrerie,* as into all
> his others, I quietly fell, giving myself up to his wild whims
> with a perfect abandon." [28]

> "An anomaly which often struck me in the character of
> my friend Sherlock Holmes was that, though in his methods
> of thought he was the neatest and most methodical of man-
> kind, and although also he affected a certain quiet primness
> of dress, he was none the less in his personal habits one of
> the most untidy men that ever drove a fellow-lodger to

[28] *The Murders in the Rue Morgue.*

distraction. Not that I am in the least conventional in that respect myself. The rough-and-tumble work in Afghanistan, coming on the top of a natural Bohemianism of disposition, has made me rather more lax than befits a medical man. But with me there is a limit, and when I find a man who keeps his cigars in the coal-scuttle, his tobacco in the toe-end of a Persian slipper, and his unanswered correspondence transfixed by a jack-knife into the every centre of his wooden mantelpiece, then I begin to give myself virtuous airs. I have always held, too, that pistol-practice should distinctly be an open-air pastime; and when Holmes in one of his queer humours would sit in an arm-chair, with his hair-trigger and a hundred Boxer cartridges, and proceed to adorn the opposite wall with a patriotic V.R. done in bullet-pocks, I felt strongly that neither the atmosphere nor the appearance of our room was improved by it." [29]

See how the sturdy independence of Watson adds salt and savour to the eccentricities of Holmes, and how flavourless beside it is the hero-worshipping self-abnegation of Dupin's friend. See, too, how the concrete details of daily life in Baker Street lift the story out of the fantastic and give it a solid reality. The Baker Street ménage has just that touch of humorous commonplace which appeals to British readers.

Another pair of parallel passages will be found in *The Purloined Letter* and *The Naval Treaty*. They show the two detectives in dramatic mood, surprising their friends by their solution of the mystery. In *The Adventure of the Priory School*, also, a similar situation occurs, though Holmes is here shown in a grimmer vein, rebuking wickedness in high places.

Compare, also, the conversational styles of Holmes and Dupin, and the reasons for Holmes's popularity become clearer than ever. Holmes has enriched English literature with more than one memorable aphorism and turn of speech.

" 'You know my methods, Watson.'
" 'A long shot, Watson—a very long shot.'

[29] *The Musgrave Ritual.*

" '—a little monograph on the hundred-and-fourteen varieties of tobacco-ash.'

" 'These are deep waters, Watson.'

" 'Excellent!' cried Mr. Acton.—'But very superficial,' said Holmes.

" 'Excellent!' I cried.—'Elementary,' said he.

" 'It is of the highest importance in the art of detection to be able to recognise out of a number of facts which are incidental and which vital.'

" 'You mentioned your name as if I should recognise it, but beyond the obvious facts that you are a bachelor, a solicitor, a Freemason and an asthmatic, I know nothing whatever about you.'

" 'Every problem becomes very childish when once it is explained to you.' "

Nor must we forget that delightful form of riposto which Father Ronald Knox has wittily christened the "Sherlockismus":

" 'I would call your attention to the curious incident of the dog in the night-time.'

" 'The dog did nothing in the night-time.'

" 'That was the curious incident.'

So, with Sherlock Holmes, the ball—the original nucleus deposited by Edgar Allan Poe nearly forty years earlier—was at last set rolling. As it went, it swelled into a vast mass—it set off others—it became a spate—a torrent—an avalanche of mystery fiction. It is impossible to keep track of all the detective-stories produced to-day. Book upon book, magazine upon magazine pour out from the Press, crammed with murders, thefts, arsons, frauds, conspiracies, problems, puzzles, mysteries, thrills, maniacs, crooks, poisoners, forgers, garrotters, police, spies, secret-service men, detectives, until it seems that half the world must be engaged in setting riddles for the other half to solve.

The Scientific Detective

The boom began in the 'nineties, when the detective short story, till then rather neglected, strode suddenly to the front and made the pace rapidly under the ægis of Sherlock Holmes. Of particular interest is the long series which appeared under various titles from the pens of L. T. Meade and her collaborators. These struck out a line—not new, indeed, for, as we have seen, it is as old as Collins and Le Fanu, but important because it was paving the way for great developments in a scientific age—the medical mystery story. Mrs. Meade opened up this fruitful vein with *Stories from the Diary of a Doctor* in 1893,[30] and pursued it in various magazines almost without a break to *The Sorceress of the Strand* [31] in 1902. These tales range from mere records of queer cases to genuine detective-stories in which the solution has a scientific or medical foundation. During this long collaboration, the authors deal with such subjects as hypnotism, catalepsy (so-called—then a favourite disease among fiction-writers), somnambulism, lunacy, murder by the use of X-rays and hydrocyanic acid gas, and a variety of other medical and scientific discoveries and inventions.

More definitely in the Holmes tradition is the sound and excellent work of Arthur Morrison in the "Martin Hewitt" books. Various authors such as John Oxenham and Manville Fenn also tried their hands at the detective-story, before turning to specialise in other work. We get also many lively tales of adventure and roguery, with a strong thread of detective interest, as, for example, the "African Millionaire" series by Grant Allen.

Now in the great roar and rush of enthusiasm which greeted Sherlock Holmes, the detective-story became swept away on a single current of development. We observed, in discussing the

[30] In collaboration with "Clifford Halifax."

[31] In collaboration with Robert Eustace. In these stories the scientific basis was provided by Robert Eustace, and the actual writing done, for the most part, by L. T. Meade. A more recent example of Mr. Eustace's collaboration, this time with Edgar Jepson, is *Mr. Belton's Immunity*.

Poe tales, that there were three types of story—the Intellectual
(*Marie Rogêt*), the Sensational (*The Gold Bug*), and the
Mixed (*Murders in the Rue Morgue*). "Sherlock Holmes"
tales, as a rule, are of the mixed type. Holmes—I regret to say
it—does not always play fair with the reader. He "picks up,"
or "pounces upon," a "minute object," and draws a brilliant
deduction from it, but the reader, however brilliant, cannot
himself anticipate that deduction because he is not told what
the "small object" is. It is Watson's fault, of course—Holmes,
indeed, remonstrated with him on at least one occasion about
his unscientific methods of narration.

An outstanding master of this "surprise" method is Melville
Davisson Post. His tales are so admirably written, and his ideas
so ingenious, that we fail at first reading to realise how strictly
sensational they are in their method. Take, for instance, *An Act
of God* from *Uncle Abner* (1911). In this tale, Uncle Abner
uses the phonetic mis-spelling in a letter supposed to be written
by a deaf mute to prove that the letter was not, in fact, written
by him. If the text of the letter were placed before the reader,
and he were given a chance to make his deduction for himself,
the tale would be a true detective-story of the Intellectual type;
but the writer keeps this clue to himself, and springs the detective's conclusions upon us like a bolt from the blue.

The Modern "Fair-play" Method

For many years, the newness of the genre and the immense
prestige of Holmes blinded readers' eyes to these feats of leger-
demain. Gradually, however, as the bedazzlement wore off, the
public became more and more exacting. The uncritical are still
catered for by the "thriller," in which nothing is explained, but
connoisseurs have come, more and more, to call for a story
which puts them on an equal footing with the detective himself,
as regards all clues and discoveries.[32]

[32] Yet even to-day the naughty tradition persists. In *The Crime at Diana's
Pool*, for instance (1927), V. L. Whitechurch sins notably, twice over; in this

Seeing that the demand for equal opportunities is coupled to-day with an insistence on strict technical accuracy in the smallest details of the story, it is obvious that the job of writing detective-stories is by no means growing easier. The reader must be given every clue—but he must not be told, surely, all the detective's deductions, lest he should see the solution too far ahead. Worse still, supposing, even without the detective's help, he interprets all the clues accurately on his own account, what becomes of the surprise? How can we at the same time show the reader everything and yet legitimately obfuscate him as to its meaning?

Various devices are used to get over the difficulty. Frequently the detective, while apparently displaying his clues openly, will keep up his sleeve some bit of special knowledge which the reader does not possess. Thus, Thorndyke can cheerfully show you all his finds. You will be none the wiser, unless you happen to have an intimate acquaintance with the fauna of local ponds; the effect of belladonna on rabbits; the physical and chemical properties of blood; optics; tropical diseases; metallurgy; hieroglyphics, and a few other trifles. Another method of misleading is to tell the reader what the detective has observed and deduced—but to make the observations and deductions turn out to be incorrect, thus leading up to a carefully manufactured surprise-packet in the last chapter.[33]

Some writers, like Mrs. Agatha Christie, still cling to the Watson formula. The story is told through the mouth, or at least through the eyes, of a Watson.[34] Others, like A. A. Milne

respect, in the course of an otherwise excellent tale. But such crimes bring their own punishment, for the modern reader is quick to detect and resent unfairness, and a stern, though kindly letter of rebuke is presently despatched to the erring author!

[33] C. E. Bentley: *Trent's Last Case;* Lord Gorell: *In the Night;* George Pleydell: *The Ware Case;* etc.

[34] An exceptional handling of the Watson theme is found in Agatha Christie's *Murder of Roger Ackroyd,* which is a *tour de force.* Some critics, as, for instance, Mr. W. H. Wright in his introduction to *The Great Detective Stories* (Scribners, 1927), consider the solution illegitimate. I fancy, however, that this

in his *Red House Mystery,* adopt a mixed method. Mr. Milne
begins by telling his tale from the positon of a detached spec-
tator; later on, we find that he has shifted round, and is telling
it through the personality of Bill Beverley (a simple-minded
but not unintelligent Watson); at another moment we find ourselves actually looking out through the eyes of Anthony Gillingham, the detective himself.

Importance of the Viewpoint

The skill of a modern detective novelist is largely shown by
the play he makes with these various viewpoints.[35] Let us see
how it is done in an acknowledged masterpiece of the genre.
We will examine for the purpose a page of Mr. A. C. Bentley's
Trent's Last Case. Viewpoint No. 1 is what we may call the
Watson viewpoint; the detective's external actions only are
seen by the reader. Viewpoint No. 2 is the middle viewpoint; we
see what the detective sees, but are not told what he observes.
Viewpoint No. 3 is that of close intimacy with the detective;
we see all he sees, and are at once told his conclusions.

We begin from Viewpoint No. 2.

"Two bedroom doors faced him on the other side of the
passage. He opened that which was immediately opposite,
and entered a bedroom by no means austerely tidy. Some
sticks and fishing-rods stood confusedly in one corner, a pile
of books in another. The housemaid's hand had failed to give
a look of order to the jumble of heterogeneous objects left on
the dressing-table and on the mantel-shelf—pipes, penknives,
pencils, keys, golf-balls, old letters, photographs, small boxes,
tins, and bottles. Two fine etchings and some water-colour

opinion merely represents a natural resentment at having been ingeniously bam-
boozled. All the necessary data are given. The reader ought to be able to guess
the criminal, if he is sharp enough, and nobody can ask for more than this.
It is, after all, the reader's job to keep his wits about him, and, like the perfect
detective, to suspect *everybody.*

[35] For a most fascinating and illuminating discussion of this question of viewpoint in fiction, see Mr. Percy Lubbock: *The Craft of Fiction.*

sketches hung on the walls; leaning against the end of the wardrobe, unhung, were a few framed engravings."

First Shift: Viewpoint No. 1.

"A row of shoes and boots was ranged beneath the window. Trent crossed the room and studied them intently; then he measured some of them with his tape, whistling very softly. This done, he sat on the side of the bed, and his eyes roamed gloomily about the room."

Here we observe Trent walking, studying, measuring, whistling, looking gloomy; but we do not know what was peculiar about the boots, nor what the measurements were. From our knowledge of Trent's character we may suppose that his conclusions are unfavourable to the amiable suspect, Marlowe, but we are not ourselves allowed to handle the material evidence.

Second Shift: Back to Viewpoint No. 2.

"The photographs on the mantel-shelf attracted him presently. He rose and examined one representing Marlowe and Manderson on horseback. Two others were views of famous peaks in the Alps. There was a faded print of three youths—one of them unmistakably his acquaintance of the haggard blue eyes [i.e. Marlowe]—clothed in tatterdemalion soldier's gear of the sixteenth century. Another was a portrait of a majestic old lady, slightly resembling Marlowe. Trent, mechanically taking a cigarette from an open box on the mantel-shelf, lit it and stared at the photographs."

Here, as at the opening of the paragraph, we are promoted to a more privileged position. We see all the evidence, and have an equal opportunity with Trent of singling out the significant detail—the fancy-costume portrait—and deducting from it that Marlowe was an active member of the O.U.D.S., and, by inference, capable of acting a part at a pinch.

Third Shift: Viewpoint No. 3.

"Next he turned his attention to a flat leathern case that lay by the cigarette-box. It opened easily. A small and light revolver, of beautiful workmanship, was disclosed, with a score or so of loose cartridges. On the stock were engraved the initials 'J. M.' . . .

"With the pistol in its case between them, Trent and the Inspector looked into each other's eyes for some moments. Trent was the first to speak. 'This mystery is all wrong,' he observed. 'It is insanity. The symptoms of mania are very marked. Let us see how we stand.' "

Throughout the rest of this scene we are taken into Trent's confidence. The revolver is described, we learn what Trent thinks about it from his own lips.

Thus, in a single page, the viewpoint is completely shifted three times, but so delicately that, unless we are looking for it, we do not notice the change.

In a later chapter, we get the final shift to a fourth viewpoint—that of complete mental identification with the detective:

"Mrs. Manderson had talked herself into a more emotional mood than she had yet shown to Trent. Her words flowed freely, and her voice had begun to ring and give play to a natural expressiveness that must hitherto have been dulled, he thought, by the shock and self-restraint of the past few days."

Here the words "had yet shown to Trent" clinch the identification of viewpoint. Throughout the book, we always, in fact, see Mrs. Manderson through Trent's emotions, and the whole second half of the story, when Trent has abandoned his own enquiries and is receiving the true explanation from Marlowe and Cupples, is told from Viewpoint No. 4.

The modern evolution in the direction of "fair play" [36] is to a great extent a revolution. It is a recoil from the Holmes influence and a turning back to *The Moonstone* and its contemporaries. There is no mystification about *The Moonstone*—no mystification of the reader, that is. With such scrupulous care has Collins laid the clues that the "ideal reasoner" might guess the entire outline of the story at the end of the first ten chapters of Betteredge's first narrative.[37]

Artistic Status of the Detective-Story

As the detective ceases to be impenetrable and infallible and becomes a man touched with the feeling of our infirmities, so the rigid technique of the art necessarily expands a little. In its severest form, the mystery-story is a pure analytical exercise, and, as such, may be a highly finished work of art, within its highly artificial limits. There is one respect, at least, in which the detective-story has an advantage over every other kind of novel. It possesses an Aristotelian perfection of beginning, middle, and end. A definite and single problem is set, worked out, and solved; its conclusion is not arbitrarily conditioned by

[36] It is needless to add that the detectives must be given fair play, too. Once they are embarked upon an investigation, no episode must ever be described which does not come within their cognisance. It is artistically shocking that the reader should be taken into the author's confidence behind the investigator's back. Thus, the reader's interest in *The Deductions of Colonel Gore* (Lynn Brock) is sensibly diminished by the fact of his knowing (as Gore does not) that it was Cecil Arndale who witnessed the scene between Mrs. Melhuish and Barrington near the beginning of the book. Those tales in which the action is frequently punctuated by eavesdropping of this kind on the reader's part belong to the merely Sensational class of detective-story, and rapidly decline into melodrama.

[37] Poe performed a similar feat in the case of *Barnaby Rudge,* of which he correctly prognosticated the whole development after reading the first serial part. Unhappily, he was not alive to perform the same office for *Edwin Drood!* Dickens came more and more to hanker after plot and mystery. His early efforts in this style are crude, and the mystery as a rule pretty transparent. In *Edwin Drood* he hoped that the "story would turn upon an interest suspended until the end," and the hope was only too thoroughly fulfilled. Undoubtedly his close friendship with Collins helped to influence him in the direction of mystery fiction; in the previous year (1867) he had pronounced *The Moonstone:* "Much better than anything he [Collins] has done."

marriage or death.[38] It has the rounded (though limited) perfection of a triolet. The farther it escapes from pure analysis, the more difficulty it has in achieving artistic unity.

It does not, and by hypothesis never can, attain the loftiest level of literary achievement. Though it deals with the most desperate effects of rage, jealousy, and revenge, it rarely touches the heights and depths of human passion. It presents us only with the *fait accompli,* and looks upon death and mutilation with a dispassionate eye. It does not show us the inner workings of the murderer's mind—it must not; for the identity of the murderer is hidden until the end of the book.[39] The victim is shown rather as a subject for the dissecting-table than as a husband and father. A too violent emotion flung into the glittering mechanism of the detective-story jars the movement by disturbing its delicate balance. The most successful writers are those who contrive to keep the story running from beginning to end upon the same emotional level, and it is better to err in the direction of too little feeling than too much. Here, the writer whose detective is a member of the official force has an advantage: from him a detached attitude is correct; he can suitably retain the impersonal attitude of the surgeon. The sprightly amateur must not be sprightly all the time, lest at some point we should be reminded that this is, after all, a question of somebody's being foully murdered, and that flippancy is indecent. To make the transition from the detached to the human point

[38] This should appeal to Mr. E. M. Forster who is troubled by the irrational structure of the novel from this point of view. Unhappily, he has openly avowed himself "too priggish" to enjoy detective-stories. This is bad luck, indeed.

[39] An almost unique example of the detective-story told from the point of view of the hunted instead of the hunter is *Ashes to Ashes* by Isabel Ostrander. This shows the clues being left by the murderer, who is then compelled to look on while they are picked up, one after the other, by the detectives, despite all his desperate efforts to cover them. It is a very excellent piece of work which, in the hands of a writer of a little more distinction, might have been a powerful masterpiece. Isabel Ostrander, who also wrote under the name of Robert Orr Chipperfield and other pseudonyms, was a particularly competent spinner of yarns. Her straightforward police-detective, McCarty, is always confounding the conclusions of Terhune—a "scientific" private detective, who believes in modern psycho-analytical detective apparatus.

of view is one of the writer's hardest tasks. It is especially hard when the murderer has been made human and sympathetic. A real person has then to be brought to the gallows, and this must not be done too lightheartedly. Mr. G. K. Chesterton deals with this problem by merely refusing to face it. His Father Brown (who looks at sin and crime from the religious point of view) retires from the problem before the arrest is reached. He is satisfied with a confession. The sordid details take place "off." Other authors permit sympathetic villains to commit suicide. Thus, Mr. Milne's Gillingham, whose attitude starts by being flippant and ends by being rather sentimental, warns Cayley of his approaching arrest, and Cayley shoots himself, leaving a written confession. Monsters of villainy can, of course, be brought to a bad end without compunction; but modern taste rejects monsters, therefore the modern detective-story is compelled to achieve a higher level of writing, and a more competent delineation of character. As the villain is allowed more good streaks in his composition, so the detective must achieve a tenderer human feeling beneath his frivolity or machine-like efficiency.

Love Interest

One fettering convention, from which detective fiction is only very slowly freeing itself, is that of the "love interest." Publishers and editors still labour under the delusion that all stories must have a nice young man and woman who have to be united in the last chapter. As a result, some of the finest detective-stories are marred by a conventional love-story, irrelevant to the action and perfunctorily worked in. The most harmless form of this disease is that taken, for example, in the works of Mr. Austin Freeman. His secondary characters fall in love with distressing regularity, and perform a number of conventional antics suitable to persons in their condition, but they do not interfere with the course of the story. You can skip the love-passages if you like, and nothing is lost. Far more blameworthy are the heroes who insist on fooling about after young women when they ought to be putting their minds on the job of detection. Just at the critical moment when the trap is set to catch the villain, the sleuth learns that his best girl has been spirited away. Heedlessly he drops everything, and rushes off to Chinatown or to the lonely house on the marshes or wherever it is, without even leaving a note to say where he is going. Here he is promptly sandbagged or entrapped or otherwise made a fool of, and the whole story is impeded and its logical development ruined.

The instances in which the love-story is an integral part of the plot are extremely rare. One very beautiful example occurs in *The Moonstone*. Here the entire plot hangs on the love of two women for Franklin Blake. Both Rachel Verinder and Rosanna Spearman know that he took the diamond, and the whole mystery arises from their efforts to shield him. Their conduct is, in both cases, completely natural and right, and the characters are so finely conceived as to be entirely convincing. E. C. Bentley, in *Trent's Last Case*, has dealt finely with the still harder problem of the detective in love. Trent's love for Mrs. Manderson is a legitimate part of the plot; while it does not prevent him from drawing the proper conclusion from the evidence before him, it does prevent him from acting upon his conclusions, and so prepares the way for the real explanation. Incidentally, the love-story is handled artistically and with persuasive emotion.

In *The House of the Arrow* and, still more strikingly, in *No Other Tiger*, A. E. W. Mason has written stories of strong detective interest which at the same time have the convincing psychological structure of the novel of character. The characters are presented as a novelist presents them—romantically, it is true, but without that stark insistence on classifying and explaining which turns the persons of the ordinary detective-story into a collection of museum exhibits.

Apart from such unusual instances as these, the less love in a detective-story, the better. *"L'amour au théâtre,"* says Racine, *"ne peut pas être en seconde place;"* and this holds good of detective fiction. A casual and perfunctory love-story is worse than no love-story at all, and, since the mystery must, by hypothesis, take the first place, the love is better left out.

Lynn Brock's *The Deductions of Colonel Gore* affords a curious illustration of this truth. Gore sets out, animated by an unselfish devotion to a woman, to recover some compromising letters for her, and, in so doing, becomes involved in unravelling an intricate murder plot. As the story goes on, the references to the beloved woman become chillier and more perfunctory; not only does the author seem to have lost interest, but so does Colonel Gore. At length the author notices this, and explains it in a paragraph:

> "There were moments when Gore accused himself—or, rather, felt that he ought to accuse himself—of an undue coldbloodedness in these speculations of his. The business was a horrible business. One ought to have been decently shocked by it. One ought to have been horrified by the thought that three old friends were involved in such a business.
> "But the truth was—and his apologies to himself for that truth became feebler and feebler—that the thing had now so caught hold of him that he had come to regard the actors in it as merely pieces of a puzzle baffling and engrossing to the verge of monomania."

There is the whole difficulty about allowing real human beings into a detective-story. At some point or other, either their emotions make hay of the detective interest, or the detective interest gets hold of them and makes their emotions look like pasteboard. It is, of course, a fact that we all adopt a detached attitude towards "a good murder" in the newspaper. Like Betteredge in *The Moonstone,* we get "detective fever," and forget the victim in the fun of tracking the criminal. For this reason,

it is better not to pitch the emotional key too high at the start;
the inevitable drop is thus made less jarring.

Future Developments: Fashions and Formulæ

Just at present, therefore, the fashion in detective fiction is
to have characters credible and lively; not conventional, but,
on the other hand, not too profoundly studied—people who live
more or less on the *Punch* level of emotion. A little more psychological complexity is allowed than formerly; the villain may
not be a villain from every point of view; the heroine, if there
is one, is not necessarily pure; the falsely accused innocent
need not be a sympathetic character.[40] The automata—the em-
bodied vices and virtues—the weeping fair-haired girl—the
stupid but manly young man with the biceps—even the colos-
sally evil scientist with the hypnotic eyes—are all disappearing
from the intellectual branch of the art, to be replaced by figures
having more in common with humanity.

An interesting symptom of this tendency is the arrival of a
number of books and stories which recast, under the guise of
fiction, actual murder cases drawn from real life. Thus, Mrs.
Belloc Lowndes and Mrs. Victor Rickard have both dealt with
the Braco Poisoning Mystery. Anthony Berkeley has retold
the Maybrick case; Mr. E. H. W. Meyerstein has published a
play based on the Seddon poisoning case, and Mr. Aldous Huxley, in *The Gioconda Smile*, has reinterpreted in his own manner another famous case of recent years.[41]

We are now in a position to ask ourselves the favourite question of modern times: What next? Where is the detective-story
going? Has it a future? Or will the present boom see the end of
it?

[40] e.g. in J. J. Connington's *The Tragedy at Ravensthorpe*, where the agora-
phobic Maurice is by no means an agreeable person to have about the house.
[41] *What Really Happened*, by Mrs. Belloc Lowndes; *Not Sufficient Evidence*,
by Mrs. Victor Rickard; *The Wychford Poisoning Drama*, by the Author of
The Layton Court Mystery; Heddon, by E. H. W. Meyerstein; *Mortal Coils*,
by Aldous Huxley.

The Most Unlikely Person

In early mystery fiction, the problem tends to be, *who* did the crime? At first, while readers were still unsophisticated, the formula of the Most Unlikely Person had a good run. But the reader soon learned to see through this. If there was a single person in the story who appeared to have no motive for the crime and who was allowed to amble through to the penultimate chapter free from any shadow of suspicion, that character became a marked man or woman. "I knew he must be guilty because nothing was said about him," said the cunning reader. Thus we come to a new axiom, laid down by Mr. G. K. Chesterton in a brilliant essay in the *New Statesman:* the real criminal must be suspected at least once in the course of the story. Once he is suspected, and then (apparently) cleared, he is made safe from future suspicion. This is the principle behind Mr. Wills Crofts's impregnable alibis, which are eventually broken down by painstaking enquiry. Probably the most baffling form of detective-story is still that in which suspicion is distributed equally among a number of candidates, one of whom turns out to be guilty. Other developments of the Most Unlikely Person formula make the guilty person a juror at the inquest or trial;[42] the detective himself;[43] the counsel for the prosecution;[44] and, as a supreme effort of unlikeliness, the actual narrator of the story.[45] Finally, resort has been made to the double-cross, and the person originally suspected turns out to be the right person after all.[46]

The Unexpected Means

There are signs, however, that the possibilities of the formula are becoming exhausted, and of late years much has been done

[42] Robert Orr Chipperfield: *The Man in the Jury-Box.*

[43] Bernard Capes: *The Skeleton Key;* Gaston Leroux: *Mystère de la Chambre Jaune;* etc.

[44] G. K. Chesterton: *The Mirror of the Magistrate (Innocence of Father Brown).*

[45] Agatha Christie: *The Murder of Roger Ackroyd.*

[46] Father R. Knox: *The Viaduct Murder,* and others.

in exploring the solution by the unexpected means. With recent discoveries in medical and chemical science, this field has become exceedingly fruitful, particularly in the provision of new methods of murder. It is fortunate for the mystery-monger that, whereas, up to the present, there is only one known way of getting born, there are endless ways of getting killed. Here is a brief selection of handy short cuts to the grave: Poisoned tooth-stoppings; licking poisoned stamps; shaving-brushes inoculated with dread diseases; poisoned boiled eggs (a bright thought); poison-gas; a cat with poisoned claws; poisoned mattresses; knives dropped through the ceiling; stabbing with a sharp icicle; electrocution by telephone; biting by plague-rats and typhoid-carrying lice; boiling lead in the ears (much more effective than cursed hebanon in a vial): air-bubbles injected into the arteries; explosion of a gigantic "Prince Rupert's drop"; frightening to death; hanging head-downwards; freezing to atoms in liquid air; hypodermic injections shot from air-guns; exposure, while insensible, to extreme cold; guns concealed in cameras; a thermometer which explodes a bomb when the temperature of the room reaches a certain height; and so forth.

The methods of disposing of inconvenient corpses are also varied and peculiar; burial under a false certificate obtained in a number of ways; substitution of one corpse for another (very common in fiction, though rare in real life); mummification; reduction to bone-dust; electro-plating; arson; "planting" (not in the churchyard, but on innocent parties)—a method first made famous by R. L. Stevenson.[47] Thus, of the three questions, "Who?" "How?" and "Why?", "How" is at present the one which offers most scope for surprise and ingenuity, and is capable of sustaining an entire book on its own, though a combination of all three naturally provides the best entertainment.[48]

[47] *The Wrong Box.*
[48] Mr. Austin Freeman has specialised in a detective-story which rejects all

The mystery-monger's principal difficulty is that of varying his surprises. "You know my methods, Watson," says the detective, and it is only too painfully true. The beauty of Watson was, of course, that after thirty years he still did not know Holmes's methods; but the average reader is sharper-witted. After reading half a dozen stories by one author, he is sufficiently advanced in Dupin's psychological method [49] to see with the author's eyes. He knows that, when Mr. Austin Freeman drowns somebody in a pond full of water-snails, there will be something odd and localised about those snails; he knows that, when one of Mr. Wills Crofts's characters has a cast-iron alibi, the alibi will turn out to have holes in it; he knows that if Father Knox casts suspicion on a Papist, the Papist will turn out to be innocent; instead of detecting the murderer, he is engaged in detecting the writer. That is why he gets the impression that the writer's later books are seldom or never "up to" his earlier efforts. He has become married to the writer's muse, and marriage has destroyed the mystery.

There certainly does seem a possibility that the detective-story will some time come to an end, simply because the public will have learnt all the tricks. But it has probably many years to go yet, and in the meantime a new and less rigid formula will probably have developed, linking it more closely to the novel of manners and separating it more widely from the novel of adventure. The latter will, no doubt, last as long as humanity, and while crime exists, the crime thriller will hold its place. It is, as always, the higher type that is threatened with extinction.

At the time of writing (1928) the detective-story is profiting by a reaction against novels of the static type. Mr. E. M. Forster is indeed left murmuring regretfully, "Yes, ah! yes—the

three questions. He tells the story of the crime first, and relies for his interest on the pleasure afforded by following the ingenious methods of the investigator. *The Singing Bone* contains several tales of this type. Mr. Freeman has had few followers, and appears to have himself abandoned the formula, which is rather a pity.

[49] As outlined in *The Purloined Letter*.

novel tells a story"; but the majority of the public are rediscovering that fact with cries of triumph. Sexual abnormalities are suffering a slight slump at the moment; the novel of passion still holds the first place, especially among women, but even women seem to be growing out of the simple love-story. Probably the cheerful cynicism of the detective-tale suits better with the spirit of the times than the sentimentality which ends in wedding bells. For, make no mistake about it, the detective-story is part of the literature of escape, and not of expression. We read tales of domestic unhappiness because that is the kind of thing which happens to us; but when these things gall too close to the sore, we fly to mystery and adventure because they do not, as a rule, happen to us. "The detective-story," says Philip Guedalla, "is the normal recreation of noble minds." And it is remarkable how strong is the fascination of the higher type of detective-story for the intellectually-minded, among writers as well as readers. The average detective-novel to-day is extremely well written, and there are few good living writers who have not tried their hand at it at one time or another.[50]

Tales of Mystery and Horror

Concerning mystery and horror apart from detection, it is more difficult to attempt an historical outline. The early tales in this kind belong to the region of folk-lore rather than of fiction, and are easily available for study. Certain supernatural themes—witchcraft, fairies, vampires, were-wolfs, ghosts friendly and unfriendly, wraiths of the living—appear with comparatively little variation in the traditions of all countries.

[50] Among men of letters distinguished in other lines who have turned their attention to the detective-story may be mentioned A. E. W. Mason, Eden Phillpotts, "Lynn Brock" (whose pseudonym protects the personality of a well-known writer), Somerset Maugham, Rudyard Kipling, A. A. Milne, Father R. Knox, J. D. Beresford.

It is owing to the work of such men as these that the detective-novel reaches a much higher artistic level in England than in any other country. At every turn the quality of the writing and the attention to beauty of form and structure betray the hand of the practised novelist.

In modern stories of the weird, we may trace the same themes, rationalised or semi-rationalised, to suit our altered conceptions of the relation between flesh and spirit.

Among living masters, Dr. M. R. James is one who holds to the older methods. His hauntings are real hauntings, his ghosts and demons have an actual objective reality, and he offers no explanation of their existence. The vampires of E. F. Benson and Marion Crawford, similarly, are real vampires, visibly and carnally sucking the blood of their victims. To another school of writers, of whom Algernon Blackwood and Robert Hichens may be taken as examples, the ghostly presence or elemental spirit has become rather the "thought-shell" of an earth-bound mind—a record left upon the ether by passions existing in the past. It possesses, indeed, an objective existence, but this existence has been bestowed upon it by the power of human thought, and can be dissipated by the same means. The werewolf is reinterpreted as the astral body of desire; the radiant energy released by ancient beliefs continues to vibrate wherever a psychic diaphragm is found to receive and reproduce it. The study of psychology has produced in addition a new kind of terror—the nightmare country between sanity and madness; the pressure of mind upon living mind, and the lonely horror of the dark places of the soul. In the purely human sphere of horror, spiritual cruelty now holds its place alongside with bodily cruelty, and we can place Ethel Colburn Mayne's *The Separate Room* next door to H. G. Wells's *The Cone* as examples of man's inhumanity to man.

As in every other kind of fiction, so in this: each day the public taste demands a greater subtlety of theme and treatment. The old raw-head-and-bloody-bones, with its apparatus of white sheet and clanking chains, no longer alarms us. It rouses us to ribald laughter, no less than the marvels of Otranto, and the statue from whose nose three drops of blood slowly and solemnly fall. Nor are we impressed by descriptions of hair standing on end with terror, or by flat-footed emphasis on the ghastly helped out with exclamation marks. It needs to-day the utmost cunning of the writer's craft to "put across" a ghost-story; the slightest touch of sentimentality or exaggeration is fatal to success.

In nothing is individual fancy so varied and capricious as in its perception of the horrible. To one person, E. L. White's *Lukundoo* is terrible beyond all imagination; to another, this story seems merely grotesque, and it is the imbecile endearments of the thing whose love "came to Professor Guildea" in Robert Hichens's story which arouse in him that delicious nausea we look for in a horror yarn. One cannot argue about these things. I remember reading somewhere about an old sundial, around whose face was written: IT IS LATER THAN YOU THINK. If that motto does not give you a "cauld grue," then nothing that I or any other person can say will convince you of its soul-shaking ghastliness. So that in any anthology of the horrible there must be many tales which the reader may think silly or dull; and also many gaps, representing the tales which frighten him but have not frightened the editor. In such a case, editors can but do their best and hope for the best, within the limits imposed by a three dollar volume.

It remains to be added that many tales which on their merits lay claim to inclusion have had to be left out of the present book for one unavoidable reason or another. Space has necessitated the neglect of the whole vast field of foreign literature, in order that something like a representative selection of English tales might be attempted. Difficulties connected with copyright have caused a few regrettable omissions. Sometimes, also, a many times reprinted masterpiece has been deliberately passed over in favour of something less readily available. And, finally, many lacunæ must be attributed to ignorance, madam, pure ignorance on the editor's part.

It is hoped, however, that in running through the present volume, the reader will find himself presented with a kind of bird's-eye view of the general subject, extending from the literature of pure deduction on the one hand, through various types of mystery—natural and supernatural, explained and unexplained—to tales of sheer horror, without any mystery at all. Every tale in this book is guaranteed to have puzzled or horrified *somebody;* with any luck at all, some of them may puzzle and horrify *you.*

What a piece of work is man, that he should enjoy this kind of thing!

A very odd piece of work—indeed, a mystery!

32 TWENTY RULES FOR WRITING
DETECTIVE STORIES

by *S. S. Van Dine*

THE DETECTIVE STORY is a kind of intellectual game. It is more
—it is a sporting event. And the author must play fair with the
reader. He can no more resort to trickeries and deceptions and
still retain his honesty than if he cheated in a bridge game. He
must outwit the reader, and hold the reader's interest, through
sheer ingenuity. For the writing of detective stories there are
very definite laws—unwritten, perhaps, but none the less binding: and every respectable and self-respecting concocter of
literary mysteries lives up to them.

Herewith, then, is a sort of Credo, based partly on the
promptings of the honest author's inner conscience. To wit:

1. The reader must have equal opportunity with the detective for solving the mystery. All clues must be plainly stated
and described.

2. No wilful tricks or deceptions may be played on the
reader other than those played legitimately by the criminal on
the detective himself.

3. There must be no love interest in the story. To introduce
amour is to clutter up a purely intellectual experience with irrelevant sentiment. The business in hand is to bring a criminal
to the bar of justice, not to bring a lovelorn couple to the
hymeneal altar.

4. The detective himself, or one of the official investigators,
should never turn out to be the culprit. This is bald trickery, on
a par with offering someone a bright penny for a five-dollar
gold piece. It's false pretenses.

267

5. The culprit must be determined by logical deductions—not by accident or coincidence or unmotivated confession. To solve a criminal problem in this latter fashion is like sending the reader on a deliberate wild-goose chase, and then telling him, after he has failed, that you had the object of his search up your sleeve all the time. Such an author is no better than a practical joker.

6. The detective novel must have a detective in it; and a detective is not a detective unless he detects. His function is to gather clues that will eventually lead to the person who did the dirty work in the first chapter; and if the detective does not reach his conclusions through an analysis of those clues, he has no more solved his problem than the schoolboy who gets his answer out of the back of the arithmetic book.

7. There simply must be a corpse in a detective novel, and the deader the corpse the better. No lesser crime than murder will suffice. Three hundred pages is far too much pother for a crime other than murder. After all, the reader's trouble and expenditure of energy must be rewarded. Americans are essentially humane, and therefore a tip-top murder arouses their sense of vengeance and horror. They wish to bring the perpetrator to justice; and when "murder most foul, as in the best it is," has been committed, the chase is on with all the righteous enthusiasm of which the thrice gentle reader is capable.

8. The problem of the crime must be solved by strictly naturalistic means. Such methods for learning the truth as slate-writing, ouija-boards, mind-reading, spiritualistic seances, crystal-gazing, and the like, are taboo. A reader has a chance when matching his wits with a rationalistic detective, but if he must compete with the world of spirits and go chasing about the fourth dimension of metaphysics, he is defeated ab initio.

9. There must be but one detective—that is, but one protagonist of deduction—one deus ex machina. To bring the minds of three or four, or sometimes a gang of detectives to bear on a problem is not only to disperse the interest and break

the direct thread of logic, but to take an unfair advantage of the reader, who, at the outset, pits his mind against that of the detective and proceeds to do mental battle. If there is more than one detective, the reader doesn't know who his co-deductor is. It's like making the reader run a race with a relay team.

10. The culprit must turn out to be a person who has played a more or less prominent part in the story—that is, a person with whom the reader is familiar and in whom he takes an interest. For a writer to fasten the crime, in the final chapter, on a stranger or person who has played a wholly unimportant part in the tale, is to confess to his inability to match wits with the reader.

11. Servants—such as butlers, footmen, valets, game-keepers, cooks, and the like—must not be chosen by the author as the culprit. This is begging a noble question. It is a too easy solution. It is unsatisfactory, and makes the reader feel that his time has been wasted. The culprit must be a decidedly worthwhile person—one who wouldn't ordinarily come under suspicion; for if the crime was the sordid work of a menial, the author would have had no business to embalm it in book-form.

12. There must be but one culprit, no matter how many murders are committed. The culprit may, of course, have a minor helper or co-plotter; but the entires onus must rest on one pair of shoulders: the entire indignation of the reader must be permitted to concentrate on a single black nature.

13. Secret societies, camorras, mafias, et al., have no place in a detective story. Here the author gets into adventure fiction and secret-service romance. A fascinating and truly beautiful murder is irremediably spoiled by any such wholesale culpability. To be sure, the murderer in a detective novel should be given a sporting chance, but it is going too far to grant him a secret society (with its ubiquitous havens, mass protection, etc.) to fall back on. No high-class self-respecting murderer would want such odds in his jousting-bout with the police.

14. The method of murder, and the means of detecting it,

must be rational and scientific. That is to say, pseudo-science and purely imaginative and speculative devices are not to be tolerated in the *roman policier*. For instance, the murder of a victim by a newly found element—a super-radium, let us say—is not a legitimate problem. Nor may a rare and unknown drug, which has its existence only in the author's imagination, be administered. A detective-story writer must limit himself, toxicologically speaking, to the pharmacopoeia. Once an author soars into the realm of fantasy, in the Jules Verne manner, he is outside the bounds of detective fiction, cavorting in the uncharted reaches of adventure.

15. The truth of the problem must at all times be apparent —provided the reader is shrewd enough to see it. By this I mean that if the reader, after learning the explanation for the crime, should re-read the book, he would see that the solution had, in a sense, been staring him in the face—that all the clues really pointed to the culprit—and that, if he had been as clever as the detective, he could have solved the mystery himself without going on to the final chapter. That the clever reader does often thus solve the problem goes without saying. And one of my basic theories of detective fiction is that, if a detective story is fairly and legitimately constructed, it is impossible to keep the solution from all readers. There will inevitably be a certain number of them just as shrewd as the author; and if the author has shown the proper sportsmanship and honesty in his statement and projection of the crime and its clues, these perspicacious readers will be able, by analysis, elimination and logic, to put their fingers on the culprit as soon as the detective does. And herein lies the zest of the game. Herein we have an explanation for the fact that readers who would spurn the ordinary "popular" novel will read detective stories unblushingly.

16. A detective novel should contain no long descriptive passages, no literary dallying with side-issues, no subtly worked-out character analyses, no "atmospheric" preoccupations. Such matters have no vital place in a record of crime and deduction.

They hold up the action, and introduce issues irrelevant to the main purpose, which is to state a problem, analyze it, and bring it to a successful conclusion. To be sure, there must be a sufficient descriptiveness and character delineation to give the novel verisimilitude; but when an author of a detective story has reached that literary point where he has created a gripping sense of reality and enlisted the reader's interest and sympathy in the characters and the problem, he has gone as far in the purely "literary" technique as is legitimate and compatible with the needs of a criminal-problem document. A detective story is a grim business, and the reader goes to it, not for literary furbelows and style and beautiful descriptions and the projections of moods, but for mental stimulation and intellectual activity— just as he goes to a ball game or to a cross-word puzzle. Lectures between innings at the Polo Grounds on the beauties of nature would scarcely enhance the interest in the struggle between two contesting baseball nines; and dissertations on etymology and orthography interspersed in the definitions of a cross-word puzzle would tend only to irritate the solver bent on making the words interlock correctly.

17. A professional criminal must never be shouldered with the guilt of a crime in a detective story. Crimes by house-breakers and bandits are the province of the police department—not of authors and brilliant amateur detectives. Such crimes belong to the routine work of the Homicide Bureaus. A really fascinating crime is one committed by a pillar of a church, or a spinster noted for her charities.

18. A crime in a detective story must never turn out to be an accident or a suicide. To end an odyssey of sleuthing with such an anti-climax is to play an unpardonable trick on the reader. If a book-buyer should demand his two dollars back on the ground that the crime was a fake, any court with a sense of justice would decide in his favor and add a stinging reprimand to the author who thus hoodwinked a trusting and kind-hearted reader.

19. The motives for all crimes in detective stories should be personal. International plottings and war politics belong in a different category of fiction—in secret-service tales, for instance. But a murder story must be kept *gemutlich,* so to speak. It must reflect the reader's everyday experiences, and give him a certain outlet for his own repressed desires and emotions.

20. And (to give my Credo an even score of items) I herewith list a few of the devices which no self-respecting detective-story writer will now avail himself of. They have been employed too often, and are familiar to all true lovers of literary crime. To use them is a confession of the author's ineptitude and lack of originality.

(a) Determining the identity of the culprit by comparing the butt of a cigarette left at the scene of the crime with the brand smoked by a suspect.

(b) The bogus spiritualistic seance to frighten the culprit into giving himself away.

(c) Forged finger-prints.

(d) The dummy-figure alibi:

(e) The dog that does not bark and thereby reveals the fact that the intruder is familiar.

(f) The final pinning of the crime on a twin, or a relative who looks exactly like the suspected, but innocent, person.

(g) The hypodermic syringe and the knock-out drops.

(h) The commission of the murder in a locked room after the police have actually broken in.

(i) The word-association test for guilt.

(j) The cipher, or code letter, which is eventually unravelled by the sleuth.

33 THE RULES OF THE GAME
by *Howard Haycraft*

IN THE YEARS since the police novel came of age—and it is happily no longer necessary to defend a form of literature which numbers among its devotees so many international leaders of intellectual, professional, and public life—several valuable and often amusing compilations of rules have been laid down for its conduct. They may be condensed into two main requirements: (1) The detective story must play fair. (2) The detective story must be readable. On these two commandments depend the several considerations of technique and ethics which will follow.

But first, a qualification and explanation of the initial commandment. To say that the detective story must play fair means much more to-day than the obvious necessity of laying all the clues before the reader. It means, as well, that no evidence shall be made known to the reader which remains unknown to the detective (except in intentional tours de force); that false clues are automatically forbidden; that fortuity and coincidence are outlawed as beneath the dignity of the self-respecting craftsman; that all determinative action must proceed directly and causatively from the central theme of crime-and-pursuit; and that no extraneous factors (such as stupidity or "forgetting") shall be allowed to divert or prolong the plot in any essential manner.

Similarly, the commandment of readability means not only ordinary literary competence, but that the detective novel must avoid becoming a static and immobile puzzle, on the one hand,

and that it must forswear the meretricious aid of hokum, on the other.

The whole question of the Rules of the Game (the relation of reader and writer) is so closely bound up with the problem of the author's own craftsmanship that it is difficult to know where the one leaves off and the other begins. Presumably there will be no objection to considering their several and frequently over-lapping phases in the same general discussion. Both problems, however, will be approached here primarily from the point of view of the average friendly reader, rather than of the practising technician.

Structure and Sources

Structurally speaking, the first thing to know about the detective story is that it is conceived not forward and developmentally as are most types of fiction, but *backward*. Each tale, whether novel or short story, is conceived solution-foremost in the author's mind, around a definite central or controlling idea. The controlling idea may be a unique crime method; an original way of concealing the culprit, as in Agatha Christie's arguable *Roger Ackroyd;* perhaps a point of law turned to the criminal's or sleuth's advantage; an untried departure in detective technique; or virtually any combination or variation of established formulas. Such focal points may derive from a number of sources: usually the author's own fertile brain, implemented as it may be by some external stimulus. A few writers even confess that they find their best ideas in planning imaginary murders of people they don't like!

This is as good a place as any to remark that the influence of real crime on the fictional variety is much slighter and less direct than is generally realized, for the principal reason that the two are quite different entities. The truth is that most real-life crime is duller, less ingenious, less dramatic, lacking in what Poe called "the pungent contradiction of the general idea," as compared with fictional felony; while the few exceptions to the rule are, paradoxically, usually *too* improbable to make good fiction. Too, real-life detection attains its results more often than not by means of undramatic, routine investigation, confession, "information received," or pure chance—none of which is suited to the police romance. This is not to say that detective story writers never make use of real crime and detection as source material, but only that the relationship is nearly always suggestive rather than directly imitative.

The Need for Unity

Once the motivating theme is arrived at, the next and infinitely more difficult step is making the story fit the crime. For the tyro confronted with this problem, no better single guiding principle can be laid down than Willard Huntington Wright's dictum that the detective tale must at all times possess "unity of mood." Which, of course, is only another way of saying that characters, crime, style, dialogue, setting, the person of the detective, in fact all the structural minutiae, must be kept sternly and prayerfully "in key."

The Detective

In any detective story worth the name, at once the most important and most difficult integer is the sleuth.

In all fairness, women and boys do not make satisfactory principal detectives. Some examples of each class may be produced to counter this argument, but by and large to assign either to full-fledged criminal pursuit is a violation of the probabilities if not the strict possibilities. They may, and often do, figure as important and attractive assistants. The beginner, at least, will do well to confine them to such rôles.

Under all circumstances, a single principal sleuth is advisable, else the reader's essential identification of himself with the pursuer is likely to falter.

Whether the detective-in-chief shall be professional or amateur shall depend largely on the writer's experience and background and access to information. Obviously, the police sleuth is the more plausible, but requires much greater technical knowledge. (Even the writer who employs an amateur hero, however, should study at least the standard textbooks of police procedure to avoid committing embarrassing blunders.) Another drawback of the professional policeman is his tendency, inseparable from routine, to be a little on the dull side. The amateur, on the other hand, is inherently livelier and offers much wider latitude to the author, but has become increasingly unconvincing in a mechanized and departmentalized civilization. To resolve this two-horned dilemma, several reasonably successful combinations have been devised, uniting the advantages of the respective methods while avoiding their pitfalls. Among them may be mentioned: the "gentleman policeman" (such as Ngaio Marsh's RODERICK ALLEYN or the Lockridges' LIEUTENANT WEIGAND) who is brought logically onto the scene in official capacity, but because of his social charm functions with some of the freedom and insouciance of the amateur; the semi-pro or consulting specialist (as REGGIE FORTUNE or ELLERY QUEEN) who has the backing of Scotland Yard or Centre Street, yet remains free from professional routine; the retired professional (as EX-SUPERINTENDENT WILSON); or, in quite different vein, the non-police or agency operative in the style made popular by Dashiell Hammett.

The ambitious author will find it an advantage, if he can withstand the personal boredom, to follow a single character throughout his tales. Not only is a great deal of preliminary structure eliminated because it remains standing between books; readers become devoted to familiar sleuths (indeed, know their names better than those of the authors in many cases) with consequent material benefit to their creator. There is no stronger merchandising asset than habit. Use it!

The characterization of the sleuth is an item of the utmost importance. Elaborate eccentricity is to be avoided. But the detective is in distinct need of a personality, and in a form so compressed as the police novel has necessarily become, the careful selection of significant details can not be overemphasized. The Régie cigarette, the Duesenberg automobile, a "pretty taste in wines and incunabula," a hothouse of orchids—all may seem chance details to the reader; actually, in the hands of an astute author, they replace whole chapters of description in a Scott or a Hardy.

In this connection, it is difficult to understand why so many contemporary authors neglect to give their sleuths full names and characters. "Inspector Doakes" indeed! How can a man have a face who hasn't a name? We readers want to know our heroes' names, first, last, and middle initial if any; we want to know where they live, what they wear and smoke, even what—though we mustn't be told too often—they eat for breakfast. The indifference of some writers to such matters is particularly incomprehensible, because the rewards of making a character the reader's familiar are obviously out of all proportion to the slight effort required. Moreover, the absence of such elementary details is a virtual confession of the author's lack of interest in his character. How, then, can he expect his audience to be interested?

Watson or Not?

As every detective tale was once expected to offer an Eccentric Sleuth, so too was it required to have its Watson. But styles have changed here, too. To-day the Watson method of narration, despite its patent advantages to the author, is pretty much frowned upon in the better writing circles, unless handled with great care and well disguised: partly because of its triteness, partly, perhaps, because it is a little *too easy*. The objective third-person approach, while more difficult technically, seems clearly to be better suited, logically and aesthetically, to a genus of literature in which the analytical mode is so greatly of the essence. Furthermore, it does not offer the temptation to over-writing that seems to assail many authors when they are confronted with the pronoun "I."

A word of caution to the beginner: if you *must* have a Watson, make him (or her) brash, whimsical, sceptical, critical, tart, sour; in short, anything *except* the worshipful friend of yore.

Viewpoint

Concerning the problem of viewpoint in a wider sense, the safest rule for the novice is to select one approach and stick to it. A finished literary artist may, perhaps, employ a shifting viewpoint to advantage and without loss of unity; but in the hands of lesser fry nothing is more irritating than the story seen now through the detective's eyes, now through the observation of one or more of the characters, and again from the "omnipotent" angle. Used singly, these approaches are equally valid. Combinations of them are not advisable for the tyro and are filled with traps for the unwary, more so in this type of fiction than any other.

The Crime

In a purely theoretical sense, it may be possible to have detection without crime; but such experimentation is only for the definitely established author, and even then it is seldom satisfactory. The beginner should take no such chances. Similarly, murder has come to be the accepted theme of the detective novel, for reasons too numerous and obvious to require attention. A Wilkie Collins may be able to hold our interest in lesser crime throughout a full book, but there are few Collinses writing to-day. Slighter offenses, moreover, tend to deprive the writer of the Motive string to his technical bow, leaving him only Means and Opportunity for his serenade. The motives of murder are manifold; the motive of theft—save in the unusual case—is, self-evidently, theft. . . . The writer who is overtaken by an unusual idea involving a crime of lesser degree than

homicide, or that even rarer avis, a really unique crimeless
puzzle, will do well to employ it in a short story. To attempt
to use it as the main theme of a full-length novel is almost certainly to risk months of hard work for a rejection slip.

Many critics and readers have a strong prejudice against
mass, or multiple, murder, and this is certainly an objection for
the tyro to keep in mind. To be strictly fair, however, a distinction should be drawn between additional killings dragged in to
pad out the story or extricate the author from a difficult situation; and, on the other hand, the deliberate series of murders
which is the criminal's objective or to which he is logically
driven to cover his tracks as the sleuth closes in. There can be
no legitimate objection to the latter situation; the former, however, is an unblushing confession of technical inadequacy and
can not be condemned too strongly. Nevertheless, the wise
writer will restrict his homicides to three or four at the most,
if only for the reason that undue repetition of any theme is
poor art and brings its own penalty in loss of interest on the
part of the reader. Instances will doubtless be cited where a
greater number of killings has been used without payment of
this penalty. But these will usually be found to be intentional
tours de force, of the nature of John Rhode's *Murders in Praed
Street* or Philip MacDonald's *Mystery of the Dead Police*.

The Title

The best advice to the author faced with the selection of a
title is not to worry about it. Some lucky writers arrive at their
titles before they write their books; others achieve them in
the silent watches of the night. But it is safe to say that any
author who turns out a 60,000 to 80,000 word opus will have
thought of a number of satisfactory possibilities before his
manuscript is completed. Certain elementary rules must be
obeyed, of course, such as the requirement that the title must
be in key with the nature of the book. Likewise, it is well not
to strain too much for effect. Most of the too-bright titles per-

petrated by authors and publishers in recent years have demonstrably failed to increase sales. It is helpful to study the type of title in current favor, with special attention to the better works and authors. Imitation of mediocrity is seldom beneficial.

The Plot

Plot is something that can never be taught; it must be learned. Such rules as have been formulated for its construction will be found in any good manual of fiction writing, and, in general, will apply to the detective story. In addition, the writer of this type of literature must keep in mind at all times the necessity of avoiding the use of coincidence, of making certain that every major episode subsequent to the opening crime proceeds directly and causatively from the duel between sleuth and criminal. Minor unrelated incidents may be introduced occasionally to divert or to relieve tension, but they must never be allowed to interfere with the progress of the main plot.

"Had-I-But-Known"

It is a safe guess that no single practice among present-day soi-disant detective story writers has aroused such concentrated distaste among so many readers as the style of plot-work and narration which has come to be recognized—in Ogden Nash's telling phrase—as the "Had-I-But-Known" school of writing.* The allusion will be obvious to any intelligent reader. By it is meant the type of story which is artificially stalled and prolonged by coincidence and happenstance; by characters performing senseless acts and upsetting the sleuth's carefully laid plans, or getting bashed over the head (never sufficiently hard!) and "forgetting" to tell about it, or neglecting to report or investigate the most obvious clues until it is "too late"— while the narrator (invariably first-person and feminine) chants in the fashion of a Greek chorus equipped with faultless

---

* See the following chapter, 'Don't Guess, Let Me Tell You."

if slightly dilatory logic: "If we had only known what was going to happen, we might have prevented it!"

The beginner to-day will do well to avoid this style. Not only is it phony writing; its day of doom is clearly in sight. Increasingly it is the subject of published ridicule and satire, and the words that are spoken of it in rental libraries and private homes are not fit subject for print. In time, news of this steadily growing opposition will penetrate even the cloistered sancta of the editors, and when it does it will bode ill for the unfortunate author who can not write without the aid of such meretricious crutches.

The Columbia University Press released through its weekly bulletin, *The Pleasures of Publishing,* April 14, 1941, the results of a diverting but nonetheless valuable survey of the detective story predilections of several hundred habitual readers of the form. Among the questions asked, the participants in the questionnaire were polled on their "pet dislikes." By "a large vote of guilty," according to the compilers, third place on this list of aversions went to the Had-I-But-Known school of writing. (First place was voted to "too much love and romance," which few readers need be told is one of the cardinal sins of the H.I.B.K. sorority; second place to "poor writing" generally; and fourth to the hard-boiled school, "but mostly on the basis of too much of a good thing.") While in the voting on *preferred* types of writing, the H.I.B.K. mode placed a poor last among all forms! Likewise, among the comments attached by many of the voters to their ballots, numerous unchivalrous aspersions were cast on such moth-eaten H.I.B.K. devices and trappings as "nosy spinsters," "women who gum up the plot," "super-feminine stories," and "heroines who wander around attics alone." Lest mere misogyny among the voters be suspected, the conductors of the poll point out that almost as many women readers as men replied to the questionnaire, and that the first two authors in point of popularity were women (both English, however): Dorothy Sayers and Agatha Christie. In the several "favorite" classifications on which opinion was sought—such as favorite author, favorite detective, favorite novel, etc.—not a single one of the supposedly popular H.I.B.K. authors reached the first ten! Granting that this poll may represent a rather specialized cross-section of the detection-reading public, it will nevertheless afford little aid or comfort to H.I. B.K.-minded authors or editors; but rather should serve as a valuable indication of the direction the wind is blowing to-day.

Emotion and Drama

The question of emotion presents a particularly difficult choice for the budding author who wants to stay within the detective framework. On the one hand, the detective story must have *some* element of drama and excitement if it is to satisfy its theme and readers. On the other, it is one of the unwritten rules that fortuitous personal peril must never be allowed to supersede detection as the integral motif. Such a fine balance is not easy of achievement. A familiar attempt to circumvent the dilemma is the tale in which the central character is forced to turn detective either to clear himself of accusation or to escape the machinations of the criminal. But in nine cases out of ten such an essential reversal of the rôles of pursuer and pursued is likely to result in better melodrama than detection. The method should therefore be regarded with extreme caution by the beginner who wishes to establish a reputation in legitimate detection rather than "the blood." (If he does not care, that is something else again, outside the scope of the present discussion; but he must make his choice—he can not have both.) A sounder and safer procedure, on the whole, is to retain the detective in the orthodox position of pursuer and to create drama out of the criminal's attempt to escape the encircling net of justice. Scores of superior and exciting stories have been built on exactly this premise, barren as it may appear in the unadorned statement. A little intensive study of the better authors will reveal some of the specific methods employed.

The Puzzle Element

The antithesis of excessive emotion and drama, of course, is to have too little—and this is equally perilous. We have heard far too much in some circles about the detective story as a "game" between author and reader. This is certainly true insofar as it means that the writer must not cheat or unfairly hoodwink his audience. But carried to an extreme, this conception of the genre as primarily a competitive contest tends to deprive it of literary entity and relegate it to the realm of mechanical puzzles, to its eventual stagnation. As Philip Van Doren Stern has accurately remarked: "Were the detective story *only* a puzzle, there would be no need to make it a book." Such a tendency was alarmingly observable in the British detective story in the mid-1920's, but has since happily given way to a large extent, even in England, to more liberal conceptions. For to-day, it seems safe to say, more readers come to the detective novel to pursue crime *with* the author and his sleuth than to challenge them to a duel of wits; to escape the woes of a cruelly competitive world in the forgetful bliss of the purely vicarious chase, rather than to invent new competitions.

All of which is simply to say that writers should never forget the necessity of the detective story to be dynamic, not static; to move continually *forward;* to entertain as well as perplex. There is more than a grain of truth in B. J. R. Stolper's humorous "recipe" for the tasty police novel:

> ½ Sherlock Holmes
> ¼ P. G. Wodehouse
> ⅛ sheer adventure
> ⅛ anything you know best [1]

With the addition of only one other ingredient—a liberal portion of salt—this is a formula well adapted to the beginner's needs.

[1] *Scholastic,* October 22, 1938.

Background and Setting

Approaching the problem of background and setting, a dependable rule is to select something the author knows well. There are virtually no limitations, save that the *less* exotic the scenes, the better they will serve the essential interest of verisimilitude. Chesterton remarked somewhere that the detective story is at its best when it "stays at home"—or words to that general effect. But, on the opposite hand, the setting should not be *too* drab or commonplace or sordid: the confirmed addict does not come to the detective story in search of Dostoevsky. Most successful are those backdrops known to the average reader, yet "touched up" by artful brushwork; for it is the "semblance of reality" which is desired, rather than reality itself.

As Carolyn Wells has said, the detective story must *seem* real in the same sense that fairy tales *seem* real to children; while Marjorie Nicolson demands that it be "photographically real though never realistic." For this reason one ventures to differ with Willard Huntington Wright's pronouncement of a few years ago in favor of elaborate floor-plans and diagrams. The well-plotted tale to-day will avoid the involutions which make such adjuncts of mere criminology necessary. A sizable group of readers, in fact, flatly refuses to read novels in which such charts are found, maintaining with some cause that their presence confesses either to lack of descriptive skill on the author's part or to a plot too complex to be entertaining. (Maps, for some reason, are received more tolerantly.) A variation of this objection would seem to account for the short life of several attempts at picturized detective stories: such embellishments only quarrel with the mental image the audience has formed.

In setting, as in all other departments of the genre, the author must be on constant guard against triteness. Several standard backdrops have been so overworked that a faint odor of the bogus has begun to exude from them: among them, weird old mansions and castles, or for that matter anything partaking of the Gothic mode. Such trappings have long since been relegated to the less critical mode of mystery, and even there they have lost much of the power they once possessed to astonish and excite. In slightly different vein, the country estate and its inevitable accompaniment, the week-end party, are due for a rest. A little intelligent reading will warn the beginner of other scenes-of-action which have grown wearisome through too frequent repetition.

We have spoken in an earlier paragraph of the curious failure of many writers to equip their sleuths with full names and recognizable traits. Equally hard to comprehend is the predilection of other authors for artificial settings—when *real* streets, buildings, neighborhoods, even trains and tram-cars, add so greatly to the believability, nay, the fascination, of narratives particularly dependent on verisimilitude for their success. It is not essential that the audience should be personally familiar with the settings for them to produce this effect. Thousands of readers who have never visited New York believe implicitly in the better PHILO VANCE cases, if for no other reason than that the topographical details are as readily recognizable as this morning's newspaper. And millions who have never seen London can picture Baker Street as vividly as their own homes.

Some day, perhaps, an inquisitive statistician will enumerate the number of police novels which use these two cities as their scenes. Apart from the circumstance that they are the residence of many of the practitioners and readers, there is a solid reason for their predominance: their world-wide familiarity to all peoples through picture, song, and story—as the saying goes. Since the coming of the moving picture, particularly, there is scarcely a reader who can not readily visualize at least the general appearance and topography of both metropolises.

This is not to suggest that the writer who lives in, say, Nebraska, should attempt to lay his story in the purlieus of Manhattan. He will do far better to stick to the Nebraska he knows.

Characters and Characterization

Like so many of the other conventions, treatment of character in the detective novel has undergone considerable change in recent years. Formerly there existed something of an unwritten law that the personae, apart from the central sleuth, should be purposely "played down." To do otherwise, it was argued, would distract attention from the integral problem (this was in the days when the "puzzle" aspect of the detective story was receiving its greatest support); and for whole decades shadowy, faceless stencils floated in and out of a multitude of murder chambers, leaving little trace of their passing in the mind of the reader. Whatever merit this fashion may have had began to decline as the police novel, even in its more routine concepts, slowly turned from mechanical crime toward something approaching the psychological. This does not mean that every writer should attempt the all out character novel of detection—for it is given to only a few to write with the penetration of a Francis Iles or a Margery Allingham—but the beginner will do well to set as his goal at least the standards of contemporary magazine fiction of the better class. The old days of cardboard heroes and hissing villains have gone with the gaslight, and nothing will so quickly doom the novice's chances of acceptance by reputable publishers as failure to comprehend the circumstance.

Admittedly, not all characters can be drawn with the same amount of detail as is devoted to the central sleuth in a form as compressed as the modern detective story. But they must be made clearly recognizable in outline—just as a clever caricaturist or shadowgraph artist can identify his subjects in a few strokes. This situation requires even greater care in the selection of significant detail than does delineation of the detective.

Contrast, too, is of the greatest importance: in physical appearance, in traits of speech and behavior, in age, particularly in name. If any two names convey the slightest similarity, either to the eye or the ear, confusion of the characters is almost sure to result. Recurrent references to the contrasting traits should be employed to help the reader (and the author!) keep the characters sharply in mind.

As in the case of the sleuth himself, full names should be given to all the principal figures. An excellent device is the printed cast of characters, with an identifying phrase for each, published in the front of the book for the reader's convenience. Both S. S. Van Dine and Ellery Queen—among several—have used this with high effectiveness. Such a list or table will also be highly useful to the author during the actual writing.

Inasmuch as the culprit is concealed among the characters in the modern detective novel, the temptation to the novice is to hide him by the very multitude of personae. But this device is likely to backfire; the author will quickly find that he has weakened the effectiveness of the tale and increased and complicated his own structural problems. In general, eight or ten principal characters should be the limit; with the number of actual suspects held to five or six. Incidental actors, in the form of servants, medical examiners, police sergeants, etc., may be added to taste and within reason.

Some critics hold that there should always be a secondary hero or heroine, in addition to the sleuth, to engage the reader's sympathy. This is on the whole a sound principle, though it may be obviated by certain unusual plots and circumstances.

Style

In style, again, the developments of recent years have belied even so astute a critic as Willard Huntington Wright, who declared in 1927 that style had no more excuse in the detective story than in the cross-word puzzle. It is necessary to cite no more than Mr. Wright's own best novels, written as "S. S. Van Dine," to disprove this thesis. Perhaps, however, his premise may be qualified, in the light of later custom, to read that too great *pretentiousness* of style is still as fatal to the detective novel as is any other distracting element. (Oddly enough, it is mainly this fault which makes the later Van Dine novels so distinctly inferior to the earlier ones.)

But if there is no room for over-writing in the form, there is always a place, indeed, a clamoring necessity, for those indefinable qualities of statement that have ever distinguished good fiction of all sorts from bad. Whatever else the detective story may or may not do to-day, it definitely must not be—to borrow a term from another glossary—"corny," either in style or device.

The Devices of Detection

A respectable book might be written on the devices of the detective story alone. Seeking a single guide-post in a wilderness of detail, we can do no better than to prescribe simplicity as the chief desideratum. A prime reason for the failure of many excellent and ingenious plots is their very involution and excessive elaborateness. In general, it may be said that the detective novel which requires a long and detailed explanatory chapter at the end has failed in its purpose. A few valedictory remarks by the detective are always permissible, to explain the thought processes by which he arrived at his conclusion. But in the really well constructed story, the "denunciation" should of itself answer all the determinative questions ("how") and show, besides, why *only* the culprit ("who"), out of all the characters, can be guilty. (A plague, in passing, on all stuffy tales in which the criminal's sole qualification is his least-likelihood!) If the dénouement has been sufficiently prepared, and if no evidence has been withheld from the reader, relatively few additional paragraphs will be required for the detective to tell us what he observed and deduced that we did not as we followed him down the path.

A good secondary rule might be to require of all prospective writers of detective fiction a thorough course of critical reading in their chosen subject: S. S. Van Dine read more than 2,000 stories before he tried to write one! Only in this way may all the pitfalls of the overworked and hackneyed be successfully skirted.

It is in the matter of evidence, of course, that most of the dangers and clichés lurk. In her still helpful manual, *The Technique of the Mystery Story,* Carolyn Wells more than a decade ago made an amusing catalogue of evidential devices which were taboo even then, including "gravity clues," "shredded evidence," and similar means and methods outlawed either because of over-use or because of far-fetchedness. One of the illuminating differences, incidentally, which will strike the reader who compares to-day's detective story with that of a quarter-century ago is the prevalence of material clues in the older form and the predominance of what may be called "behavioristic" evidence in the new. This is not to imply that physical evidence no longer has a legitimate function; only that if it is to whet the jaded appetite of to-day's reader it must be served up with piquant sauces. The best single example, perhaps, of the modern method of handling the material clue is Philip MacDonald's brilliantly simple *Rasp*. Still other instances particularly suited to the beginner's study are the radio adventures (even more than the book appearances) of ELLERY QUEEN.

Some random *do's* and *don'ts* for the beginner concerning device and general technique:

Avoid the Locked Room puzzle. Only a genius can invest it with novelty or interest to-day.

Eschew footprints, tobacco ash, and ballistics. Don't expect your reader to be excited by fingerprints, either!

Use plenty of conversation but only a minimum of description, save where it serves a definite rather than a decorative purpose. Atmosphere is important; but convey it economically, suggestively.

Disguise, of course, went out with the bustle.

Love, once barred from the premises, is permissible in moderation to-day (indeed, is essential for the women's-magazine market) but it must not be allowed to interrupt or divert the directional flow of crime-and-detection any more than any other incidental factor.

The least-likely-person theme, in the old sense, is stale stuff. Give the reader cause to suspect every one, including the culprit, but *apparently* clear him in the early stages. An infinite number of variations on this formula can be—and constantly are—worked out.

A related rule proclaims that the criminal must be some one who has appeared throughout the story. Father Knox adds the further qualification that the culprit "must not be any one whose thoughts the reader has been permitted to follow": a justifiable if lock-the-stable-door rule obviously inspired by *Roger Ackroyd*—and at the same time an argument for the "constant" viewpoint in narration.

Make your crime method, whatever else it may be, "practically demonstrable." To this dictum one is tempted to add a remonstrance against all methods of killing so complex, so dependent on the exact juxtaposition of a multitude of factors and persons, that they have about the same chance of success as a hole-in-one in golf—yet which always come off to perfection! Remember that plausibility is your best friend!

Don't introduce a "trick" murder device unless you are certain that it is both original and plausible. The ice-bullet, the ice-dagger, and similar "sells" so popular a decade ago are to-day as archaic as the Florentine paper-cutter of an earlier era. The same objection applies to mechanical alibis of the nature of the phonograph to simulate conversation, doors unlocked from the inside by Rube Goldberg-ish contraptions, and similar over-ingenious inventions. Even the skill of a John Dickson

Carr can not quite carry off such far-fetched contrivances to-day, and the unknown beginner will only handicap his chances by attempting them. . . . An additional weakness of the mechanical mode is its requirement of some special knowedge or aptitude on the part of the perpetrator, thereby narrowing the field of suspects—for the rules of fair-play demand that the reader be duly informed of all such special abilities.

The better fictional homicides to-day are accomplished—like those in real life—by shooting, strangling, stabbing, pushing (off cliffs and buildings and into water), bashing, and poisoning; not necessarily in the order named.

Poison is an increasingly popular modern murder weapon, concurrent with the intensified emphasis on psychology and character in the detective story. In all psychology there is no more fascinating study than the warped mentality of the poisoner. But beware, young author, of unusual poisons requiring expert medical knowledge, and *never, never* succumb to that trade-mark of the hopeless hack, the poison-that-leaves-no-trace! Choose an ordinary poison, not too difficult to obtain, and make your puzzle out of the mentality of the murderer, or the circumstances of administering, or both.

Like unto the method, the motive of the crime must be strictly plausible. It must also be adequate. Murder, as some one may have remarked before, is a serious business, for all the nonchalance with which the detective story customarily treats it. No mean or trivial motive—frequently as these occur in real life—will satisfy the artistic verities of the fictional form. Avarice is acceptable, if on a sufficiently large scale, but is somewhat difficult to conceal for the reason that the person who gains by the death of another is usually quite readily discoverable. For this reason many writers have come to employ financial gain only as a subsidiary or false-suspicion motive. Revenge, jealousy, ambition, passion, are all motives which seem somehow more suited to the nature of the crime, at least in its fictive guise. In connection, again, with the new emphasis on psychology and character, numerous writers are finding fear-of-exposure at once a most convincing motive and one capable of wide variation. It also lends itself to combination with virtually all the other motives.

But so much emphasis on the criminal phases of the subject must not lead the would-be writer to forget (as too often happens) that the crime in a detective story is only the means to an end, which is—detection. All too many originally intriguing crime-plots have turned out to be weak sisters in the bookstores solely because the authors failed to match their starting ideas with equally brilliant deduction. Concerning this aspect, little general advice can be offered aside from Poe's twin and initial dicta: that whenever all the impossibilities have been eliminated, that which remains, however improbable, will be the truth; and that the more outré the crime in appearance, the easier the solution. (And the demand by modern readers that the solution must be brought about by the detective's reasoning and actions—never by chance or coincidence.) As for specific methods and styles of deduction, the beginner can only be advised to read, read, and read again until he is thoroughly saturated with his subject.

A few more Pearls of Wisdom and we shall be finished:

Let your readers and characters become acquainted before the killings set in. To be introduced to a corpse is not an exhilarating or even interesting experience. A few unpleasant traits distributed among the victims-to-be will prevent the intrusion of undue grief when the homicides begin.

Forget your social and political prejudices; or, if you can't, at least express them obliquely and with caution. The detective story may be a novel of manners, even a novel of character; but it can not, without losing its essential form, become a novel of ideas.

Shun the "master-mind" criminal—as trite as he is implausible in fiction. To be sure, "crime syndicates" exist in real life (some even control entire continents!) but they are pursued and brought to bay by *mass* methods, not by lone-wolf sleuths. The unities of fictional detection demand a single principal criminal and a single principal detective. Both should be believable human beings, of superior and closely matched intelligence.

The supernatural in a detective story may be "evoked only to be dispelled," to quote Dorothy Sayers. All incidents and circumstances must have physical explanations, and *all* must be explained.

Try to close your case without recourse to legal procedure. Not only do the legal aspects of crime offer the most difficult technical problems and pitfalls for the novice—the excessive craze for court-room plays, novels, and motion pictures in recent years has, temporarily at least, worn out the dramatic possibilities of even the coroner's inquest. Many of the better contemporary writers have resorted to reporting all such proceedings (when inescapable) off-stage, while creating a diversion on the actual scene.

Avoid as you would the plague long lists and tabulations of clues and evidence. There is no quicker way to antagonize friends and lose readers. If a résumé seems unavoidable, handle it conversationally. Better still, start an argument among your characters and introduce your rehashing in the disguise of debate. . . . Leave railway and other time-tables to Freeman Wills Crofts.

Similarly, a transcript of evidence is not fiction. Don't seat your detective at a table and parade the witnesses before him. Move him around, mix evidence with events—or else you will have a Yawning Reader on your hands. (British writers please note!)

Trace the insidious false clue to its lair and eliminate it— remembering that by this term is meant the clue that has no explicable connection with the crime. The false clue should not be confused with the legitimate clue which the writer, by exercise of his skill, persuades his audience to *misinterpret,* and which is quite within the rules of the game. The distinction is a delicate and deceptive but highly important one, and should be watched carefully by the author who wishes to avoid giving offense.

The list might be continued indefinitely to include a whole host of minor rules, such as the familiar prohibitions against secret passages, sinister Orientals, twin brothers from Australia, concealment of information, intuitional solutions, unmotivated confession, and similar matters. But these are largely canons of good taste and as such are easily acquirable by all readers and writers of average perception and discrimination. It has therefore been the purpose of the present discussion less to set forth such specific statutes than to attempt to establish some of the larger principles from which they derive.

The Physical Boundaries

A word must be said somewhere about the physical limitations of the detective story manuscript. These are determined chiefly by certain commercial considerations, which will be more fully examined in the next chapter. But it may be said briefly here that the beginner who submits a detective novel longer than, say, 80,000 words, is courting almost certain rejection. The established author, with an assured volume of sales, or whose books might conceivably fetch a higher retail price, is of course in a more favorable and flexible position.

Some detective novels total no more than 40,000 or 50,000 words in length. But such an extreme of abbreviation is scarcely to be recommended, either. A book that does not fill at least an evening of the reader's time is likely to leave him with the resentful feeling that he has somehow been cheated of his due— and his rental fee.

If an author is interested in attempting short-story selling in the magazine field, he should begin by careful study of editorial needs and lengths. These vary so greatly with the individual periodical that no attempt will be made to elaborate on them here.

One word in conclusion. The detective story, while admittedly a form of escape literature and unlikely ever to become anything else, has nevertheless made a respectable place for itself in contemporary letters. This position was not won without a struggle, in which, it must be conceded, English authorship has to date played a considerably more important rôle than has American. But, as these lines are written, it seems only too likely that the future of the detective story (as, perhaps, of all literature) will rest in non-European hands for at least the next few years. Thus the very survival of the genre in a troubled world (assuming this, as we do, to be desirable) may depend on the clarity and completeness of American understanding of the basic principles responsible for the present eminence of the detective story and necessary for its continuance. Regrettably, such a realization is not held as widely as could be desired. In the absence of pronouncements by better qualified authorities, the attempt will be made here, as briefly and simply as possible, to remedy the difficulty with a final summarizing statement:

Stripped of its decorations and embellishments, the detective story is at bottom one thing only: a conflict of wits between criminal and sleuth, in which the detective is traditionally victorious by out-thinking his adversary. Each important plot incident, every structural step of the story, must be the perfect and logical consequence and result of this central conflict of crime and pursuit, just as each move in a chess game determines and is determined by a counter-move. The formula is capable of infinite variation, as is chess. It may be adorned and disguised in almost any fashion the author chooses, whether gaudy or sober. But in basic structure it must never vary by so much as a hairsbreadth from absolute logicality. Beside this one simple rule, all other rules pale to relative unimportance. This *is* the detective story.

Conversely, the one completely unforgivable sin in the detective story is the substitution, at any point, of accident, chance, or coincidence for logical deduction. If this uncomfortable shoe may seem to fit certain dainty American feet—well, let it be put on, and high time too!

34

CASUAL NOTES ON THE MYSTERY NOVEL

by *Raymond Chandler*

(1) The mystery novel must be credibly motivated both as to the original situation and the denouement. It must consist of the plausible actions of plausible people in plausible circumstances, it being remembered that plausibility is largely a matter of style. This rules out most trick endings and the so-called 'closed circle' stories in which the least likely character is forcibly made over into the criminal without convincing anyone. It also rules out such elaborate mise-en-scènes as Christie's *Murder in the Calais Coach,* in which the whole set-up for the crime reveals such a fluky set of events that nobody could ever really believe them. Here, as everywhere of course, plausibility is a matter of effect, not of fact, and one writer will succeed with a pattern which in the hands of a lesser artist would just seem foolish.

(2) The mystery story must be technically sound about methods of murder and detection. No fantastic poisons or improper effects such as death from improper doses, etc. No silencers on revolvers (they won't work because chamber and barrel are not continuous), no snakes climbing bellropes. If the detective is a trained policeman, he must act like one and have the mental and physical equipment to go with the job. If he is a private investigator or amateur, he must at least know enough of police routine not to make a fool of himself. The mystery story must take into account the cultural stage of its

Reprinted, by special permission, from *Raymond Chandler Speaking,* edited by Dorothy Gardiner and Kathrine Sorley Walker, Hamish Hamilton and Four Winds, publishers. Copyright © 1962 by the Helga Greene Literary Agency (London).

readers; things that were acceptable in Sherlock Holmes are not acceptable in Sayers or Christie or Carter Dickson.

(3) It must be realistic as to character, setting and atmosphere. It must be about real people in a real world. There is of course an element of fantasy in the mystery story. It outrages probability by telescoping time and space. Hence the more exaggerated the basic premise the more literal and exact must be the proceedings that flow from it. Very few mystery writers have any talent for character work, but that does not mean it is superfluous. Those who say the problem overrides everything are merely trying to cover up their own inability to create character and atmosphere. Character can be created in various ways: by the subjective method of entering into the character's thoughts and emotions; by the objective or dramatic method as on the stage, that is, by the appearance, behavior, speech and actions of the character; and by the case history method in what is now known as the documentary style. This last is particularly applicable to the kind of detective novel which tries to be as factual and unemotional as an official report. But whatever the method, character must be created, if any kind of distinction is to be achieved.

(4) The mystery novel must have a sound story value apart from the mystery element. The idea is revolutionary to some of the classicists and most distasteful to all second-rate performers. Nevertheless it is sound. All really good mysteries are reread, some of them many times. Obviously this would not happen if the puzzle were the only motive for the reader's interest. The mysteries that survive over the years invariably have the qualities of good fiction. The mystery story must have color, lift, and a reasonable amount of dash. It takes an enormous amount of technical adroitness to compensate for a dull style, although the trick has been turned occasionally, especially in England.

(5) The mystery novel must have enough essential simplicity of structure to be explained easily when the time comes.

The ideal denouement is the one in which everything is made clear in a brief flash of action. Ideas as good as this are always rare, and a writer who can achieve this once is to be congratulated. The explanation need not be short (except on the screen) and often cannot be short. The important thing is that it should be interesting in itself, something the reader is anxious to hear, not a new story with a new or unrecognizable set of characters dragged in to justify a leaky plot. It must not be merely a long-winded assembling of minute circumstances that the reader could not possibly be expected to remember.

There is nothing more difficult to manage than an explanation. If you say enough to assuage the stupid reader, you will have said enough to infuriate the intelligent one, but this merely points up one of the essential dilemmas of the mystery writer, that the mystery novel has to appeal to a cross section of the entire reading public and cannot possibly appeal to all of these by the same devices. Not since the early days of the three-decker novel has any one type of fiction been read by so many different sorts of people. Semi-literates don't read Flaubert and intellectuals don't as a rule read the current fat slab of goosed history masquerading as an historical novel. But everyone reads mysteries from time to time—or almost everyone—and a surprising number of people read almost nothing else. The handling of the explanation vis-à-vis this variously educated public is an almost insoluble problem. Possibly, except for the dyed-in-the-wool aficionado who will stand anything, the best solution is the Hollywood rule: 'No exposition except under heat, and break it up at that.' (This means that an explanation must always be an accompaniment to some kind of action, and that it must be given in short doses rather than all at once.)

(6) The mystery must elude a reasonably intelligent reader. This, and the problem of honesty, are the two most baffling elements in mystery writing. Some of the best detective stories ever written do not elude an intelligent reader to the end (those

of Austin Freeman, for instance). But it is one thing to guess the murderer and quite another to be able to justify the guess by reasoning. Since readers are of many minds, some will guess a cleverly-hidden solution and some will be fooled by the most transparent plot. (Could *any* modern reader be fooled by Conan Doyle's "The Red-Headed League"? Could any modern police routine miss Edgar Allan Poe's "The Purloined Letter"?) But it is not necessary or even desirable to fool to the hilt the real aficionado of mystery fiction. A half-guessed mystery is more intriguing than one in which the reader is entirely at sea. It ministers to the reader's self-esteem to have penetrated some of the fog. The essential is that there be a little fog left at the end for the author to blow away.

(7) The solution, once revealed, must seem to have been inevitable. At least half of all the mystery novels published violate this law. Their solutions are not only not inevitable, they are very obviously trumped-up because the writer had realized that his original murderer had become too apparent.

(8) The mystery novel must not try to do everything at once. If it is a puzzle story operating in a cool mental climate, it cannot also be a story of violent adventure or passionate romance. An atmosphere of terror destroys logical thinking. If the story is about the intricate psychological pressures that drive people to commit murder, it cannot also contain the dispassionate analysis of the trained investigator. The detective cannot be hero and menace at the same time; the murderer cannot be a tormented victim of circumstances and also a heavy villain.

(9) The mystery novel must punish the criminal in one way or another, not necessarily by operation of the law courts. Contrary to popular belief, this has nothing to do with morality. It is part of the logic of the form. Without this the story is like an unresolved chord in music. It leaves a sense of irritation.

(10) The mystery novel must be reasonably honest with the reader. This is always said, but the full implications are seldom

realized. What is honesty in this connection? It is not enough that the facts be stated. They must be fairly stated, and they must be the sort of facts that can be reasoned from. Not only must important (or any) clues not be concealed from the reader, but they must not be distorted by false emphasis. Unimportant facts must not be presented in such a way as to make them portentous. Inferences from the facts are the detective's stock in trade, but he should disclose enough of his thinking to keep the reader's mind thinking along with him. It is the basic theory of all mystery writing that at some stage of the proceedings the reader could, given the necessary acuteness, have closed the book and revealed the essence of the denouement. But this implies more than mere possession of the facts; it implies that the ordinary lay reader could honestly be expected to draw the right conclusions from these facts. The reader cannot be charged with special and rare knowledge nor with an abnormal memory for insignificant details. For if such were necessary, the reader did not in fact have the materials for the solution, he merely had the unopened packages they came in.

The submerging of the big clue in a puddle of talk about nothing is a permissible trick when the movement of the story has created enough tension to put the reader on guard. If the reader has to know as much as Dr. Thorndyke to solve a mystery, obviously he cannot solve it. If the premise of *Trent's Last Case,* by E. C. Bentley, is plausible, then logic and realism have no meaning. If the actual time when a murder was committed is conditioned by the murdered person having been a hemophiliac, then the reader cannot be expected to deal with the matter intelligently until he knows of the hemophilia; when he does (the story I refer to is Dorothy Sayers' *Have His Carcase*) the mystery disappears because the alibis no longer apply to the necessary times.

Obviously it is much more than a trick, acceptable or otherwise, for the detective to turn out to be the criminal, since the detective by tradition and definition is the seeker after the truth. There is always an implied guarantee to the reader that the detective is on the level, and this rule should of course be extended to include any first-person narrator or any character from whose point of view the story is told. The suppression of facts by the narrator as such, or by the author when pretending to show the facts as seen by a particular character, is a flagrant dishonesty. (For two reasons I have always been quite unmoved to indignation by Agatha Christie's violation of this rule in *The Murder of Roger Ackroyd*. (a) The dishonesty is rather cleverly explained and (b) the whole arrangement of the story and of its dramatis personae make it clear that the narrator is the only possible murderer, so that to an intelligent reader the challenge of this story is not 'Who committed the murder?' but 'Watch me closely and catch me out if you can'.)

Intention and Emphasis

It seems evident by this time that the whole question of dishonesty is a matter of intention and emphasis. The reader expects to be fooled, but not by a trifle. He expects to misinterpret some clue but not because he failed to master chemistry, geology, biology, pathology, metallurgy and half a dozen other sciences at the same time. He expects to forget some detail that later turns out to be important, but not if the price of remembering it is to remember a thousand trivialities which have no importance whatsoever. And if, as in some of Austin Freeman's stories, the matter of exact proof turns on scientific knowledge, the reader expects that the detection of the criminal may be achieved by an ordinary attentive brain, even though the specialist is needed to drive the guilt home.

There are, of course, subtle dishonesties which are intrinsic in the form itself. Mary Roberts Rinehart, I think it was, once remarked that the point of the mystery story was that it was two stories in one: the story of what happened and the story of what appeared to have happened. Since a concealment of the truth is implied, there must be some means of effecting that concealment. It is all a question of degree. Some tricks are offensive because they are blatant and because, once they are shown up, there is nothing left. Some are pleasing because they are insidious and subtle, like a caught glance the meaning of which one does not quite know although one is suspicious that it is not flattering. All first-person narration, for example, could be accused of a subtle dishonesty because of its appearance of candor and its ability to suppress the detective's ratiocination while giving a clear account of his words and acts and many of his emotional reactions. There must come a time when the detective has made up his mind and has not given the reader this bit of news, a point as it were (and many old hands recognize it without much difficulty) when the detective suddenly stops thinking out loud and ever so gently closes the door of his mind in the reader's face. Back in the days when the audience was still innocent and had to be hit in the face with a stale flounder in order to realize that something was fishy, the detective used to do this by saying, for example: 'Well, there are the facts. If you give them your careful attention, I am sure your thoughts will be rich in possible explanations of these strange events.' Nowadays it is done with less parade, but the effect of a closing door is just as unmistakable.

Subtle Disguise of Truth

It ought to be added to close this subject that the question of fair play in a mystery story is purely professional and artistic and has no moral significance at all. The point is whether the reader was misled within the rules of fair play or whether he was hit below the belt. There is no possibility of perfection. Complete frankness would destroy the mystery. The better the writer the farther he will go with the truth, the more subtly he will disguise that which cannot be told. And not only is this game of skill without moral laws, but it is constantly changing the laws by which it does act. It has to; the reader is growing wiser by the minute. It may be that in Sherlock Holmes' day if the butler skulked outside the library window with a shawl over his head, he became a suspect. Today that course of action would instantly eliminate him from all suspicion. For not only does the contemporary reader refuse to follow any such will o' the wisp as a matter of course, but he is constantly alert to the writer's effort to make him look at the wrong things and not look at the right ones. Anything passed over lightly becomes suspicious, any character not mentioned as a suspect *is* a suspect, and anything which causes the detective to chew the ends of his mustache and look grave is by the alert reader suitably dismissed as of no importance. It often seems to this particular writer that the only reasonably honest and effective method of fooling the reader that remains is to make the reader exercise his mind about the wrong problem, to make him, as it were, solve a mystery (since he is almost sure to solve something) which will land him in a bypath because it is only tangential to the central problem. And even this takes a bit of cheating here and there.

Addenda

(1) The perfect mystery cannot be written. Something must always be sacrificed. You can have only one paramount value. This is my complaint against the deductive story. Its paramount value is something which does not exist: a problem which will stand up against the kind of analysis that a good lawyer gives to a legal problem. It is not that such stories are not intriguing, but that they have no way of compensating for their soft spots.

(2) It has been said that "nobody cares about the corpse." This is nonsense, it is throwing away a valuable element. It is like saying that the murder of your aunt means no more to you than the murder of an unknown man in a city you never visited.

(3) A mystery serial seldom makes a good mystery novel.

The curtains depend for their effect on your not having the next chapter. When the chapters are put together the moments of false suspense are merely annoying.

(4) Love interest nearly always weakens a mystery because it introduces a type of suspense that is antagonistic to the detective's struggle to solve the problem. It stacks the cards, and, in nine cases out of ten, it eliminates at least two useful suspects. The only effective kind of love interest is that which creates a personal hazard for the detective—but which, at the same time, you instinctively feel to be a mere episode. A really good detective never gets married.

(5) It is the paradox of the mystery novel that while its structure will seldom if ever stand up under the close scrutiny of an analytical mind, it is precisely to that type of mind that it makes its greatest appeal. There is of course the blood-lust type of reader just as there is the worrier-about-the-character type of reader and the vicarious-sex-experience type of reader. But all of these put together would probably be a smallish minority compared with the alert kind of people who love the mystery story precisely because of its imperfections.

It is, that is to say, a form which has never really been licked, and those who have prophesied its decline and fall have been wrong for that exact reason. Since its form has never been perfected, it has never become fixed. The academicians have never got their dead hands on it. It is still fluid, still too various for easy classification, still putting out shoots in all directions. Nobody knows exactly what makes it tick and there is no one quality you can attribute to it that is not found to be missing in some successful example. It has produced more bad art than any type of fiction except the love story and probably more good art than any other form so widely accepted and liked.

35 DON'T GUESS, LET ME TELL YOU

by *Ogden Nash*

Personally I don't care whether a detective story writer was
    educated in night school or day school
So long as they don't belong to the H.I.B.K. school.
The H.I.B.K. being a device to which too many detective story
    writers are prone,
Namely the Had I But Known.
Sometimes it is the Had I But Known what grim secret lurked
    behind that smiling exterior I would never have set foot
    within the door,
Sometimes the Had I But Known then what I know now I could
    have saved at least three lives by revealing to the Inspec-
    tor the conversation I heard through that fortuitous hole
    in the floor.
Had-I-But-Known narrators are the ones who hear a stealthy
    creak at midnight in the tower where the body lies, and,
    instead of locking their door or arousing the drowsy police-
    man posted outside their room, sneak off by themselves to
    the tower and suddenly they hear a breath exhaled behind
    them,
And they have no time to scream, they know nothing else till
    the men from the D.A.'s office come in next morning and
    find them.
Had I But Known-ers are quick to assume the prerogatives of
    the Deity,
For they will suppress evidence that doesn't suit their theories
    with appalling spontaneity,
And when the killer is finally trapped into a confession by some

elaborate device of the Had I But Known-er some hundred
pages later than if they hadn't held their knowledge aloof,
Why they say Why Inspector I knew all along it was he but I
couldn't tell you, you would have laughed at me unless I
had absolute proof.
Would you like a nice detective story for your library which I
am sorry to say I didn't rent but owns?
I wouldn't have bought it had I but known it was impregnated
with Had I But Knowns.

SUPPLEMENT AND GLOSSARY

36 A LAYMAN'S GUIDE TO LAW AND THE COURTS

WRITERS of suspense and mystery fiction will find the following information a valuable reference tool for use in describing points of law, courtroom procedures, criminal actions, legal transactions, and arrest procedures. This is a condensation of *Law and the Courts,* prepared by the American Bar Association.—*Ed.*

The processes of the law and the courts are baffling and mysterious to many laymen. The following material traces the steps normally involved in a civil case and in a criminal case, explaining the procedures common to most of them. It was prepared for use by nonlawyers (writers and others). The Standing Committee on Association Communications of the American Bar Association will, upon request, be pleased to offer assistance to writers in reviewing articles, scripts, and other material, for accuracy in legal procedure. The ABA Public Information Department also will be glad to help answer questions or direct inquiries to knowledgeable sources.

Some variations of procedure exist among the various state courts, and among the federal courts as well. When the occasion requires, details of procedure in particular courts, or in special

---

This chapter is a condensation of *Law and the Courts:* A Layman's Handbook of Court Procedures, and is reprinted by permission of the American Bar Association. The complete booklet is available for 50¢ from the American Bar Association, Circulation Department 4030, 1155 East 60th Street, Chicago, Illinois 60637. Copyright © 1974 American Bar Association.

types of litigation, can be supplied by local attorneys, by court public information officers or other court officials.

Criminal cases

BRINGING THE CHARGE. Criminal charges are instituted against an individual in one of two ways:

1) Through an *indictment,* or *true bill,* voted by a grand jury, or
2) Through the filing of an *information* in court by the prosecuting attorney (sometimes called the county, district or state's attorney), alleging the commission of a crime.

In either case, the charge must set forth the time, date and place of the alleged criminal act as well as the nature of the charge.

In most states, crimes of a serious nature, such as murder or treason, may be charged by indictment only. In some states, the prosecutor has the option in any case to proceed by way of indictment or information.

THE GRAND JURY. The grand jury is a body of citizens (usually 16, but varying in number from state to state) summoned by the court to inquire into crimes committed in the county or, in the case of federal grand juries, in the federal court district.

Grand jury proceedings are private and secret. Prospective defendants are not entitled to be present at the proceedings, and no one appears to cross-examine witnesses on the defendants' behalf.

However, a witness before a federal grand jury is free to describe his testimony to anyone he pleases, after he leaves the grand jury room. To this extent, such proceedings are not secret.

Although all states have provision for impaneling a grand jury, only about half use it as a regular arm of law enforcement. In the others, the prosecutor, on his own responsibility, is empowered to make formal accusation of all, or of all but the most serious, crimes.

In states where the grand jury is utilized, it is convened at regular intervals, or it may be impaneled at special times by the court to consider important cases.

The grand jury has broad investigative powers: it may compel the attendance of witnesses; require the taking of oaths, and compel answers to questions and the submission of records.

Ordinarily, however, the grand jury hears such witnesses as the prosecutor calls before it and considers only the cases presented to it by the prosecutor.

Nevertheless, a grand jury may undertake inquiries of its own, in effect taking the initiative away from the prosecutor. In common parlance, this is known as a "runaway" grand jury.

The grand jury's traditional function is to determine whether information elicited by the prosecutor, or by its own inquiries, is adequate to warrant the return of an indictment or true bill charging a person or persons with a particular crime. If the grand jury concludes that the evidence does not warrant a formal charge, it may return a *no bill*.

In several states, powers of investigation similar to those of the grand jury are conferred by law upon a single person, a judicial officer or a deputy appointed by him, known as a "one man grand jury."

ARREST PROCEDURE. When an indictment is returned by a grand jury, or an information is filed by the prosecuting attorney, the clerk of the court issues a *warrant* for the arrest of the person charged, if he has not already been arrested and taken into custody.

The law usually requires in a *felony* case (generally, a crime for which a person may be confined in the penitentiary) that the defendant must promptly be brought before a magistrate or justice of the peace (in federal cases, the U.S. Commissioner) and be permitted to post bond, in order to secure release from custody, and either request or waive a *preliminary hearing*. When the grand jury indicts, there is no preliminary hearing. In most states, however, persons charged with murder are not eligible for release on a bail bond.

Many jurisdictions permit law enforcement officials to hold a person without formal charge up to 24 hours for the purpose of investigation. But he may not be held for an unreasonable time unless a criminal charge is filed. In addition, the defendant formally charged with a crime is entitled to an attorney at all times. If he is unable to procure an attorney and if he requests counsel, the court will appoint an attorney to represent him, at public expense and without cost to him.

Special Note

Under the so-called Miranda decision of the United States Supreme Court, the following "basic Miranda procedure" and "typical Miranda statement given by an officer" are used:

I. Typical Miranda statement given by officer

Before we ask you any questions, you must understand what your rights are.

You have the right to remain silent. You are not required to say anything to us at any time or to answer any questions. Anything you say can and will be used against you in court.

You have the right to talk to a lawyer for advice before we question you and to have him with you during questioning.

If you cannot afford a lawyer and want one, a lawyer will be provided for you free of charge.

If you want to answer questions now without a lawyer present, you will still have the right to stop answering at any time. You also have the right to stop answering at any time until you talk to a lawyer.

II. Basic Miranda procedure

1. Warnings given *before* questioning a suspect who is *in custody* (custody = focus of interrogation + not permitted to move on).

2. Warnings always given when—
    a. subject is placed under *arrest.*
    b. interrogation in police *presence,* i.e., in station, or in squad car.
    c. if it is clear to officer that suspect thinks he has to answer.

3. Warnings not necessary for a mere witness (even grand jury witness who is not yet focus of investigation).

4. Warnings should be repeated after delay in questioning. Warning should be repeated when questioning officer changes.

5. Officer should immediately *stop* questions when suspect becomes silent *or* requests lawyer. If suspect agrees to talk and then goes silent, questions should stop.

6. Officer should give warning even to suspect who claims to make a statement that will show his innocence.

PRELIMINARY HEARING. If the individual charged with a crime requests a preliminary hearing before a magistrate, the court will set a hearing within a reasonably short time. At the hearing, the state must present sufficient evidence to convince the magistrate that there is reason to believe the defendant has committed the crime with which he is charged. The defendant must be present at this hearing, and he may or may not present evidence on his own behalf.

If the magistrate believes the evidence justifies it, he will order the defendant *bound over* for trial in the proper court—that is, placed under bond for appearance at trial, or held in jail if the charge involved is not a bailable offense or if the defendant is unable to post bond. The magistrate also may decide that even without bond the accused will most likely appear in court for his trial and therefore will release him on his *own recognizance,* that is, on his own promise to appear. If he concludes the state has failed to produce sufficient evidence in the preliminary hearing, the magistrate may dismiss the charge and order the defendant released.

ARRAIGNMENT. In most instances, a criminal case is placed on the court's calendar for *arraignment*. On the date fixed, the accused appears, the indictment or information is read to him, his rights are explained by the judge, and he is asked whether he pleads *guilty* or *not guilty* to the charge.

If he pleads not guilty, his case will be set later for trial; if he pleads guilty, his case ordinarily will be set later for sentencing. In cases of minor offenses, sentences may be imposed immediately. But in some states, arraignment and plea are separate proceedings, held on different days.

PREPARATION FOR TRIAL. As in civil cases, very careful preparation on the part of the state and the defense precedes the trial.

However, the defense may first enter a motion challenging the jurisdiction of the court over the particular offense involved, or over the particular defendant. The defense attorney also may file a *demurrer,* or motion for dismissal, as in a civil suit.

In preparing for trial, attorneys for both sides will interview prospective witnesses and, if deemed necessary, secure expert evidence, and gather testimony concerning ballistics, chemical tests, casts and other similar data.

Trials: civil or criminal

While in detail there are minor differences in trial procedure between civil and criminal cases, the basic pattern in the courtroom is the same. Consequently, this section treats the trial steps collectively.

OFFICERS OF THE COURT. The *judge* is the officer who is either elected or appointed to preside over the court. If the case is tried before a jury, the judge rules upon points of law dealing with trial procedure, presentation of the evidence and the law of the case. If the case is tried before the judge alone, he will determine the facts in addition to performing the aforementioned duties.

The *court clerk* is an officer of the court, also either elected or appointed, who at the beginning of the trial, upon the judge's instruction, gives the entire panel of prospective jurors (*veniremen*) an oath. By this oath, the venireman promises that, if called, he will truly answer any question concerning his qualifications to sit as a juror in the case.

Any venireman who is disqualified by law, or has a valid reason to be excused under the law, ordinarily is excused by the judge at this time. A person may be disqualified from jury duty because he is not a resident voter or householder, because of age, hearing defects, or because he has served recently on a jury.

Then the court clerk will draw names of the remaining veniremen from a box, and they will take seats in the jury box. After twelve veniremen have been approved as jurors by the judge and the attorneys, the court clerk will administer an oath to the persons so chosen "to well and truly try the cause."

The *bailiff* is an officer of the court whose duties are to keep order in the courtroom, to call witnesses, and to take charge of the jury as instructed by the court at such times as the jury may not be in the courtroom, and particularly when, having received the case, the jury is deliberating upon its decision. It is the duty of the bailiff to see that no one talks with or attempts to influence the jurors in any manner.

The *court reporter* has the duty of recording all proceedings in the courtroom, and listing and marking for identification any exhibits offered or introduced into evidence. In some states, the clerk of the court has charge of exhibits.

The *attorneys* are officers of the court whose duties are to represent their respective clients and present the evidence on their behalf.

The role of the attorney is sometimes misunderstood, particularly in criminal proceedings. Our system of criminal jurisprudence presumes every defendant to be innocent until proved guilty beyond a *reasonable doubt*. Every defendant is entitled to be represented by legal counsel, regardless of the unpopularity of his cause. This is a constitutional safeguard.

It is entirely ethical for an attorney to represent a defendant whom the community may assume to be guilty. The accused is entitled to counsel in order that he be protected from conviction on insufficient evidence, and he is entitled to every protection which the law affords.

JURY LIST. The trial jury in either a civil or criminal case is called a *petit jury*. It is chosen by lot by the court clerk from a previously compiled list called a *venire,* or in some places the *jury array*.

Many persons are exempted from jury duty by reason of their occupations. These exemptions differ from state to state, but in some jurisdictions those automatically exempted include lawyers, physicians, dentists, pharmacists, teachers and clergymen. In a number of others, nurses, journalists, printers, railroad, telephone and telegraph employees, government officials, firemen and policemen are among the exempt occupational groups.

On occasion, the qualification of all the jurors may be challenged. This is called a *challenge to the array* and generally is based on the allegation that the officers charged with selecting the jurors did so in an illegal manner.

SELECTING THE JURY. In most cases, a jury of twelve is required in either a civil or criminal proceeding. In some courts, alternate jurors are selected to take the places of members of the regular panel who may become disabled during the trial. These alternate jurors hear the evidence just as do the regular jurors, but do not participate in the deliberations unless a regular juror or jurors become disabled.

The jury selection begins with the calling by the court clerk of twelve veniremen whose names are selected at random from a box, to take their places in the jury enclosure. The attorneys for the parties, or sometimes the judge, may then make a brief statement of the facts involved, for the purpose of acquainting the jurors with sufficient facts so that they may intelligently answer the questions put to them by the judge and the attorneys. The questions elicit information such as the name, the occupation, the place of business and residence of the prospective juror, and any personal knowledge he may have of the case. This questioning of the jurors is known as the *voir dire*.

If the venireman expresses an opinion or prejudice which will affect his judgment in the case, the court will dismiss him for *cause,* and a substitute juror will be called by the court clerk. There is no limit on the number of jurors who may be excused *for cause.*

In addition to the challenges for cause, each party has the right to exercise a specific number of *peremptory challenges*. This permits an attorney to excuse a particular juror without having to state a cause. If a peremptory challenge is exercised, another juror then is called until attorneys on both sides have exercised all of the peremptory challenges permitted by law, or they have waived further challenges. The number of peremptory challenges is limited and varies with the type of case.

The jury is then sworn in by the court clerk to try the case. The remaining members of the jury panel are excused and directed to report at a future date when another case will be called, or excused and directed to report to another court in session at the time.

SEPARATING THE WITNESSES. In certain cases, civil or criminal, the attorney on either side may advise the court that he is *calling for the rule* on witnesses. This means that, except for the plaintiff or complaining witness and the defendant, all witnesses who may testify for either party will be excluded from the courtroom until they are called to testify. These witnesses are admonished by the judge not to discuss the case or their testimony with other witnesses or persons, except the attorneys. This is sometimes called a *separation of witnesses*. If the rule is not called for, the witnesses may remain in the courtroom if they desire.

OPENING STATEMENTS. After selection of the jury, the plaintiff's attorney, or attorney for the state in a criminal case, may make an opening statement to advise the jury what he intends to prove in the case. This statement must be confined to facts intended to be elicited in evidence and cannot be argumentative. The attorney for the defendant also may make an opening statement for the same purpose or, in some states, may reserve the opening statement until the end of the plaintiff's or state's case. Either party may waive his opening statement if he desires.

PRESENTATION OF EVIDENCE. The plaintiff in a civil case, or the state in a criminal case, will begin the presentation of evidence with their *witnesses*. These usually will include the plaintiff in a civil case or complaining witness in a criminal case, although they are not required to testify.

A witness may testify to a matter of fact. He can tell what he saw, heard (unless it is hearsay as explained below), felt, smelled or touched through the use of his physical senses.

A witness also may be used to identify documents, pictures or other physical exhibits in the trial.

Generally, he cannot state his opinion or give his conclusion unless he is an expert or especially qualified to do so. In some instances, a witness may be permitted to express an opinion, for example, as to the speed an auto was traveling or whether a person was intoxicated.

A witness who has been qualified in a particular field as an *expert* may give his opinion based upon the facts in evidence and may state the reasons for that opinion. Sometimes the facts in evidence are put to the expert in a question called a *hypothetical question*. The question assumes the truth of the facts contained in it. Other times, an expert is asked to state an opinion based on personal knowledge of the facts through his own examination or investigation.

Generally, a witness cannot testify to *hearsay*, that is, what someone else has told him outside the presence of the parties to the action.

Also, a witness is not permitted to testify about matters that are too remote to have any bearing on the decision of the case, or matters that are irrelevant or immaterial.

Usually, an attorney may not ask *leading questions* of his own witness, although an attorney is sometimes allowed to elicit routine, noncontroversial information. A leading question is one which suggests the answer desired.

Objections may be made by the opposing counsel to leading questions, or to questions that call for an opinion or conclusion on the part of the witness, or require an answer based on hearsay. There are many other reasons for objections under the rules of evidence.

Objections are often made in the following form: "I object to that question on the ground that it is irrelevant and immaterial and for the further reason that it calls for an opinion and conclusion of the witness." Many jurisdictions require that the objection specify why the question is not proper. The judge will thereupon sustain or deny the objection. If sustained, another question must then be asked, or the same question be rephrased in proper form.

If an objection to a question is sustained on either direct or cross-examination, the attorney asking the question may make an *offer to prove*. This offer is dictated to the court reporter away from the hearing of the jury. In it, the attorney states the answer which the witness would have given if permitted. The offer forms part of the record if the case is subsequently appealed.

If the objection is overruled, the witness may then answer. The attorney who made the objection may thereupon take an *exception*, which simply means that he is preserving a record so that, if the case is appealed, he may argue that the court erred in overruling the objection. In some states, the rules permit an automatic exception to an adverse ruling without its being asked for in each instance.

CROSS-EXAMINATION. When plaintiff's attorney or the state's attorney has finished his direct examination of the witness, the defendant's attorney or opposing counsel may then cross-examine the witness on any matter about which the witness has been questioned initially in direct examination. The cross-examining attorney may ask leading questions for the purpose of inducing the witness to testify about matters which he may otherwise have chosen to ignore.

On cross-examination, the attorney may try to bring out prejudice or bias of the witness, such as his relationship or friendship to the party, or other interest in the case. The witness can be asked if he has been convicted of a felony or crime involving moral turpitude, since this bears upon his credibility.

The plaintiff's attorney may object to certain questions asked on cross-examination on previously mentioned grounds or because they deal with facts not touched upon in direct examination.

RE-DIRECT EXAMINATION. After the opposing attorney is finished with his cross-examination, the attorney who called the witness has the right to ask questions on *re-direct examination*. The re-direct examination covers new matters brought out on cross-examination and generally is an effort to rehabilitate a witness whose testimony on direct examination has been weakened by cross-examination.

Then the opposing attorney may re-cross-examine.

DEMURRER TO PLAINTIFF'S OR STATE'S CASE, OR MOTION FOR DIRECTED VERDICT. At the conclusion of the plaintiff's or state's evidence, the attorney will announce that the plaintiff or state *rests*.

Then, away from the presence of the jury, the defendant's counsel may demur to the plaintiff's or state's case on the ground that a cause of action or that the commission of a crime has not been proven. In many states, this is known as a *motion for a direct verdict*, that is, a verdict which the judge orders the jury to return.

The judge will either sustain or overrule the demurrer or motion. If it is sustained, the case is concluded. If it is overruled, the defendant then is given the opportunity to present his evidence.

PRESENTATION OF EVIDENCE BY THE DEFENDANT. The defense attorney may elect to present no evidence, or he may present certain evidence but not place the defendant upon the stand.

In a criminal case, the defendant need not take the stand unless he wishes to do so. The defendant has constitutional protection against self-incrimination. He is not required to prove his innocence. The plaintiff or the state has the *burden of proof*.

In a civil case, the plaintiff must prove his case by a *preponderance of the evidence*. This means the greater weight of the evidence.

In a criminal case, the evidence of guilt must be *beyond a reasonable doubt*.

The defendant is presumed to be not negligent or liable in a civil case, and not guilty in a criminal case.

The defense attorney may feel that the burden of proof has not been sustained, or that presentation of the defendant's witnesses might strengthen the plaintiff's case. If the defendant does present evidence, he does so in the same manner as the plaintiff or the state, as described above, and the plaintiff or state will cross-examine the defendant's witnesses.

REBUTTAL EVIDENCE. At the conclusion of the defendant's case, the plaintiff or state's attorney may then present rebuttal witnesses or evidence designed to refute the testimony and evidence presented by the defendant. The matter covered is evidence on which the plaintiff or state did not present evidence in its *case in chief* initially; or it may be a new witness to contradict the defendant's witness. If there is a so-called *surprise witness*, this is often where you will find him.

After rebuttal evidence, the defendant may present additional evidence to contradict it.

FINAL MOTIONS. At the conclusion of all the evidence, the defendant may again renew his demurrer or motion for directed verdict.

The motion is made away from the presence of the jury. If the demurrer or motion is sustained, the case is concluded. If over-ruled, the trial proceeds.

Thus, the case has now been concluded on the evidence, and it is ready to be submitted to the jury.

CONFERENCES DURING THE TRIAL. Occasionally during the trial, the lawyers will ask permission to approach the bench and speak to the judge, or the judge may call them to the bench. They whisper about admissibility of certain evidence, irregularities in the trial or other matters. The judge and lawyers speak in inaudible tones because the jurors might be prejudiced by what they hear. The question of admissibility of evidence is a matter of law for the judge, not the jury, to decide. If the ruling cannot be made quickly, the judge will order the jury to retire, and will hear the attorneys' arguments outside the jury's presence.

Whenever the jury leaves the courtroom, the judge will ad-monish them not to form or express an opinion or discuss the case with anyone.

CLOSING ARGUMENTS. The attorney for the plaintiff or state will present the first argument in closing the case. Generally, he will summarize and comment on the evidence in the most favorable light for his side. He may talk about the facts and properly drawn inferences.

He cannot talk about issues outside the case or about evidence that was not presented. He is not allowed to comment on the defendant's failure to take the stand as a witness in a criminal case.

If he does talk about improper matters, the opposing attorney may object, and the judge will rule on the objection. If the offend-ing remarks are deemed seriously prejudicial, the opposing at-torney will ask that the jury be instructed to disregard them, and in some instances may move for a *mistrial,* that is, ask that the present trial be terminated and the case be set for retrial at a later date.

Ordinarily, before closing arguments, the judge will indicate to the attorneys the instructions he will give the jury, and it is proper for the attorneys in closing argument to comment on them and to relate them to the evidence.

The defendant's attorney will next present his arguments. He usually answers statements made in opening argument, points out defects in the plaintiff's case, and summarizes the facts favorable to his client.

Then the plaintiff or state is entitled to the concluding argument to answer the defendant's argument and to make a final appeal to the jury.

If the defendant chooses not to make a closing argument, which sometimes occurs, then the plaintiff or state loses the right to the last argument.

INSTRUCTIONS TO THE JURY. Although giving instructions to the jury is the function of the judge, in many states attorneys for each side submit a number of instructions designed to apply the law to the facts in evidence. The judge will indicate which instructions he will accept and which he will refuse. The attorneys may make objections to such rulings for the purpose of the record in any appeal.

The judge reads these instructions to the jury. This is commonly referred to as the judge's *charge* to the jury. The instructions cover the law as applicable to the case.

In most cases, only the judge may determine what the law is. In some states, however, in criminal cases the jurors are judges of both the facts and the law.

In giving the instructions, the judge will state the issues in the case and define any terms or words necessary. He will tell the jury what it must decide on the issues, if it is to find for the plaintiff or state, or for the defendant. He will advise the jury that it is the sole judge of the facts and of the credibility of witnesses; that upon leaving the courtroom to reach a verdict, it must elect a *foreman* of the jury and then reach a decision based upon the judgment of each individual juror. In some states, the first juror chosen automatically becomes the foreman.

IN THE JURY ROOM. After the instructions, the bailiff will take the jury to the jury room to begin deliberations.

The bailiff will sit outside and not permit anyone to enter or leave the jury room. No one may attempt to *tamper* with the jury in any way while it is deliberating.

Ordinarily, the court furnishes the jury with written forms of all possible verdicts so that when a decision is reached, the jury can choose the proper verdict form.

The decision will be signed by the foreman of the jury and be returned to the courtroom.

Ordinarily, in a criminal case the decision must be unanimous. In some jurisdictions, in civil cases, only nine or ten out of twelve jurors need agree to reach a verdict. However, all federal courts require a unanimous verdict.

If the jurors cannot agree on a verdict, the jury is called a *hung jury*, and the case may be retried before a new jury at a later date.

In some states, the jury may take the judge's instructions and the exhibits introduced in evidence to the jury room.

If necessary, the jury may return to the courtroom in the presence of counsel to ask a question of the judge about his instructions. In such instances, the judge may reread all or certain of the instructions previously given, or supplement or clarify them by further instructions.

If the jury is out overnight, the members often will be housed in a hotel and secluded from all contacts with other persons. In many cases, the jury will be excused to go home at night, especially if there is no objection by either party.

VERDICT. Upon reaching a verdict, the jury returns to the courtroom with the bailiff and, in the presence of the judge, the parties and their respective attorneys, the verdict is read or announced aloud in open court. The reading or announcement may be made by the jury foreman or the court clerk.

Attorneys for either party, but usually the losing party, may ask that the jury be *polled*, in which case each individual juror will be asked if the verdict is his verdict. It is rare for a juror to say that it is not his verdict.

When the verdict is read and accepted by the court, the jury is dismissed, and the trial is concluded.

MOTIONS AFTER VERDICT. Motions permitted to be made after the verdict is rendered will vary from state to state.

A *motion in arrest of judgment* attacks the sufficiency of the indictment or information in a criminal case.

A *motion for judgment non obstante verdicto* may be made after the verdict and before the judgment. This motion requests the judge to enter a judgment for one party, notwithstanding the verdict of the jury in favor of the other side. Ordinarily, this motion raises the same questions as could be raised by a motion for directed verdict.

A *motion for a new trial* sets out alleged errors committed in the trial and asks the trial judge to grant a new trial. In some states, the filing of a motion for a new trial is a condition precedent to an appeal.

JUDGMENT. The verdict of the jury is ineffective until the judge enters *judgment* upon the verdict. In a civil damage action, this judgment might read:
"It is, therefore, ordered, adjudged and decreed that the plaintiff do have and recover the sum of $1,000 of and from the defendant."

At the request of the plaintiff's lawyer, the clerk of the court in such a case will deliver a paper called an *execution* to the sheriff, commanding him to take and sell the property of the defendant and apply the proceeds to the amount of the judgment.

SENTENCING. In a criminal case, if the defendant is convicted, the judge will set a date for sentencing. At that time, the judge may consider mitigating facts in determining the appropriate sentence.

In the great majority of states and in the federal courts, the function of imposing sentence is exclusively that of the judge. But in some states the jury is called upon to determine the sentences for some, or all, crimes, In these states, the judge merely imposes the sentence as determined by the jury.

RIGHTS OF APPEAL. In a civil case, either party may appeal to a higher court. But in a criminal case this right is limited to the defendant. Appeals in either civil or criminal cases may be on such grounds as errors in trial procedure and errors in *substantive law*—that is, in the interpretation of the law by the trial judge. These are the most common grounds for appeals to higher courts, although there are others.

The right of appeal does not extend to the prosecution in a criminal case, even if the prosecutor should discover new evidence of the defendant's guilt after his acquittal. Moreover, the state is powerless to bring the defendant to trial again on the same charge. The U.S. and most state constitutions prevent retrial under provisions known as *double jeopardy* clauses.

Criminal defendants have a further appellate safeguard. Those convicted in state courts may appeal to the federal courts on grounds of violation of constitutional rights, if such grounds exist. This privilege serves to impose the powerful check of the federal judicial system upon abuses that may occur in state criminal procedures.

The record on appeal consists of the papers filed in the trial court and the court reporter's transcript of the evidence. The latter is called a *bill of exceptions* or *transcript on appeal* and must be certified by the trial judge to be true and correct. In most states, only that much of the record need be included as will properly present the questions to be raised on appeal.

APPEAL. Statutes or rules of court provide for procedure on appeals. Ordinarily, the party appealing is called the *appellant*, and the other party the *appellee*.

The appeal is initiated by filing the transcript of the trial court record with the appellate court within the time prescribed. This filing marks the beginning of the time period within which the appellant must file his *brief* setting forth the reasons and the law upon which he relies in seeking a reversal of the trial court.

The appellee then has a specified time within which to file his answer brief. Following this, the appellant may file a second brief, or brief in reply to the appellee's brief.

When the appeal has been fully briefed, the case may be set for hearing on *oral argument* before the appellate court. Sometimes the court itself will ask for argument; otherwise, one of the parties may petition for it. Often, appeals are submitted *on the briefs* without argument.

Courts of appeal do not hear further evidence, and it is unusual for any of the parties to the case to attend the hearing of the oral argument.

Generally, the case has been assigned to one of the judges of the appellate court, although the full court will hear the argument. Thereafter, it is customary for all the judges to confer on the issues presented, and then the judge who has been assigned the case will write an opinion. If a judge or judges disagree with the result, they may dissent and file a *dissenting opinion*. In many states, a written opinion is required.

An appellate court will not weigh evidence and generally will reverse a trial court for errors of law only.

Not every error of law will warrant a reversal. Some are *harmless errors*—that is, the rights of a party to a fair trial were not prejudiced by them.

However, an error of law, such as the admission of improper and persuasive evidence on a material issue, may and often does constitute a *prejudicial* and *reversible error*.

After the opinion is *handed down* and time for the filing of a petition for rehearing—or a petition for transfer, or a petition for *writ of certiorari* (if there is a higher appellate court)—has expired, the appellate court will send its *mandate* to the trial court for further action in the case.

If the lower court is *affirmed*, the case is ended; if reversed, the appellate court may direct that a new trial be held, or that the judgment of the trial court be modified and corrected as prescribed in the opinion.

The taking of an appeal ordinarily does not suspend the operation of a judgment obtained in a civil action in a trial court. Thus, the party prevailing in the trial court may order an execution issued on the judgment, unless the party appealing files an *appeal* or *supersedeas bond*, which binds the party and his surety to pay or perform the judgment in the event it is affirmed on appeal. The filing of this bond will *stay* further action on the judgment until the appeal has been concluded.

37 GLOSSARY OF LEGAL TERMS

accumulative sentence—A sentence, additional to others, imposed at the same time for several distinct offenses; one sentence to begin at the expiration of another.

adjudication—Giving or pronouncing a judgment or decree; also the judgment given.

adversary system—The system of trial practice in the U.S. and some other countries in which each of the opposing, or adversary, parties has full opportunity to present and establish its opposing contentions before the court.

allegation—The assertion, declaration, or statement of a party to an action, made in a pleading, setting out what he expects to prove.

amicus curiae (a-mī′kus kū′ri-ē)—A friend of the court; one who interposes and volunteers information upon some matter of law.

appearance—The formal proceeding by which a defendant submits himself to the jurisdiction of the court.

appellant (a-pel′ant)—The party appealing a decision or judgment to a higher court.

appellate court—A court having jurisdiction of appeal and review; not a "trial court."

arraignment—In criminal practice, to bring a prisoner to the bar of the court to answer to a criminal charge.

This list, which is a sampling of commonly used legal terms, is reprinted by permission of the American Bar Association from *Law and the Courts: A Layman's Handbook of Court Procedures*. The complete booklet is available for 50¢ from the American Bar Association, Circulation Department 4030, 1155 East 60th Street, Chicago, Illinois 60637. Copyright © 1974, American Bar Association.

attachment—A remedy by which plaintiff is enabled to acquire a lien upon property or effects of defendant for satisfaction of judgment which plaintiff may obtain in the future.

attorney of record—Attorney whose name appears in the permanent records or files of a case.

bail—To set at liberty a person arrested or imprisoned, on security being taken, for his appearance on a specified day and place.

bail bond—An obligation signed by the accused, with sureties, to secure his presence in court.

bailiff—A court attendant whose duties are to keep order in the courtroom and to have custody of the jury.

best evidence—Primary evidence; the best evidence which is available; any evidence falling short of this standard is secondary; i.e., an original letter is best evidence compared to a copy.

bind over—To hold on bail for trial.

brief—A written or printed document prepared by counsel to file in court, usually setting forth both facts and law in support of his case.

burden of proof—In the law of evidence, the necessity or duty of affirmatively proving a fact or facts in dispute.

cause—A suit, litigation or action—civil or criminal.

certiorari (ser'shi-ō-ra'rī)—An original writ commanding judges or officers of inferior courts to certify or to return records of proceedings in a cause for judicial review.

chambers—Private office or room of a judge.

change of venue—The removal of a suit begun in one county or district, to another, for trial, or from one court to another in the same county or district.

circuit courts—Originally, courts whose jurisdiction extended over several counties or districts, and whose sessions were held in such counties or districts alternately; today, a circuit court may hold all its sessions in one county.

circumstantial evidence—All evidence of indirect nature; the process of decision by which court or jury may reason from circumstances known or proved to establish by inference the principal fact.

codicil (kod'i-sil)—A supplement or an addition to a will.

commit—To send a person to prison, an asylum, workhouse, or reformatory by lawful authority.

common law—Law which derives its authority solely from usages and customs of immemorial antiquity, or from the judgments and decrees of courts. Also called "case law."

commutation—The change of a punishment from a greater degree to a lesser degree, as from death to life imprisonment.

competency—In the law of evidence, the presence of those characteristics which render a witness legally fit and qualified to give testimony.

complainant—Synonymous with "plaintiff."

complaint—The first or initiatory pleading on the part of the complainant, or plaintiff, in a civil action.

concurrent sentence—Sentences for more than one crime in which the time of each is to be served concurrently, rather than successively.

condemnation—The legal process by which real estate of a private owner is taken for public use without his consent, but upon the award and payment of just compensation.

contempt of court—Any act calculated to embarrass, hinder, or obstruct a court in the administration of justice, or calculated to lessen its authority or dignity. Contempts are of two kinds: direct and indirect. Direct contempts are those committed in the immediate presence of the court; indirect is the term chiefly used with reference to the failure or refusal to obey a lawful order.

corpus delicti (kor′pus dē-lik′tī)—The body (material substance) upon which a crime has been committed, e.g., the corpse of a murdered man, the charred remains of a burned house.

corroborating evidence—Evidence supplementary to that already given and tending to strengthen or confirm it.

costs—An allowance for expenses in prosecuting or defending a suit. Ordinarily does not include attorney's fees.

counterclaim—A claim presented by a defendant in opposition to the claim of a plaintiff.

criminal insanity—Lack of mental capacity to do or abstain from doing a particular act; inability to distinguish right from wrong.

cross-examination—The questioning of a witness in a trial, or in the taking of a deposition, by the party opposed to the one who produced the witness.

cumulative sentence—Separate sentences (each additional to the others) imposed against a person convicted upon an indictment containing several counts, each charging a different offense. (Same as accumulative sentence.)

damages—Pecuniary compensation which may be recovered in the courts by any person who has suffered loss, detriment, or injury to his person, property or rights, through the unlawful act or negligence of another.

de novo (dē nō′vō)—Anew, afresh. A "trial de novo" is the retrial of a case.

declaratory judgment—One which declares the rights of the parties or expresses the opinion of the court on a question of law, without ordering anything to be done.

decree—A decision or order of the court. A final decree is one which fully and finally disposes of the litigation; an interlocutory decree is a provisional or preliminary decree which is not final.

default—A "default" in an action of law occurs when a defendant omits to plead within the time allowed or fails to appear at the trial.

demur (dē-mer′)—To file a pleading (called "a demurrer") admitting the truth of the facts in the complaint, or answer, but contending they are legally insufficient.

deposition—The testimony of a witness not taken in open court but in pursuance of authority given by statute or rule of court to take testimony elsewhere.

direct evidence—Proof of facts by witnesses who saw acts done or heard words spoken, as distinguished from circumstantial evidence, which is called indirect.

direct examination—The first interrogation of a witness by the party on whose behalf he is called.

directed verdict—An instruction by the judge to the jury to return a specific verdict.

dismissal without prejudice—Permits the complainant to sue again on the same cause of action, while dismissal "with prejudice" bars the right to bring or maintain an action on the same claim or cause.

double jeopardy—Common-law and constitutional prohibition against more than one prosecution for the same crime, transaction or omission.

due process—Law in its regular course of administration through the courts of justice. The guarantee of due process requires that every man have the protection of a fair trial.

embezzlement—The fraudulent appropriation by a person to his own use or benefit of property or money entrusted to him by another.

eminent domain—The power to take private property for public use by condemnation.

enjoin—To require a person, by writ of injunction from a court of equity, to perform, or to abstain or desist from, some act.

entrapment—The act of officers or agents of a government in inducing a person to commit a crime not contemplated by him, for the purpose of instituting a criminal prosecution against him.

escrow (es'krō)—A writing, or deed, delivered by the grantor into the hands of a third person, to be held by the latter until the happening of a contingency or performance of a condition.

ex post facto (ex pōst fak'to)—After the fact; an act or fact occurring after some previous act or fact, and relating thereto.

exception—A formal objection to an action of the court, during the trial of a case, in refusing a request or overruling an objection; implying that the party excepting does not acquiesce in the decision of the court, but will seek to procure its reversal.

exhibit—A paper, document or other article produced and exhibited to a court during a trial or hearing.

expert evidence—Testimony given in relation to some scientific, technical, or professional matter by experts, i.e., persons qualified to speak authoritatively by reason of their special training, skill, or familiarity with the subject.

extenuating circumstances—Circumstances which render a crime less aggravated, heinous, or reprehensible than it would otherwise be.

extradition—The surrender by one state to another of an individual accused or convicted of an offense outside its own territory, and within the territorial jurisdiction of the other.

fair comment—A term used in the law of libel, applying to statements made by a writer in an honest belief of their truth, relating to official act, even though the statements are not true in fact.

false arrest—Any unlawful physical restraint of another's liberty, whether in prison or elsewhere.

felony—A crime of a graver nature than a misdemeanor. Generally, an offense punishable by death or imprisonment in a penitentiary.

forcible entry and detainer—A summary proceeding for restoring possession of land to one who has been wrongfully deprived of possession.

forgery—The false making or material altering, with intent to defraud, of any writing which, if genuine, might be the foundation of a legal liability.

fraud—An intentional perversion of truth; deceitful practice or device resorted to with intent to deprive another of property or other right, or in some manner to do him injury.

garnishment—A proceeding whereby property, money or credits of a debtor, in possession of another (the garnishee), are applied to the debts of the debtor.

gratuitous guest—In automobile law, a person riding at the invitation of the owner of a vehicle, or his authorized agent, without payment of a consideration or a fare.

guardian ad litem (ad lī'tem)—A person appointed by a court to look after the interests of an infant whose property is involved in litigation.

habeas corpus (hā' be-as kor' pus)—"You have the body." The name given a variety of writs whose object is to bring a person before a court or judge. In most common usage, it is directed to the official or person detaining another, commanding him to produce the body of the prisoner or person detained so the court may determine if such person has been denied his liberty without due process of law.

hearsay—Evidence not proceeding from the personal knowledge of the witness.

holographic will (hol-ō-graf'ik)—A testamentary instrument entirely written, dated and signed by the testator in his own handwriting.

hostile witness—A witness who is subject to cross-examination by the party who called him to testify, because of his evident antagonism toward that party as exhibited in his direct examination.

hypothetical question—A combination of facts and circumstances, assumed or proved, stated in such a form as to constitute a coherent state of facts upon which the opinion of an expert can be asked by way of evidence in a trial.

impeachment of witness—An attack on the credibility of a witness by the testimony of other witnesses.

inadmissible—That which, under the established rules of evidence, cannot be admitted or received.

in camera (in kam' e-ra)—In chambers; in private.

incompetent evidence—Evidence which is not admissible under the established rules of evidence.

indeterminate sentence—An indefinite sentence of "not less than" and "not more than" so many years, the exact term to be served being afterwards determined by parole authorities within the minimum and maximum limits set by the court or by statute.

indictment—An accusation in writing found and presented by a grand jury, charging that a person therein named has done some act, or been guilty of some omission, which, by law, is a crime.

injunction—A mandatory or prohibitive writ issued by a court.

instruction—A direction given by the judge to the jury concerning the law of the case.

interlocutory—Provisional; temporary; not final. Refers to orders and decrees of a court.

interrogatories—Written questions propounded by one party and served on an adversary, who must provide written answers thereto under oath.

intervention—A proceeding in a suit or action by which a third person is permitted by the court to make himself a party.

intestate—One who dies without leaving a will.

irrelevant—Evidence not relating or applicable to the matter in issue; not supporting the issue.

jury—A certain number of persons, selected according to law, and sworn to inquire of certain matters of fact, and declare the truth upon evidence laid before them.

grand jury—A jury of inquiry whose duty is to receive complaints and accusations in criminal cases, hear the evidence and find bills of indictment in cases where they are satisfied that there is probable cause that a crime was committed and that a trial ought to be held.

petit jury—The ordinary jury of twelve (or fewer) persons for the trial of a civil or criminal case. So called to distinguish it from the grand jury.

leading question—One which instructs a witness how to answer or puts into his mouth words to be echoed back; one which suggests to the witness the answer desired. Prohibited on direct examination.

libel—A method of defamation expressed by print, writing, pictures, or signs. In its most general sense, any publication that is injurious to the reputation of another.

limitation—A certain time allowed by statute in which litigation must be brought.

malfeasance (mal-fē′zans)—Evil doing; ill conduct; the commission of some act which is positively prohibited by law.

mandamus (man-dā′mus)—The name of a writ which issues from a court of superior jurisdiction, directed to an inferior court, commanding the performance of a particular act.

mandate—A judicial command or precept proceeding from a court or judicial officer, directing the proper officer to enforce a judgment, sentence, or decree.

manslaughter—The unlawful killing of another without malice; may be either voluntary, upon a sudden impulse, or involuntary in the commission of some unlawful act.

material evidence—Such as is relevant and goes to the substantial issues in dispute.

misdemeanor—Offenses less than felonies; generally those punishable by fine or imprisonment otherwise than in penitentiaries.

misfeasance—A misdeed or trespass; the improper performance of some act which a person may lawfully do.

mistrial—An erroneous or invalid trial; a trial which cannot stand in law because of lack of jurisdiction, wrong drawing of jurors, or disregard of some other fundamental requisite.

mitigating circumstance—One which does not constitute a justification or excuse for an offense, but which may be considered as reducing the degree of moral culpability.

moot—Unsettled; undecided. A moot point is one not settled by judicial decisions.

moral turpitude—Conduct contrary to honesty, modesty, or good morals.

murder—The unlawful killing of a human being by another with malice aforethought, either expressed or implied.

negligence—The failure to do something which a reasonable man, guided by ordinary considerations, would do; or the doing of something which a reasonable and prudent man would not do.

nolo contendere (nō′lō kon-ten′de-rē)—A pleading usually used by defendants in criminal cases, which literally means "I will not contest it."

objection—The act of taking exception to some statement or procedure in trial. Used to call the court's attention to improper evidence or procedure.

of counsel—A phrase commonly applied to counsel employed to assist in the preparation or management of the case, or its presentation on appeal, but who is not the principal attorney of record.

out of court—One who has no legal status in court is said to be "out of court," i.e., he is not before the court. For example, when a plaintiff, by some act of omission or commission, shows that he is unable to maintain his action, he is frequently said to have put himself "out of court."

panel—A list of jurors to serve in a particular court, or for the trial of a particular action; denotes either the whole body of persons summoned as jurors for a particular term of court or those selected by the clerk by lot.

parole—The conditional release from prison of a convict before the expiration of his sentence. If he observes the conditions, the parolee need not serve the remainder of his sentence.

parties—The persons who are actively concerned in the prosecution or defense of a legal proceeding.

peremptory challenge—The challenge which the prosecution or defense may use to reject a certain number of prospective jurors without assigning any cause.

plaintiff—A person who brings an action; the party who complains or sues in a personal action and is so named on the record.

plaintiff in error—The party who obtains a writ of error to have a judgment or other proceeding at law reviewed by an appellate court.

pleading—The process by which the parties in a suit or action alternately present written statements of their contentions, each responsive to that which precedes, and each serving to narrow the field of controversy, until there evolves a single point, affirmed on one side and denied on the other, called the "issue" upon which they then go to trial.

polling the jury—A practice whereby the jurors are asked individually whether they assented, and still assent, to the verdict.

power of attorney—An instrument authorizing another to act as one's agent or attorney.

prejudicial error—Synonymous with "reversible error"; an error which warrants the appellate court to reverse the judgment before it.

preliminary hearing—Synonymous with "preliminary examination"; the hearing given a person charged with a crime by a magistrate or judge to determine whether he should be held for trial. Since the Constitution states that a man cannot be accused in secret, a preliminary hearing is open to the public unless the defendant himself requests that it be closed. The accused person must be present at this hearing and must be accompanied by his attorney.

presumption of fact—An inference as to the truth or falsity of any proposition of fact, drawn by a process of reasoning in the absence of actual certainty of its truth or falsity, or until such certainty can be ascertained.

presumption of law—A rule of law that courts and judges shall draw a particular inference from a particular fact, or from particular evidence.

probate—The act or process of proving a will.

probation—In modern criminal administration, allowing a person convicted of some minor offense (particularly juvenile offenders) to go at large, under a suspension of sentence, during good behavior, and generally under the supervision or guardianship of a probation officer.

prosecutor—One who instigates the prosecution upon which an accused is arrested or one who brings an accusation against the party whom he suspects to be guilty; also, one who takes charge of a case and performs the function of trial lawyer for the people.

quash—To overthrow; vacate; to annul or void a summons or indictment.

quasi judicial (kwā'sī)—Authority or discretion vested in an officer, wherein his acts partake of a judicial character.

reasonable doubt—An accused person is entitled to acquittal if, in the minds of the jury, his guilt has not been proved beyond a "reasonable doubt"; that state of the minds of jurors in which they cannot say they feel an abiding conviction as to the truth of the charge.

rebuttal—The introduction of rebutting evidence; the showing that statements of witnesses as to what occurred is not true; the stage of a trial at which such evidence may be introduced.

redirect examination—Follows cross-examination and is exercised by the party who first examined the witness.

referee—A person to whom a cause pending in a court is referred by the court to take testimony, hear the parties, and report thereon to the court. He is an officer exercising judicial powers and is an arm of the court for a specific purpose.

rest—A party is said to "rest" or "rest his case" when he has presented all the evidence he intends to offer.

retainer—Act of the client in employing his attorney or counsel, and also denotes the fee which the client pays when he retains the attorney to act for him.

search and seizure, unreasonable—In general, an examination without authority of law of one's premises or person with a view to discovering stolen contraband or illicit property or some evidence of guilt to be used in prosecuting a crime.

search warrant—An order in writing, issued by a justice or magistrate, in the name of the state, directing an officer to search a specified house or other premises for stolen property. Usually required as a condition precedent to a legal search and seizure.

self-defense—The protection of one's person or property against some injury attempted by another. The law of "self defense" justifies an act done in the reasonable belief of immediate danger. When acting in justifiable self-defense, a person may not be punished criminally nor held responsible for civil damages.

separate maintenance—Allowance granted for support to a married party, and any children, while the party is living apart from the spouse, but not divorced.

slander—Base and defamatory spoken words tending to harm another's reputation, business or means of livelihood. Both "libel" and "slander" are methods of defamation—the former being expressed by print, writings, pictures or signs; the latter orally.

state's evidence—Testimony given by an accomplice or participant in a crime, tending to convict others.

statute—The written law in contradistinction to the unwritten law.

stay—A stopping or arresting of a judicial proceeding by order of the court.

stipulation—An agreement by attorneys on opposite sides of a case as to any matter pertaining to the proceedings or trial. It is not binding unless assented to by the parties, and most stipulations must be in writing.

subpoena (su-pē′nä)—A process to cause a witness to appear and give testimony before a court or magistrate.

subpoena duces tecum (su-pē′nä dū′sēz tē′kum)—A process by which the court commands a witness to produce certain documents or records in a trial.

summons—A writ directing the sheriff or other officer to notify the named person that an action has been commenced against him in court and that he is required to appear, on the day named, and answer the complaint in such action.

testimony—Evidence given by a competent witness, under oath; as distinguished from evidence derived from writings and other sources.

tort—An injury or wrong committed, either with or without force, to the person or property of another.

transcript—The official record of proceedings in a trial or hearing.

trial de novo (dē nō′vō)—A new trial or retrial held in a higher court in which the whole case is gone into as if no trial had been held in a lower court.

true bill—In criminal practice, the endorsement made by a grand jury upon a bill of indictment when they find sufficient evidence to warrant a criminal charge.

undue influence—Whatever destroys free will and causes a person to do something he would not do if left to himself.

venire (vē-nī'rē)—Technically, a writ summoning persons to court to act as jurors; popularly used as meaning the body of names thus summoned.

veniremen (vē-nī'rē-men)—Members of a panel of jurors.

venue (ven'ū)—The particular county, city or geographical area in which a court with jurisdiction may hear and determine a case.

verdict—In practice, the formal and unanimous decision or finding made by a jury, reported to the court and accepted by it.

waiver of immunity—A means authorized by statutes by which a witness, in advance of giving testimony or producing evidence, may renounce the fundamental right guaranteed by the Constitution that no person shall be compelled to be a witness against himself.

warrant of arrest—A writ issued by a magistrate, justice, or other competent authority, to a sheriff, or other officer, requiring him to arrest a person therein named and bring him before the magistrate or court to answer to a specified charge.

weight of evidence—The balance or preponderance of evidence; the inclination of the greater amount of credible evidence, offered in a trial, to support one side of the issue rather than the other.

willful—A "willful" act is one done intentionally, without justifiable cause, as distinguished from an act done carelessly or inadvertently.

with prejudice—The term, as applied to judgment of dismissal, is as conclusive of rights of parties as if action had been prosecuted to final adjudication adverse to the plaintiff.

without prejudice—A dismissal "without prejudice" allows a new suit to be brought on the same cause of action.

witness—One who testifies to what he has seen, heard, or otherwise observed.

writ—An order issuing from a court of justice and requiring the performance of a specified act, or giving authority and commission to have it done.